D0872197

THE
INCEST
PERPETRATOR

THE
INCEST
PERPETRATOR
A FAMILY MEMBER NO ONE
WANTS TO TREAT

ANNE L. HORTON
BARRY L. JOHNSON
LYNN M. ROUNDY
DORAN WILLIAMS
editors

SAGE PUBLICATIONS
The Publishers of Professional Social Science
Newbury Park   London   New Delhi

To Judy Williamson (1951–1987)

For information address:

SAGE Publications, Inc.
2111 West Hillcrest Drive
Newbury Park, California 91320

SAGE Publications Ltd.
28 Banner Street
London EC1Y 8QE
England

SAGE Publications India Pvt. Ltd.
M-32 Market
Greater Kailash I
New Delhi 110 048 India

Printed in the United States of America

Library of Congress Cataloging-in-Publication Data

Main entry under title:

The incest perpetrator : a family member no one wants to treat /
edited by Anne L. Horton . . . [et al.].
p.   cm.
Includes bibliographical references.
Includes Index
ISBN 0-8039-3391-6.—ISBN 0-8039-3392-4 (pbk.)
1. Incest—Treatment. 2. Psychotherapy. I. Horton, Anne L.
RC560.I53I53 1990   89-37648
616.85′83—dc20   CIP

FIRST PRINTING, 1990

Contents

Preface

Today there are a number of social problems that are generally not welcomed by the treatment community. The problem of incest—particularly the incest perpetrator—has certainly met head on with this resistance and wrestled with the subsequent difficulties that such discomfort produces in clinical settings. The taint of moral judgments, family rejection, lack of ready solutions, and the coercive character of these interventions make incest perpetrators the pariahs of society's major institutions, even those specifically designated to assist them. This key actor in the incestuous family has been generally condemned, but the obligation of the treatment community remains constant for all service recipients—to help them seek solutions and change as well as to develop strategies to alleviate suffering. To do this, the incest perpetrator has been selected as the subject of analysis for this book, and the emphasis is on help and correction.

This book is a collection of informative pieces on incest perpetrators: the result of a comprehensive, combined effort on the part of incest perpetrators themselves, clinicians, researchers, and other involved helping professionals. This project focuses specifically on the incest offender and the basic information necessary for responsible treatment. Who is the incest perpetrator? What treatment options are available? Who treats them? What services do they want? What advice do they, the service consumers, have for the treatment community?

Thousands of incest victims will be coming forward voluntarily this year, seeking treatment for their past suffering or a remedy for their situation. For every victim there must also be a perpetrator, but the perpetrators will not reach out for help. Although the perpetrator is the family member who would be making, at least initially, the greatest behavioral and psychological change, this population is being offered

fewer treatment options, less trained service providers, and no positive incentives toward intervention. When public identification makes
remedial measures mandatory, many still decline services, or approach
them reluctantly.

In a recent study (see Chapter 3) it was demonstrated that most
perpetrators recognize, before anyone else does, that their behavior
or intent is "wrong, immoral or unacceptable"; yet they do not seek
help. Most also believe that early intervention and treatment would
have been beneficial; yet it was not pursued. The large majority
of incest perpetrators in less restrictive settings are married and remain with the family in which the incest occurred. What can be
done?

Conte (1984) stated that the greatest unmet need in cases involving
incest is that of the treatment of perpetrators. This book is dedicated
to narrowing that gap. A direct, practical approach to this population
provides a basic profile of the perpetrator, identification indicators,
treatment opportunities, and appropriate referrals. Experts in the
criminal justice area and treatment communities have joined forces
with the perpetrators to unravel the critical issues of remedial concern, including legal and other ethical issues. Until adequate treatment and prevention issues are focused on perpetrators, the entire
family unit and the community will suffer emotionally, economically,
and intergenerationally.

It is important to note that this book is aimed at the needs of "incest" perpetrators specifically and does not use a more generic approach to pedophiles or child sexual abuse as many of the recent publications have. This emphasis, which results from a growing trend
toward placing incest perpetrators in less restrictive settings, is particularly important to a broad cross section of treatment providers as they
encounter these family problems in the community. Therefore, while
the similarities and differences between these sex offenders and others
will be noted and reported, the treatment emphasis focuses on a more
holistic systems approach that involve other family members more in
the change process, as opposed to a strictly individual focus. Whether
these families remain together or not, familial issues are always an
important treatment dynamic. As a result, relationship concerns figure
in clinical assessments, treatment plans, and recommendations as a
factor in a way that does not affect other sex offenders or unrelated
pedophiles.

The book has been divided into three basic sections: (a) defining the problem, (b) profiles and identification, and (c) treatment. Jon Conte lends his considerable expertise and insight to the opening chapter with an overview of the particular concerns and need for treatment experience and sensitivity toward this population. The second chapter attempts to clarify and define major treatment dilemmas—whose problem is it? While the legal system is responsible for enforcing the law, it cannot guarantee that treatment, particularly involuntary treatment, will be effective. This new legal, social, and moral partnership is discussed, emphasizing the considerable demands and resources of each area to effect responsible support for these troubled individuals and their families. In Chapter 2, Frank and Susan Bolton discuss those important legal issues from a criminal justice perspective.

Chapters 3, 10, 11, and 14 reflect material drawn primarily from four national studies in different treatment settings, and reflect the work of the major investigator, three coeditors and authors, and ten research assistants. Anne Horton, Barry Johnson, Lynn Roundy and Doran Williams have been actively involved in the research, writing, and editing. However, the research assistants have had the major responsibility of reporting their individual research areas. Other outside experts in the field have contributed research and treatment material in their specific areas of expertise. Kathleen Coulborn Faller clarifies important distinctions with respect to familial relationships that impact directly on clinical decisions and the understanding of positional dynamics. Jane Gilgun and Teresa Connor discuss isolation and clinical concerns with respect to offenders. John Christiansen and Reed Blake discuss the important clinical phases of the "grooming process" and introduce practical guidelines for therapeutic application.

Special populations of offenders—adolescents and women—receive careful coverage by researchers who are specifically working on the most up-to-date research in each area, Robert and Lois Pierce and Craig Allen. Because treatment issues are the major focus of this book, Pat Carnes's work on sexual addiction was included as a valuable and timely contribution that directly influences the clinician in making a total assessment of the perpetrator. The influence of his work will be extremely helpful to those working at all levels with these offenders in various settings.

The final section on treatment occupies a major portion of this book and has been the thrust of our research efforts for the past two years. With increased numbers of incest offenders entering treatment programs and facilities, it is essential for professionals to know and understand the perpetrators' clinical needs and opinion of and feelings toward the treatment options currently offered.

Our 1987 national survey of 274 perpetrators currently involved in Parents United showed that 69% of these families elected to remain together, and thus, that treatment resources are needed, not only for the perpetrator but to help all members of the family. These services need to be anticipated at the outset and be part of a planned and coordinated total intervention to incestuous families. Such intervention necessitates a pool of efforts on the part of the helping community and the criminal justice system. Initiating this complex process requires new knowledge and appreciation for the legal aspects of this social problem. Chapters 10 and 11 on the identification, resources, and treatment issues of offenders, offer guidelines for clinicians. A final review of clinical concerns and considerations, which discusses the considerable importance of victim safety issues, is the focus of Chapter 12 by Vicki D. Granowitz, Nodie Cox Davis, and Deena D. Levi. Current treatment providers who are working in the field with offenders offer suggestions and firsthand observations in Chapter 13.

In keeping with the concern for total intervention, Henry and Anna Giarretto describe their integrated family approach to treatment (see Chapter 14). An innovative program set up for military families offers a model step-by-step design for program development. Charlotte Schuler discusses how they developed a protocol and established services (see Chapter 15). A limited resource directory is also included at the close of the book.

While the needs of all incest perpetrators cannot be addressed within the scope of this book, it does attempt to provide proscriptive treatment information and relevant clinical findings specifically for the conscientious treatment provider. No one agent alone has the ability to remedy this complex scenario of interacting human beings. With additional knowledge and training, it is hoped that we can add significantly to the correction of this serious family problem.

We, the editors, are indebted to many who have influenced and joined us in the pursuit of this project. All the contributors, research assistants, and local and national agencies and organizations who participated, as well as our own families, have been exceedingly generous with their time, expertise, and caring. We are also particularly indebted to the clinicians and the incest perpetrators and their families who have shared this information and who are committed to providing the best care, education, and treatment to those suffering from incest in their lives. We wish to thank the Women's Research Institute and the College of Family, Home, and Social Sciences at Brigham Young University for their grant and funding support of this project. In addition, special acknowledgments must be extended to the B.Y.U. School of Social Work, C.Y. Roby, Diane Gonzalez, Craig Chadwick, LaDawn Johansen, Wendy Helms, and Martha Webster for their considerable personal contributions.

Our aim is to end family violence, pain, and fear in the home. As helping professionals we are committed to help our clients make meaningful changes in their lives and to promote the best interests of society. As none of us will be safe until all are provided for, it is to this common effort that this book is dedicated.

REFERENCE

Conte, J. R. (1984, December). The justice system and sexual abuse of children. *Social Science Review*, 556–568.

Editors' Note

This book consists of chapters written by concerned and sensitive authors. The title itself speaks of the difficulty the authors encountered in writing and researching this challenging issue as they tried to explore treatment options at both a micro and macro level. Throughout the text there has been considerable effort made to avoid sexist language. Obviously, this imposes a hardship as a common pronoun that is suitable to both sexes has not been found. Therefore, victims will commonly be referred to in the feminine gender, and perpetrators, or offenders, in the masculine gender. In some instances, when discussing therapists or clinicians, "he/she," and "him/her," will be used. Treatment providers, mental health professionals, clinicians, and so on, will be used interchangeably throughout the text. The editors have selected this format in an effort to maintain uniformity, but it is not meant to indicate a lack of sensitivity to male victims or homosexual and lesbian relationships.

These authors represent various disciplines and institutions. All contributors have had full license to express their own views, and this diversity of style, content, and philosophy will hopefully enrich and educate the reader from many varying perspectives.

PART I

Defining the Problem

1

The Incest Offender: *An Overview and Introduction*

Jon R. Conte

INTRODUCTION

For many generations parents have warned children to "beware of strangers." However, recently researchers have suggested that sexual assault by strangers is a relatively rare occurrence. For example, in the clinical sample described by Conte and Schuerman (1987), only 4% of child victims were abused by adults unrelated and not previously known by the child or family. Children are more likely to be sexually abused by members of their own families and by acquaintances than by strangers.

THE PROBLEM

Many of us have difficulty understanding how older persons are able to have sex with a child. Such behavior is generally believed to inflict pain and emotional harm, violate acceptable standards of adult conduct toward children, and be incongruent with how most adults see themselves. It is especially hard for us to understand how members of a family can behave in these ways with one another. As cases of child sexual abuse have come to light in our own communities, schools, churches, workplaces, even in our own families, we have been forced to recognize that, in terms of appearance, sexual offenders look very much like ourselves. They are of our own race, religion, profession, socioeconomic group, and usually (for those of us who are men) our own gender.

These two dynamics (our difficulty in understanding how anyone could sexually abuse a child, and the apparent similarity between ourselves and incest offenders); our efforts to deal with the anxiety they create through defensive operations of minimization, rationalization, and denial; and the relative lack of scientific data on incest have created a professional literature and social policy that is ambivalent, contradictory, and potentially dangerous—dangerous in that the literature and social policies dealing with incestuous sexual abuse may be inaccurate and not lead to the therapeutic and social policy goals that best serve the interests of sexually abused children, the adults who share and influence their lives, or society.

CONFLICTING CONCERNS IN THE LITERATURE

Who are these men? Two distinct literatures have developed that, until very recently, appeared to describe two quite distinct types of adult sexual offenders. One literature has focused on the nonfamily offender, that is, the pedophile (for review see, e.g., Quinsey, 1984, in press). Pedophilia involves recurrent, intense sexual urges and sexually arousing fantasies of at least six months duration involving sexual activity with a prepubescent child (generally 13 years or younger). Some individuals with this diagnosis may be sexually attracted to children (exclusive type), while others may also be attracted to adults (nonexclusive type). Pedophiles may be attracted to only boys, only girls, or both. In many cases, where interest in violence or infliction of pain is absent, the pedophile may be "generous and very attentive to the child's needs in all respects other than the sexual victimization in order to gain the child's affection, interests, and loyalty, and prevent the child from reporting the sexual activity" (American Psychiatric Association, 1987).

A second literature, spanning over three decades of sporadic work, has focused on the family of the incest offender (for review, see Conte, 1986). Definitions of incest vary, but incest is generally recognized as sexual contact between persons who are biologically related (e.g., father-daughter, mother-son, grandparent-grandchild, or brother-sister) or between stepparents and stepchildren (e.g., stepfather-daughter abuse). Much of the professional literature to date has focused on father or stepfather and daughter abuse.

TREATMENT ASSUMPTIONS

Although there is as much variation within family-oriented views of adult sexual use of children as there is between family and nonfamily views, Conte (1986) has suggested that all family views of the problem rest on two key assumptions: incestuous fathers and stepfathers do not act out sexually outside of the home and incest is the sexual expression of nonsexual needs. These core assumptions directly influence how professionals and society have chosen to respond to the incest offender.

The belief that incest offenders do not act out outside of the family is both a statement about reality and a statement about the nature of incest. Incest is a family problem in which every member of the family contributes to the development and maintenance of the sexual relationship between father or stepfather and daughter. This belief is the basis for the assumption that incest offenders are not dangerous to children who live outside of their homes and therefore, in most cases, can be left in the community (although perhaps not in the same house) during treatment.

Recent data reported by Abel, Becker, Cunningham-Rathner, Mittelman, and Rouleau (1988) indicates that 49% of the incestuous fathers and stepfathers referred for outpatient treatment at their clinics abused female children outside of the family at the same time they were abusing their own children (19% of these men were raping adult women at the same time they were sexually abusing their own children). While these data are from a single study and replication is critical in understanding how generalizable they are, they do raise questions about the validity of the assumption that the initial referral diagnosis (e.g., father or stepfather incest) has any significance in understanding the nature, etiology, or factors associated with the clinical problem presented by these men. More critically, it raises questions about one of the core assumptions about incestuous abuse for almost half of incestuous offenders.

The assumption that incest is the sexual expression of nonsexual needs has led generations of professionals to direct attention toward nonsexual problems typically found in incestuous offenders (e.g., depression, poor self-esteem, difficulties in relationships with adult women). Virtually all sexual behavior may include sexual (i.e., tactile, physiological) and nonsexual (e.g., affectional, recreational) aspects. Little empirical evaluation exists on the sexual arousal of incest offenders. In an early study, Quinsey, Chaplin, and Carrigan (1979) evaluated nine incestuous and seven nonincestuous child molesters and found that incestuous (father or stepfather) offenders exhibited more appropriate (i.e., adult) sexual arousal than nonincestuous child molesters.

Currently, it is not clear what proportion of incestuous offenders are

sexually aroused to children or exactly what factors are sexually arousing about children. Some time ago, Abel, Barlow, Blanchard, and
Guild (1977) demonstrated that rapists were sexually aroused (i.e.,
physiology) to violence against (i.e., a nonsexual dimension) women.
Recently, Quinsey and Chaplin (1988) have reported that in laboratory
assessments, child molesters who have injured their victims were
more sexually responsive to audiotape descriptions of violent sex de-
picting gratuitous infliction of physical violence than were child molesters who had not inflicted injury. It would not be surprising to learn
in the future that the components of sexual arousal to children can be
identified and may include physical features (e.g., softness of skin, size
and appearance of sex organs) and emotional features (e.g., domina-
tion, control, naivete). At the moment, these are matters of clinical
speculation. Future empirical evaluation of the extent and nature (i.e.,
what is sexually arousing about children) will be extremely important
in understanding the nature of incestuous abuse. Nevertheless, it is
likely that sexual arousal to children will be regarded as part of the
problem of incestuous abuse. The degree of this arousal and what
other partners or behaviors are arousing will likely vary among incestuous offenders.

FIXATED OR REGRESSED

Among the more popular notions about men who have sex with children is that there are two distinct types, fixated and regressed (Groth,
Hobson, & Gary, 1982). The fixated offender has a primary sexual orientation toward children. This interest usually begins in adolescence,
and there appears to be no precipitating event associated with the onset of the orientation; male victims are primary targets. The regressed
offender develops a primary sexual orientation to age-mates. The sexual involvement with a child represents a clear change in interest and
behavior, usually occurs at times of stress, may be more episodic; female victims are the primary targets.

While this typology may have been useful in the late seventies and
early eighties to a field and a society trying to understand adult sexual
interest in children, it appears to have lost much of its clinical value.
A number of problems exist with it. It was primarily developed on an
incarcerated sample of sexual offenders. Men in prison may be quite
psychologically distinct from men with the same problem who are not
in prison. To date, no empirical evidence exists for the accuracy of the

typology in classifying adult sexual offenders. Indeed, community therapists report that many offenders have characteristics of both the regressed and the fixated types. It appears that the largest group of offenders is a mixed group, combining certain characteristics of both the fixated and the regressed. For example, in the sample of offenders described by Abel et al. (1988), of the 159 incestuous offenders referred for sexual abuse of a daughter, 12% had abused nonrelated male children, 49% had abused nonrelated female children, and 19% had raped adult females.

A MORE FUNCTIONAL VIEW

It appears that many of the currently accepted concepts about incestuous offenders should be viewed quite cautiously as untested theories. It is premature to make assumptions about the number and sex of victims, the sexual or nonsexual nature of the interest that drives sexual abuse, or the associated features of the clinical problem based on an initial presenting problem of incestuous sexual abuse. Conte (1985) has suggested that, until additional research is available, a more functional view of the common clinical dimensions of adult sexual use of children be taken. This framework suggests that all offenders be assessed for the extent to which they present the following dimensions that appear to be consistent with sexual abuse of children: denial, sexual arousal, sexual fantasies, cognitive distortions (e.g., "it's OK for an adult to rub a child's genitals to make her more sexually responsive when she grows up"), social skills deficits, and other mental health problems (e.g., drug abuse, depression).

Given the apparent lack of reliability in many of the concepts used to direct clinical practice with incestuous offenders in the past, it appears to be quite important for the clinician to be aware that some, if not all, of these clinical dimensions may be present in someone who presents as an incestuous offender. For example, knowledge about the extent to which the adult is sexually aroused to children is vital information in helping the clinician understand what has to be done to help the adult control the behavior that places him at serious legal risk. Knowing the number, relationship, and location of an adult's victims not only tells the clinician what children are at risk, but can be helpful to the clinician and offender in structuring the offender's life early in treatment to help prevent a recurrence until therapy has a chance to be successful in altering the condition.

While it is generally recognized that sexual offenders, like many clients who exhibit negatively balanced behaviors, tend to minimize, rationalize, or distort reports of their behavior, it is fundamentally clear that the first task of assessment is for the clinician to be aware of the possible dynamics and components of the problem that is to be assessed. It is unlikely that an offender will report behavior that the clinician does not ask questions about, seek information on, or otherwise try to elicit. In a study by Abel, Becker, Cunningham-Rathner, and McHugh (1983), offenders increased by 20% the number of types of sexual deviancy they described simply by being reinterviewed by experienced clinicians aware of the tendency for offenders to be involved in more than one type of deviancy. While these results are less than those obtained from the laboratory assessment of the nature of sexual arousal (62%), they do indicate the importance of the clinician's awareness of the nature of sexual offenses and interview efforts to obtain information from the client.

DIFFERENCES IN TREATMENT BETWEEN INCEST PERPETRATORS AND PEDOPHILES

What is different about the treatment of the incest offender? While the material above should raise some questions about the traditional views of the incest offender—especially those that automatically view the incest offender as clinically distinct from the pedophile—there are aspects of the treatment of incestuous fathers, stepfathers, and their families that can be quite unique.

The fact that the offender and victim live in the same house (all or some of the time) and the offender has abused his relationship with the victim places the victim at ongoing risk. The family will consist of a web of relationships (e.g., dyads or triads) and the accompanying emotions, hidden motives, and needs. Family members' reactions to incest can vary across individuals, and within individuals, across time. For example, anger may be directed toward the offender, then the victim, then her mother, and back and forth by each member of the family.

Mental health and social service problems, which may be associated with the sexual abuse or at least must be resolved to protect the child in the future, can vary from family to family. For example, in some families the mother may have few personal or work skills for independent living. Indeed, in some of these families husbands have discouraged efforts to gain independence. Dominance and dependency facilitate helplessness, which assures the husbands' continued sexual access to the children. In such cases, efforts to help the mother gain mastery and living skills will be the key to her ability to protect and care for the children over time. In other families, alcohol or drug use may have been associated with the sexual abuse and thus require intervention if the children are to be protected in the future.

Treatment of family members can involve any of the following: (a) crisis intervention during the early part of disclosure, (b) individual or couple treatment focusing on unresolved or new issues raised by the victimization, (c) supportive psychotherapy as the family deals with the intervention processes of child protection, law enforcement, or medicine, and (d) psychoeducational efforts to teach and help family members learn about sexual abuse and how to be helpful to the member of their family who has been sexually abused. In many cases, the mental health professional must serve as an advocate with other systems to ensure that the family and child are appropriately treated. Many families will require social services, financial help, or other resources (e.g., food stamps, vouchers for treatment, transportation) to make it possible for them to help the child victim.

CHALLENGES IN TREATING OFFENDERS

The treatment of the incest offender brings its own complexity. Based on the initial assessment (e.g., How pervasive is the sexual interest in children? How out of control is the offender? How will the community react to the disclosure?) intervention should be designed to protect society from the offender and the offender from a recurrence of the abuse during the early months of treatment. Decisions about removal of the offender from the home rest, in part, on local practice, but removal may be an important statement to the offender about who is responsible for the abuse. Removal also makes it possible for the therapist to begin working with the family to make those changes essential for restructuring the family to prevent future abuse and to resolve their own individual problems (Wolf, Conte, & Engel-Meinig, 1988).

Treatment of the incest offender will not only have to deal with those problems known to be part of the sexual abuse of children (e.g., sexual arousal to children, cognitive distortions supporting sexual use of a child), but also the range of other problems associated with sexual abuse (e.g., substance use, authoritarian family behaviors, trauma from one's own abuse) and disclosure (e.g., depression, guilt, suicidal ideation).

Incest cases can be quite complex as individual family members present competing needs, feelings, behaviors, or problems at the same time. There has been virtually no examination of the extent to which the individuals or dyads (e.g., the marital couple or mother-victim) in the family and the needs of the family as a group are successfully managed. It is also not known what the effects of certain management strategies are on the victim or other family members (e.g., couple therapy or family group therapy versus individual therapy for each family member). It is not currently known what the ideal assignment of therapists is to these cases or how many therapists can or should work with these cases. Nor is it clear what practice models or theories of therapy are most successful with these cases and which produce no change or may even support continued sexual abuse of children. For the time, it is clear that the therapist should be acutely aware of the importance of keeping treatment focused on ultimate goals and on managing the complexity inherent in the treatment of incest cases.

POLICY ISSUES

What should our policy be toward incest offenders? Social policies are often fragmented with different views of the ultimate objectives being held and implemented by different social actors. There is no single social policy regarding incest offenders held in common by the public, elected officials, and professionals in mental health, social service, and law enforcement. Furthermore, it is virtually impossible, at present, to describe the actual practices dealing with incest offenders that are implemented at state and local levels because there are no descriptive data currently available on how incest offenders are handled (e.g., how many receive treatment, how many are removed from the home, or how many stand trial).

Debates range over whether it is more desirable to remove the incest victim or offender from the home, whether incest offenders should be criminally charged and receive treatment as a condition of probation, or whether the effects of state intervention are worse or as bad as the effects of incest. Such questions are rarely raised when the topic is the nonincestuous offender.

The reasons for society's viewing the incestuous and nonincestuous offender in different terms are complex. They likely include the long-held views (outlined above) in the professional literature that incest is a different kind of clinical problem and that incest offenders are not generally dangerous to nonfamily members. Deeply held views about the sanctity of the family and the rights of parents over children are also partly responsible. Adult narcissism, which identifies with the adult rather than the child, may be part of the dynamic underlying this view. Many of us, when viewing the adult members of our families and communities who abuse their own children, and noting the resemblances between those adults and ourselves, tend to overidentify with the offender and thereby minimize what they do. As a result, we connect not with the pain of their victims or the needs of adult sexual offenders to be helped to control their own behavior, but rather with what it would feel like if we were removed from our homes, lost contact with our family, or had to experience the other logistical and emotional problems that the incest offender faces when the abuse is disclosed.

One of the social policy challenges of this age is to view the incest offender for what he is. To do this we will have to identify with his victims at least as much as we do with him. More critically, we will have to rely on developing knowledge (some of which is outlined above) about the nature of incestuous sexual abuse and a clear understanding of what is in society's best interest. This is not the place to make a complete argument for what that best interest is. However, it seems to me that society is best served if the incest offender stops having sex with children, helps bear the consequences of his behavior, which means that he must suffer most of the hassles that result from disclosure (e.g., leaving the home, reducing his standard of living to support his family and their treatment), enters and remains in treatment himself, and supports the treatment of those whom he has abused. These expectations are not all that different for the nonincestuous offender judged to be appropriate for community-based treatment (Wolf et al., 1988). Implementing such expectations is likely to have significant implications for how incest offenders are handled by the justice system and how mental health professionals respond to these adults.

In the near future, our knowledge and practice with incest offenders is likely to undergo considerable challenge and (one hopes) change. The efforts of researchers, practitioners, and policymakers to deal with the incest offender are likely to set the stage for how society deals with the entire problem of child sexual abuse. This is quite a responsibility!

REFERENCES

Abel, G. G., Barlow, D. H., Blanchard, E. D., & Guild, D. (1977). The components of rapists' sexual arousal. *Archives of General Psychiatry, 34,* 895–903.

Abel, G., Becker, J., Cunningham-Rathner, J., & McHugh, J. (1983). *Motivating sex offenders for treatment with feedback of their psychophysical assessment.* Paper presented at the World Congress of Behavior Therapy, Washington, DC.

Abel, G., Becker, J., Cunningham-Rathner, J., Mittleman, M., & Rouleau, J. L. (1988). Multiple paraphiliac diagnoses among sex offenders. *Bulletin of the American Academy of Psychiatry and the Law, 16*(2), 153–168.

American Psychiatric Association. (1987). *Diagnostic and statistical manual of mental disorders* (3rd ed.). Washington, DC: Author.

Conte, J. R. (1986). Child sexual abuse and the family: A critical analysis. *Journal of Psychotherapy and the Family, 2,* 113–126.

Conte, J. R. (1985). Clinical dimensions of adult sexual use of children. *Behavioral Sciences and the Law, 3,* 341–354.

Conte, J. R., & Schuerman, J. R. (1987). Factors associated with an increased impact of child sexual abuse. *Child Abuse and Neglect: The International Journal, 11,* 201–211.

Groth, A. N., Hobson, W. F., & Gary, T. S. (1982). The child molester: Clinical observations. *Social Work and Human Sexuality, 1,* 129–144.

Quinsey, V. L. (1984). Sexual aggression: Studies of offenders against women. In D. Weisstub (Ed.), *Law and mental health: International perspectives* (Vol. 1). New York: Pergamon.

Quinsey, V. L. (in press). Men who have sex with children. In D. Weisstub (Ed.), *Law and mental health: International perspectives* (Vol. 2). New York: Pergamon.

Quinsey, V. L., & Chaplin, T. C. (1988). Penile responses of child molesters and normals to descriptions of encounters with children involving sex and violence. *Journal of Interpersonal Violence, 3,* 259–274.

Quinsey, V. L., Chaplin, T. C., & Carrigan, W. F. (1979). Sexual preferences among incestuous and nonincestuous child molesters. *Behavior Therapy, 10,* 562–565.

Wolf, S., Conte, J. R., & Engel-Meinig, M. (1988). Assessment and treatment of sexual offenders in a community setting. In L. Walker (Ed.), *A handbook on sexual abuse of children.* New York: Springer.

2

Meeting the Challenge: *Legal Dilemmas and Considerations in Working with the Perpetrator*

Susan R. Bolton
Frank G. Bolton, Jr.

INTRODUCTION

If there were a single descriptive term for the juncture of legal mandates and clinical needs in working with the perpetrator, it might be *ambiguity*. It is not the law that is ambiguous. The law is all too clear and certain in some cases. It is the clinician's role in bringing that law into a therapeutic alliance with a positive outcome for the entire family and community that is ambiguous and, sometimes, impossible. History suggests that when hard legal mandates and softer clinical requirements are tested against each other in a courtroom, it is the clinician who has been most loyal to the law who will more frequently deliver the most positive outcome for all concerned.

Today's uneasy peace between the law and the clinician, in the case of the perpetrator, grows out of fundamental incompatibilities between the two. Yet, both are necessary. The law sponsors life as a society. Clinical work focuses on the needs of individuals, small groups, and families. In this, "the greater good" may clash with "individual need." Again, in more cases than not, "the greater good" will serve as the foundation of the court's decision.

Gelles (1982) has described points of friction between research and the clinician. These same stressors will be found in the juxtapositioning of the law with clinical needs in treating the perpetrator. Legal mandates are nomothetic (broad) and clinical practice is idiographic (individualized). Additionally, legal definitions are often too general to capture the subtle differences in individual matters—differences known to be critical in clinical decision making. Finally, the law seeks closure (i.e., an action or an answer) while the clinician seeks to remain open to new learning on the part of the client or to new information in which to guide the treatment plan. There is no arguing that both the law and clinical thinking are required in working with the perpetrator. To believe that these two separate and necessary elements will be brought into perfect balance is unrealistic. For the clinician, this "balancing act" becomes obvious from the first contact with the suspected perpetrator.

CLINICAL VERSUS LEGAL DEFINITIONS

The clinician or the attorney dealing with the perpetrator is trapped in a definitional quandary. Because the issue is at the same time a criminal, social, behavioral, and medical problem (Conte, 1981), no single profession's definition of the matter will be sufficient. Multiple systems influence definitions here, and these are systems that vary in perspective (Wolfe, Fairbank, Kelly, & Bradlyn, 1981). The result is a lack of consensus (Faller, 1981), definitions that are more abstract than operational, and clinical and statutory definitions that conflict (Bourne & Newberger, 1979). As these inconsistencies are played out in a courtroom, the clinician will soon understand that the law seeks precision in order to offer control, even while the clinician demands a more open definition to allow room for compassion. It is not that the law lacks compassion, it merely demands a clear starting point.

Clinically, legal clarity of the sexually abusive act will mean that some perpetrators will have been seen as sexually abusive when the "clinical sense" seems to deny that intent on the part of the perpetrator. This is especially true in the early phases of community recognition of the problem. During these periods, there is often a feeling among community clinicians that the public and legal professionals are on a "witch hunt" that includes even the slightest physical contact as evidence of inappropriate sexual behavior. The opposite may be true within the legal community. This is a community that may feel the more accepting definitions adopted within clinical practice to be overly compassionate. This compassion may be seen as allowing guilty perpetrators to "walk." At this intersection of the law and clinical work, there is also the criminal defense attorney. These attorneys may intertwine legal matters external to the event in a way that allows a perpetrator, known to both clinician and prosecutor, to escape prosecution. Anger at "the system" from both clinical and legal sectors is the result.

The reality is that no uniform definition based on behavioral indices that are legally defensible will be consistently available to either the attorney or the clinician working with perpetrators. At this point in the art and science that melds legal and clinical work, too many nuances and variables exist that color the court's response in an individual perpetrator's case. Consider the following as only a sample of the variables that "define" an individual case:

- Age of the victim
- Age discrepancy between the victim and the perpetrator (i.e., is this age difference sufficient to create a "power imbalance"?)
- Age of the perpetrator (e.g., juvenile offender)
- Relationship in perpetrator-victim dyad (e.g., relative, nonrelative, sibling, acquaintance, or stranger?)
- Degree of physical contact (e.g., what actions, how much contact, what frequency is sufficient to qualify as an assault?)
- Degree of impact (i.e., behavior change, seriousness, or absence of overt indications in the victim)
- Parallel terminology (i.e., sexual abuse, sexual assault, sexual exploitation)
- Diagnostic discriminations (i.e., pedophilia or not)
- Etiological discriminations (i.e., character disorders, mental disorders, habit formation, or previous victimization)

The expectation that a legal system will meet these needs and provide prior consideration of these variables in an anticipatory way is not a rational hope. For some time to come, the clinician will serve as the gatekeeper for these issues, a role that provides additional frustration.

THE DUTY TO REPORT

Often, it is the clinician who is called on to place the individual behavioral complexities of a family together into a meaningful whole. In the case of sexually aberrant behavior, the court must be told. Clinicians would, in some cases, prefer to rely on the "therapeutic alliance" to deal with the sexually aberrant behavior in a less official and presumably more nurturing way. Plainly spoken, this is not an acceptable strategy under the law, and those who select it will be prosecuted. In each state of the United States, persons who have some responsibility for children and who have reasonable grounds to believe that a child is or has been a victim of sexual abuse must report that information to the appropriate authorities.

There is no question that the disclosure of sexual abuse perpetration that occurs in the context of a therapeutic relationship conflicts with the clinician's confidentiality mandate. There is no question that such disclosure may terminate the therapeutic relationship or result in lost therapeutic ground. There are those who would argue for specific situations that would allow the clinician to elect not to report. But courts that have considered the question have been less than open to that allowance. The decision of these courts has been that reporting will be mandated despite the assumed disruption of confidentiality or the presumptive destruction of the therapeutic effort. The court believes that the potential disruption to the child's life takes precedence over the disruption of the therapy. It is also important to the clinician to recognize that additional elements of the therapeutic process may be negated.

Many child abuse reporting statutes reach beyond mere reporting and abrogate the testimonial privilege between the physician or psychologist and patient. Although the language varies from state to state, there is a certain message that the physician-patient, husband-wife, and psychologist-client privilege (except the attorney-client privilege) shall not pertain. The core of this language is that clinical confidentiality is removed for the purposes of any civil, criminal, administrative, or judicial proceeding that pertains to suspected child maltreatment.

Statutes abrogating the privilege between client and therapist may result in the clinician being required to testify about the content of the communications that took place during therapy, as well as disclosing any testing or other records that were maintained. Clinicians who attempt to circumvent this mandate by failing to keep records will find themselves, in many cases, in violation of state licensure or certification laws. And, the failure to maintain written records does not remove the clinician's likelihood of being called to testify.

Some states have interpreted reporting statutes so broadly that clinicians have been compelled to testify in private civil cases for damages in situations in which the claim for damage originated in a sexually abusive incident. For example, in *Carson v. Jackson* (1985), a Florida appellate court required a clinician to testify concerning a baby-sitter's confession of sexual abuse in a civil action brought by the child victim's parents against the baby-sitter. This court specifically rejected the argument that the statute should be limited to administrative and judicial proceedings brought by the child protection agency of the state. In contrast, the California statute abrogating the privilege between psychologist and client applies only to the initial report of abuse mandated by the child abuse reporting law as seen in *People v. Stritzinger* (1983). The fact of the matter is that the clinician must be prepared to testify if a confession or a report is an element of the therapeutic work with the family. The single intra-therapeutic insulation against this fact is a warning at the outset that any disclosure may result in reporting and possible testimony. Such a warning does provide the client an option. Such a warning is appropriate, but it will serve to frustrate therapeutic progress for clinician and client alike. This legal intrusion upon therapy has not escaped the attention of critics.

Smith and Meyer (1984) have argued that child abuse reporting laws should be reconsidered due to their potential for interfering with successful therapy. Noting that "protecting the communications of therapy has been called a sine qua non for successful therapy" (p.358), they argue that reporting laws interfere with voluntary treatment of child abusers. One of the purposes of the reporting laws is to encourage treatment to stop the abuse and to keep the families together. The mandatory reporting by clinicians is counterproductive when the disclosure occurs during a voluntary treatment sought before the authorities were aware of the abuse. Smith and Meyer also argued that the requirement that clinicians testify about information revealed in therapy further damages the therapeutic relationship. This lessens the possibility, and likelihood, of voluntary treatment. They propose that the clinician's duty to report should be narrowed. Beyond mere reporting, disclosures in therapy should be absolutely confidential as in the attorney-client privilege.

Hurley (1985), writing of California's mandatory reporting law, noted that California law requires reporting not only of direct observation of children, but of situations where clinicians gain facts that would cause a reasonable person to suspect abuse of children. While these statutes probably pass constitutional muster due to the court's compelling state interest in protecting children outweighing the individual right of privacy of the client, a question remains. Hurley noted that, without the assurance of confidential communication, therapy may not be sought, or the client may be less honest based on a feared loss of the children or of criminal prosecution.

Coleman (1986), writing specifically of incest offenders, proposed that, in situations where treatment was sought voluntarily, mandatory reporting statutes unjustifiably weigh the protection of the child more heavily than other important interests that might exist.

When the perpetrator, rather than the victim, is the client, Coleman (1986) believed that reporting by clinicians should be permissive rather than mandatory, but this liberal inclusion of "optional" reporting is not recommended when the client is a sexually abused child who remains at risk. In this situation, Coleman recommended that the mandatory reporting requirement be retained. The argument made in support of permissive reporting is a familiar one to clinicians: The confidentiality provided in the psychotherapeutic relationship is necessary to ensure the proper diagnosis and treatment through the availability of full disclosure in a safe environment. If (as is generally accepted in clinical settings) the foundation of treatment is the agreement of confidentiality, and if effective treatment is in the best interest of all concerned, Coleman believed that confidentiality must be returned to the clinician.

Miller and Weinstock (1987) echoed the concern that state laws fail to adequately weigh the benefits of reporting against the costs of breaching confidentiality when evidence of the abuse originates with the perpetrator during the course of therapy. The specific suggestions that follow their argument include the requirement of reporting if the victim is not in treatment or if the clinician's suspicion is that the abuse is ongoing. However, under their suggestion only the identity of the victim, and not that of the perpetrator, would be disclosed if the perpetrator is currently in an abuse-directed therapeutic relationship. If the abuse is continuing despite the therapy, or if the therapy is inappropriately terminated, the perpetrator would then be reported. In the case of the inpatient program, the perpetrator would only be reported if that were a condition for the receipt of services.

There are both legal and clinical advocates on both sides of the arguments. Those advocating statutory change appear to be having little impact on recent legislation. There is no evidence that state statutes are being tempered. In fact, the past 20 years of reporting statute development has found this area of the law to be liberalized in the opposite direction, requiring that increasing numbers and descriptions of individuals be required to report and testify. A summary view would warn the clinician that reporting will be mandated, record keeping is advised, and testimony will be a likely requirement. Failure to recognize these aspects of working with the perpetrator could result in civil liability.

FAILURE TO REPORT

Most clinicians are familiar with the 1976 *Tarasof* decision in California. Attorney and child maltreatment specialist Besharov (1986) suggested that this decision applies directly to a clinician's work with perpetrators. *Tarasof v. Regents of the University of California* (1976) established a cause of action against a psychologist who failed to warn of an impending danger he learned of in the course of therapy. His client disclosed the intent to kill an individual, and he later killed her. In language that is important to all who work with possible perpetrators of violence against others, the court found:

> Defendant therapists cannot escape liability merely because (the victim) herself was not their patient. When a therapist determines, or pursuant to the standards of his profession should determine that his patient presents a serious danger of violence to another, he incurs an obligation to use reasonable care to protect the intended victim against such danger. The discharge of this duty may require the therapist to take one or more of various steps depending upon the nature of the case. Thus it may call for him to warn the intended victim or others likely to apprise the victim of the danger, to notify the police or to take whatever other steps are reasonably necessary under the circumstance. (551 P.2d at 340)

This case did not involve a sexual abuse perpetrator, but it is difficult to argue against the concept that the suspected or known perpetrator is not one who "represents a serious danger of violence to another."

A related failure to report circumstance is civil liability for injuries sustained by children for negligent failure to diagnose and report the Battered Child Syndrome. In a California case (*Landeros v. Flood*, 1976), the Supreme Court of California held that proper treatment of a child's Battered Child Syndrome would have included a report to local law enforcement. This report would have resulted in an investigation followed by protective custody. Since the defendant in the case failed to make such a report, the child was returned to her parents and was later severely abused. This resulted in a claim of negligence against both the physician and the hospital. The conclusion must be that the clinician may be subject to both civil and criminal liability if he/she fails to take steps to protect a child known or reasonably known to be at risk for future harm at the hands of his/her client. The clinical question here is that of the veracity of what is being reported to the clinician. This is a question for which few solid answers exist.

The Reporter's Credibility

The clinician working with the perpetrator plays two competing roles. The mandate exists for both clinical assessment and for forensic assessment. The clinical assessment establishes empathy. The forensic assessment establishes truth within the parameters of the law, a demand that requires fact finding as well as collection and interpretation of evidence. Many clinicians are underprepared to play the investigator role required by the court.

Much of the information in clinical work such as this originates in the child. There is a strong suggestion that, with some exceptions (e.g., the domestic relations case), children tend to be more truthful than untruthful about these circumstances. However, like all others, children may sometimes be less than completely accurate or show some weakened memory capacity regarding the event(s). Research indicates that children are no better or worse in eyewitness accuracy than adults, but this research cannot replicate the trauma of the sexually abusive event. Research is continuing in the divorce-related sexual abuse allegation, but the win/lose orientation of the parental relationship may influence child testimony in unanticipated ways. In all of these situations, the court seems likely to be extra protective of the child, a position easily supported. The clinician who supports the perpetrator's testimony against what appears to be reasonable information from the child victim must be on very solid ground; a "feeling" that the client is truthful is not sufficient.

If information in support of the perpetrator is to be brought forward in contradiction to the child's testimony, a minimal evaluation/investigation will include an understanding of social supports, family structure, family interaction, geographic isolation, household density, social participation, family decision making, roles and tasks of individual family members, attachment histories, communication and disciplinary strategies, the quality of the marital and sexual relationship of the adults, personality variables, sexual attitudes and knowledge, impulse control capacities, hostility levels, self-concept of all family members, previous victimization experiences, and capacity for affection. Even this may not be sufficient.

In the truthful, innocent perpetrator's favor has been the increasing belief in false allegations of sexual abuse. In a recent work, Bulkley

(1988) noted that claims of increasing false accusations of sexual abuse are unsupported by the data. Quinn (1988) noted that current estimates of false reporting range from 3% to 8% of sexual abuse complaints received by social service departments. An ongoing survey of domestic relations courts, reported on by Quinn, estimated that 2.5% of contested custody and visitation cases include a sexual abuse allegation, and 22% of these were probably false. Current work in new child interviewing strategies (Bolton & Bolton, 1987) offer some hope to the clinician in this area, but there are still unanswered problems.

The clinician must understand that children have moved from a position of being viewed as incompetent and unworthy of credibility in complaints of sexual abuse (Goodman & Helgeson, 1985) to being seen as infallible witnesses (Quinn, 1988). The courts recognize that neither extreme is appropriate and will consider evidence fully. The credibility of today's child witness, in allegations of sexual abuse, is strong in the eyes of the court. The clinician working with the perpetrator must feel the weight of some extra responsibility and preparation if he/she is to establish the most responsible advocacy for the client.

THE CRIMINAL PROSECUTION

Currently, there is a trend toward criminal prosecution of incest perpetrators (U.S. Attorney General, 1984). The discovery of sexual abuse or incest more frequently leads to criminal prosecution than other forms of child maltreatment. Writers in the field have suggested the importance of this prosecution rests with the associated protection of the victim, the compelling of an admission or finding of guilt, and the obtaining of the necessary authority to mandate treatment for the perpetrator. The entire area of sexual abuse has a greater criminal justice "flavor" than the other areas of child maltreatment. This is a direction that may come as a surprise for the clinician first prepared to work in the related family violence arenas.

The clinician in the sexual abuse case may be asked to take on the additional evaluative questions of whether criminal prosecution would be successful, whether it would be helpful, its possible impact on the perpetrator, the possible impact on the balance of the family, and the differential impact depending on the success or failure of the prosecution. These are not questions easily answered by traditional clinical training, and additional training is an immediate demand. These are not questions easily answered by the information usually at hand, and, finally, the process of acquiring answers may be unfamiliar to the clinician. The courtroom is the workplace of the attorney, not the clinician. This difference may sometimes result in the underprepared clinician working against the perpetrator despite the best of intentions.

In a typical prosecution involving a child sexual abuse or incest perpetrator, there will be no physical evidence. The success or failure of prosecution will often be based on some credibility balance among the child witness, the experts, and the alleged perpetrator. The court's protectiveness of this child witness may frustrate a clinician called on to support the perpetrator.

Trauma experienced by child victims is a topic of heated discussion in legal and clinical circles. This is never more true than in the child sexual abuse or incest prosecution. Problems associated with child witnesses in face-to-face confrontations with perpetrators in the courtroom have been a significant impediment to prosecution. Many writers have proposed alternative strategies intended to shield child witnesses from this confrontation. Recently, the United States Supreme Court faced this issue squarely. While not completely closing the door on alternatives to face-to-face confrontation between the perpetrator and the child witness, the Supreme Court has resoundingly affirmed the Sixth Amendment's requirements for face-to-face confrontation, by rejecting the use of a screen to physically shield the child witness from the alleged perpetrator while testifying in the courtroom (*Coy v. Iowa*, 1988).

In this decision, the Court reiterated that the confrontation clause rights are not absolute and may give way to other important interests. But the Supreme Court has clearly held, as a matter of routine, that alternatives to face-to-face confrontation cannot be afforded to child witnesses in sexual abuse prosecutions. The Court noted: "We leave for another day the question whether any exceptions exist. Whatever they may be, they would surely be allowed only when necessary to further an important public policy" (101 L.Ed.2d at 867).

In a concurring opinion, Justice Sandra Day O'Connor, joined by Justice White, wrote of the appropriate situations in which other competing interests would allow the use of procedural devices to shield a child witness from courtroom trauma. She offered, "nothing in today's decision necessarily dooms such efforts by state legislatures to protect child witnesses" (101 Ed.2d at 868). Justice O'Connor noted that she would permit use of a device if it was necessary to further important public policies, but that decisions must be made on a case-by-case basis as to whether there was a necessity to protect the child witness from face-to-face confrontation.

The presumed trauma to the child witness brought about by face-to-face confrontation with the perpetrator may lead to criminal prosecution being brought less often and may allow less successful prosecutions when they are attempted. The vindication of the alleged perpetrator in a criminal court, through the vehicle of a jury's "not guilty" verdict, may become a factor in a therapeutic relationship. Therapeutic continuation is at issue; progress toward disclosure is at issue. The jury's failure to believe the child witness may impose additional stress on the child and all other family members. It is only the most skilled and the most committed clinician who is able to maintain a therapeutic alliance under these trying circumstances. Whether the perpetrator will retain physical participation and accept intellectual and emotional responsibility for his/her role in the events despite legal outcomes is the true measure of the clinician's capacity.

SUMMARY

It is clear that the clinician attempting to work with the perpetrator in the sexual abuse or incest situation holds an extra measure of responsibility. That responsibility extends to all members of the perpetrator's family, to the victim's family if separate, and to the community at large. The role is that of empathic evaluator and forensically sophisticated investigator. Information becomes evidence. Confidences become public record. The privacy of the clinician's questions and answers is removed and made the subject of scrutiny by other clinicians, the media, and the public at large. The dark questions that arise in the clinician himself/herself, as well as those imposed by outsiders, weigh heavily. In this, the legal system may at times be a partner and at times, an opponent. Both roles are necessary for justice to be served.

REFERENCES

Besharov, D. (1986). Child abuse: Arrest and prosecution decision making. *American Criminal Law Review, 24*, 315–377.

Bolton, F. G., & Bolton, S. R. (1987). *Working with violent families: A guide for clinical and legal practitioners.* Newbury Park, CA: Sage.

Bourne, R., & Newberger, E. H. (Eds.). (1979). *Critical perspectives on child abuse.* Lexington, MA: D. C. Heath.

Bulkley, J. (1988). Legal proceedings, reforms, and emerging issues in child sexual abuse cases. *Behavioral Sciences and the Law, 6*, 153–180.

Carson v. Jackson, 466 So.2d 1188 (Fla. App. 1985).

Coleman, P. (1986). Creating therapist-incest offender exception to mandatory child abuse reporting statutes: When the psychiatrist knows best. *University of Cincinnati Law Review, 54*, 1113–1152.

Conte, J. (1981). Sexual abuse of children: Enduring issues for social work. In J. R. Conte & D. Shore (Eds), *Social work and child sexual abuse*. New York: Haworth.

Coy v. Iowa, 108 S.Ct. 2798.

Faller, K. C. (1981). *Social work with abused and neglected children: A manual of interdisciplinary practice*. New York: Free Press.

Gelles, R. J. (1982). Applying research on family violence to clinical practice. *Journal of Marriage and the Family, 44*, 2–9.

Goodman, G. S., & Helgeson, V. S. (1985). Child sexual assault: Children's memory and the law. In American Bar Association (Ed.), *National policy conference on legal reforms in child sexual abuse cases*. Washington, DC: National Legal Resource Center for Child Advocacy and Protection.

Hurley, M. M. (1985). Duties in conflict: Must psychotherapists report child abuse inflicted by clients and confided in therapy? *San Diego Law Review, 22*, 645–668.

Landeros v. Flood, 131 Cal. Rptr. 69, 551 P.2d 389 (1976).

Miller, R. D., & Weinstock, R. (1987). Conflict of interest between therapist-patient confidentiality and the duty to report sexual abuse of children. *Behavioral Sciences and the Law, 5*, 161–174.

People v. Stritzinger, 194 Cal. Rptr. 431, 668 P.2d 738 (1983).

Quinn, K. M. (1988). The credibility of children's allegations of sexual abuse. *Behavioral Sciences and the Law, 6*, 181–199.

Smith, S. R., & Meyer, R. G. (1984). Reporting laws and psychotherapy: A time for reconsideration. *International Journal of Law and Psychiatry, 7*, 351–366.

Tarasof v. Regents of the University of California, 131 Cal. Rptr. 14, 551 P.2d 334 (1976).

U.S. Attorney General. (1984). *Family violence in America: The final report of the Attorney General's Task Force on family violence*. Washington, DC: Attorney General's Office.

Wolfe, D. A., Fairbank, J. A., Kelly, J. A., & Bradlyn, D. (1981). *Child abuser's response to stressful and non-stressful parent-child interactions*. Paper presented at the First Family Violence Researchers Conference, Durham, NH.

PART II

Profiles and Identification

3

A Comparative Profile of the Incest Perpetrator: *Background Characteristics, Abuse History, and Use of Social Skills*

David T. Ballard
Gary D. Blair
Sterling Devereaux
Logan K. Valentine
Anne L. Horton
Barry L. Johnson

INTRODUCTION

The more we study incest, the more we realize offenders look like everyone else, making identification and treatment all the more challenging. According to Herman's study (1981), the casual observer would not suspect that these perpetrators would commit incest, due to the ofttimes exemplary image they project—church-going, respected, hardworking, competent, often successful men, who were admired as perfect patriarchs. Groth (1978), however, described the generally accepted view of perpetrators, which, although a myth, still serves much of the clinical community as well as the general public. Incest perpetrators were viewed as (a) dirty old men, (b) strangers to their victims, (c) retarded, (d) alcoholic or drug-addicted, (e) sexually frustrated, (f) insane, and (g) increasingly violent over time.

While those offenders housed in more highly restrictive settings (primarily prison/forensic mental health units) often may reflect a number of negative characteristics, these traits cannot be generalized to describe the "average" incest perpetrator, as has been done in the past. Subsequent research done in different settings, particularly community-based (Horton & Williams, 1988), indicates that perpetrators vary considerably in their characteristics, abuse and criminal/mental health history, and social skills. These factors, as well as the details of the specific offense, attitude, and choice of victim, impact greatly on offender placement in a specific treatment setting and their ultimate prognosis. It is also critical to note in any comparison of offenders that those in the prison sample represent only the inmates selected for the sex offender treatment program.

A HISTORICAL OVERVIEW AND BRIEF REVIEW OF THE LITERATURE

Characteristics

Traditionally, incest perpetrators have been lumped together in one homogeneous group. Current literature indicates that incest offenders tend to be a more complex, heterogeneous population (Groth, 1983; McIvor & Duthie, 1986). Finkelhor and Williams (1988) cited the critical need to evaluate treatment programs; yet treatment issues are only beginning to emerge, and agreement on approaches is further hindered by a lack of understanding of the offender himself. It stands to reason that, in order to serve this population, more accurate information must be gathered. Because Kelly (1982) has demonstrated that treatment can affect attitudes, beliefs, and sexual arousal patterns, it would appear that more input directly from the offenders would be an important link to planning services.

Constructing a reliable profile of the perpetrator is obviously difficult, and misconceptions abound. Julian, Mohr and Lapp (1980) found the offender to be middle-aged, rather than "old," and to have a lower degree of education. Other researchers challenge the reliability of these figures primarily because of the inconsistency in reporting practices. Our research was designed to assess and compare incest offenders found in prison, mental health facilities, and community-based treatment settings in an effort to get a more complete profile of the offender. Our findings emphasize the need for observing the individuality and distinctions of these clients as well as the need for developing a broader typology of offenders to serve the diagnostic and clinical community. Finkelhor and Williams (1988) reaffirmed that:

> . . . such men (incest perpetrators) are not a homogeneous group. Even a characteristic that is not widespread, like low intelligence, may be the marker for a particular subgroup that is theoretically and clinically important. (p.38)

General agreement appears to exist for factors involving certain personality types, or at least a commonality of traits. Clearly, the use of relatives for sexual purposes indicates a lack of appropriateness and the blurring of boundaries. Immaturity at some level is also almost invariably involved and, by definition, this behavior is antisocial in that it violates moral taboos and the law. The use of rationalization and compartmentalization are also universal, and, although the perpetrator may not appear to be socially impaired, there is an air of secrecy and isolation about the family's private life that must be maintained at all times. The nature and interdependence of the family almost assures this, at least initially, and defies detection. The use of alcohol and drugs is reported by researchers to vary from less than one-third (Burgess, 1978) up to two-thirds (Muldoon, 1981). In our study, again these figures were lower and were used to support minimization and denial, also common features.

While the prison population is the group that originally was the subject of much generalization, the forensic units also provided a share of the misconceptions. Attempts have been made to classify offenders into treatment categories with particular emphasis on the major psychiatric diagnoses, personality disorders, and paraphiliacs (Knopp, 1984). In Holmes's book (1983), Dr. William Erickson classified incest perpetrators as psychotic, sociopathic, or endogamous. Yet, Groth (1978) stated that it is unusual in the incest population, to find signs of hallucinations, delusions, catatonic stupors or uncontrollable manic excitement, bizarre or highly infantile behavior or any other symptoms of active, clinical psychosis. This aspect is particularly lacking in community-based treatment where Parents United does not even classify these offenders according to any pathology.

Because the psychiatric community is drawn from those showing pathological illnesses contributing to their criminal behavior, it is helpful to consider that the incest in these cases is often a secondary diagnosis. This may also be an important consideration with the prison population, as their criminal offense may have convicted them and the deviant sexual behavior may be identified as an additional problem.

Abuse History

The sexual history of offenders has also received much interest, with a great deal of focus on the theories that incest perpetrators have a sexual propensity for children and are unlikely to molest others outside the family. As with many social science theories, these results have proven inconclusive. Yet, clearly the exceptions to the rules are very important to note especially when designing treatment programs. While adult heterosexual sex is unsatisfactory to some, it is not repugnant to all, particularly the sexual addicts (See Chapter 9). And while the incest perpetrator may be statistically less likely to offend outside the family, generally it is not accurate to assume this behavior does not occur. Those perpetrators who do offend, in and out of the family, often have histories of large numbers of victims. Establishing a single pathological clinical profile is not possible. Marital and sexual satisfaction are also claimed by some to be no worse for incest perpetrators than for many other men (Parker & Parker, 1986).

Other areas of sexual and physical abuse have commanded research interest. There are numerous claims that abusers are also victims who certainly need clinical attention where this exists. The lack of empathy for the perpetrator is very evident when clinicians and others do not address his victim status as a key element of treatment. This study looks closely at the various forms of abuse and the likelihood of victims becoming perpetrators and of their perpetrating earlier and in a more deviant fashion. Again, social learning theory lends itself to possible explanations for the criminal behavior, although it fails to explain why many victims do not go on to harm others. Their ability to overcome this tendency may prove more useful than the reasons victims tend to offend. The link between physical abuse and sexual abuse is also explored.

Social Skills

Over the past decade increasing attention has been devoted to understanding social skills, particularly in respect to this clientele. Yet, many authors skip definitions assuming a generalized agreement as to the meaning of the term. Much of what we know today has come from a foundation in behavior modification (Wolpe & Lazarus, 1966). However, the terms "molar," "molecular," "social support," "social networks," "social competence," "social performance," and "interpersonal behavior" are but a few of the many offshoots of the undefined social skills concept.

Because the ability to "play the system" appears to be of considerable importance in the selection of treatment setting, a clearer understanding of this important variable is attempted here. "Playing the system" is seen by many clinical observers as the key variable to community-based placement. The system currently is emphasizing a mental health approach, so the offender who jumps on this bandwagon is seen as more compliant and insightful. While social skills appear to vary considerably, most writers and researchers agree that there is a lack of social skills, but they do not clearly explain what that means.

This study was designed to assess the social skills of offenders, based on the following criteria gathered from the literature, by observing the treatment focus of a number of in- and outpatient programs. Fifteen different variables were selected to measure the relative social skills of the incest perpetrator. The inappropriateness of the incest act (social perception), the ability to communicate verbally, and the ability to assert themselves in a variety of social situations were the broad categories used to determine the social skill level targeted for this study. The level of social isolation and social withdrawal was measured by the number of friends they had and their marital status, ratings on a self-described social activity scale, and the lack of social skills as self-reported on a semantic differential scale.

Another phase representing the social skill level of the perpetrators was their response to questions about their ability to empathize with their victims. It included whether or not they had been physically or sexually abusive to other family members, as well as their responses to questions about their satisfaction level in relationships with spouse and others. Finally, the perpetrators were asked about the reason for selecting their victim and how they became involved in the incestuous behavior. Our instrument combined these specific factors into an operational package that explored "in-depth" the level of awareness, as well as a checklist of reported behaviors and perceptions.

A final analysis of these variables combines a concern for many of the social characteristics expressed earlier, and specific references will be made to the social and abuse profiles as variables here. It is because of the complexity of defining this area without neglecting key concerns that the reader will be referred to the earlier part of the finding to avoid repetition. The emphasis on the level of restriction ordered for offenders reflects the conscious or unconscious assessment of the social skills variables. To give the reader an overview of our multilevel approach to this complex area, the specific combination of variables, including examples of the questions offenders addressed, are included in the findings and discussion.

FINDINGS AND DISCUSSION

Because of the interactional components involved in treating the incest perpetrator, the areas of diagnostic and treatment concerns are divided into three specific categories for discussion purposes: (a) demographic variables, (b) abuse history, and (c) social skills. The issues discussed in the final category overlap with the first two and should be seen as a combination of factors that work together to indicate a typology of subtypes rather than one specific profile.

Personal Characteristics of the Incest Offender

Basic demographic variables were collected on all four populations—both inpatient and community-based—and are reported here in an effort to observe the clinically important similarities and differences. The total population of 373 incest perpetrators is presented. Not surprisingly, the vast majority of perpetrators were males and of a relatively mature age (but certainly not qualifying as "old"). The tendency for offenders in the community to be slightly older may reflect the greater social abilities of these perpetrators to avoid detection. Ethnicity in this population is of interest because the prison population traditionally has an overrepresentation of nonwhite inmates, but this does not occur in this study. In fact, a larger percentage is evident in the community-based program. Overall social disapproval apparently does not consider color an important variable.

Levels of education are in keeping with other studies in that they were lower than the national average, and incarcerated offenders were statistically lower than those in the community. Income and employment records boldly reflect the economic advantages of allowing these breadwinners to continue to support their families. Because more of them remain with their families, this advantage speaks loudly to policymakers who see the economic advantages. Health status and the use of alcohol and drugs appear less dramatic than those reported in other studies. Similar to Burgess (1978), our findings indicate that the role of alcohol appears to be overemphasized, and actually less than a third could be considered involved with alcohol during the offense period, and even fewer were addicted. Our figures fell well below a third. However, treatment for alcohol and drug abuse where applicable is an important issue for those so addicted. Clinicians need to provide for these aspects specifically in the change process. This treatment can usually be best accomplished for inpatients and may account for a higher percentage being incarcerated under these circumstances, based more on their treatment needs than dangerousness. Religious affiliation is lower for the institutionalized samples and reflects not only a behavior that conflicts with a belief system, but also shows a lower level of social involvement and potential referral resources. This variable as well as other social characteristics within this section will be part of the social skills package that includes a broad consideration of these interacting factors.

Personality factors again are elusive and often misleading, but a content analysis of perpetrators' similarities reflected some commonalities. There was an almost universal need to deny their offense and to demand secrecy from their victims. And while some offenders—particularly those accepted by any treatment program, regardless of setting—do admit responsibility, they always have explanations and excuses initially. Whether their behavior was symptomatic of a fixation on young children or done for other reasons, overall the issue of "control" appears to be a primary factor. Others in the community may not view the offender as an aggressive personality at all, yet family members invariably are caught up in this issue. Self-esteem is also generally observed to be low, as a defensive response or an unclear understanding of their needs.

Many families see the victims as their father's "favorite" and leave her without familial support or maternal concern. While the oldest child is often selected, other younger siblings may move into the victim role when the original victim moves on. Overcontrol and overly restrictive behavior are common in jealous offenders, and false accusations of promiscuity and seduction are often aimed at victims. Additional feelings of guilt, self-blame, and worthlessness fall on the victim and the offender, in many cases. This tyranny is relatively common and poses an additional threat to normal development for the child and the perpetrator.

While dysfunction may originate from this aberrant behavior, it is usually other deviant behavior that is identified as needing treatment. Without alert treatment providers, this area of anomaly may be—and historically has been—overlooked and not specifically explored by untrained or uncomfortable therapists. It is still not usually offered by the offender or his family unless there is a specific inquiry. Direct and detailed questions must be asked, or a conspiracy of silence may result and holistic treatment will be aborted.

Sexual History

The tie-in between physical and sexual abuse has been a source of considerable recent interest. In this study, the prison and mental health sample are noticeably higher with respect to physical abuse and sexual acting out. This research observed some important similarities

Table 3.1 Perpetrator's Social and Marital Profiles

	INSTITUTIONAL		COMMUNITY-BASED		
VARIABLE	Prison	Mental Health	Parents United	Private Practice	TOTALS
Sample size	N = 63	N = 41	N = 240	N = 39	N = 383
Sex					
males	95.2%	100.0%	97.9%	100.0%	97.9%
females	4.8%	0.0%	2.1%	0.0%	2.1%
Age (mean yrs)	38.1	37.1	39.4	41.0	38.8
Ethnicity					
white	88.9%	92.3%	81.9%	86.5%	84.6%
nonwhite	11.1%	7.7%	18.1%	13.5%	15.4%
Education (mean no. yrs)	11.6	11.2	12.3	11.9	12.1
Current employment					
Full-time	26.3%	27.0%	80.6%	65.8%	65.1%
Part-time	0.0%	24.3%	6.5%	5.3%	7.1%
Unemployed	73.7%	48.6%	12.9%	28.9%	27.7%
Previous employment[a]					
Full-time	77.4%	65.0%	72.1%	74.4%	72.5%
Part-time	4.8%	17.5%	5.6%	10.3%	7.2%
Unemployed	17.7%	17.5%	22.3%	15.4%	20.3%
Income (monthly ave.)	$ 812	$ 746	$1413	$1100	$1236
Religious affiliation					
Protestant	38.1%	23.1%	54.1%	43.6%	47.1%
Catholic	11.1%	7.7%	19.3%	15.4%	16.3%
Other	28.6%	25.7%	9.0%	20.5%	15.3%
None	22.2%	43.6%	17.6%	20.5%	21.4%
Current health status					
Excellent	19.1%	17.5%	29.6%	18.9%	25.5%
Good	54.0%	65.0%	45.4%	43.2%	48.7%
Fair/poor	27.0%	17.5%	25.0%	37.8%	25.8%
Previous health status[a]					
Excellent	15.9%	15.0%	24.5%	23.1%	21.9%
Good	52.4%	45.0%	41.2%	48.7%	44.3%
Fair/poor	31.8%	40.0%	34.4%	28.2%	33.8%
Current use of alcohol					
Habitual	1.7%	0.0%	2.5%	0.0%	1.9%
Occasional-frequent	1.7%	10.0%	25.9%	12.9%	19.1%
Never-seldom	96.6%	90.0%	71.6%	94.9%	79.0%

(continued)

Table 3.1 (Continued)

| VARIABLE | INSTITUTIONAL | | COMMUNITY-BASED | | |
	Prison	Mental Health	Parents United	Private Practice	TOTALS
Previous use of alcohol[a]					
Habitual	27.0%	15.0%	16.3%	17.9%	18.1%
Occasional-frequent	34.9%	35.0%	35.7%	43.6%	36.3%
Never-seldom	38.1%	50.0%	48.1%	38.4%	45.6%
Current use of drugs					
Habitual	1.7%	0.0%	2.5%	0.0%	1.9%
Occasional-frequent	1.7%	0.0%	4.3%	2.6%	3.2%
Never-seldom	96.6%	100.0%	93.2%	97.4%	94.9%
Previous use of drugs[a]					
Habitual	22.2%	10.0%	7.3%	15.4%	10.9%
Occasional-frequent	19.0%	10.0%	14.2%	12.8%	14.4%
Never-seldom	58.7%	80.0%	78.5%	71.8%	74.7%
Psychiatric history					
History of	14.3%	24.4%	N/A[b]	7.7%	15.4%
Hospitalized for	25.4%	19.5%	N/A[b]	7.7%	18.9%
Current marital status					
Married	34.9%	35.9%	64.6%	59.0%	56.2%
Single/divorced/ widowed	58.8%	53.8%	31.3%	25.7%	37.5%
Other	6.3%	10.3%	4.2%	15.4%	6.3%
Previous marital status[a]					
Married	76.2%	67.5%	84.0%	73.7%	79.8%
Single/divorced/ widowed	12.7%	15.0%	9.9%	18.4%	11.8%
Other	11.1%	17.5%	6.1%	7.9%	8.3%
Number of marriages					
One	53.8%	60.7%	57.2%	51.5%	56.4%
Two	34.6%	17.9%	31.1%	27.3%	30.1%
Three	7.7%	17.9%	8.6%	18.2%	10.1%
Four or more	3.8%	3.6%	3.2%	3.0%	3.3%
Previous marital satisfaction (mean) 1 = Low 10 = High					
Sexual	5.9	5.0	4.0	5.1	4.5
Emotional	4.6	3.8	3.2	4.9	3.6
Overall	5.1	4.4	3.4	5.7	4.0

NOTE: a. These statistics refer to the time the incest was discovered.
       b. NA = not applicable

that reflect the choice and advisability of more restrictive settings for these more violent clients. Clinicians are encouraged to study these considerations as they are an important component of treatment.

A major concern and treatment issue also addresses the likelihood of abuse victims to act out toward others, particularly their own children. Pelto (1981) found ten times as many and Langevin (1983) over five times as many childhood sexual abuse experiences in the histories of incest offenders as compared to nonoffender controls. Groth, Hobson, and Gary (1982), in an attempt to partially explain why the phenomenon of sexual victimization is so commonly found to have occurred with perpetrators, theorized that the former incest victim becomes a perpetrator in an effort to resolve sexual trauma that is unresolved. In other words, the male child may try to combat feelings of powerlessness inherent in being a victim by eventually identifying with the perpetrator and reversing roles. He becomes the powerful one rather than the victim. He is then reenacting, in his own perpetrating, the characteristics of his own victimization in an attempt to restore to himself the feeling of being in control. It may also reflect repressed anger and the need to be rejected.

The affect that this theorizing might have on the social learning and socialization theories that have been developed might prove meaningful in helping to anticipate what kinds of beliefs and behaviors could be expected from perpetrators. McBroom (1979) reviewed the well-established theories of socializing agents and role learning: Children learn specific types of behavior and roles from socializing agents, parents usually being the most prominent agents. It has also been argued that child sexual conduct, the perceptions of child sexuality in society, and changes in conduct and status "are more the result of cultural-social factors than they are the result of biological-hormonal or physiological factors."

It has been shown that children tend to modify their standards of moral evaluation in the direction of a model's judgments. Expounders of different theories agree that moral reasoning can be modified through exposure to divergent views. Modeling, however, serves as the major vehicle for transmitting new behaviors (Bandura, 1977). Holmes (1983) discussed a story of a young man, now an inmate in a state prison. The young man tells how he was regularly sodomized by his father until he was old enough to reject the advances. He is now in prison because he raped and sodomized over 22 young people. Stories similar to this could be told and retold by almost any clinical therapist involved in treating incest perpetrators and victims.

Table 3.2 Perpetrator's Abuse Histories

	INSTITUTIONAL		COMMUNITY-BASED		
		Mental	Parents	Private	
VARIABLE	Prison	Health	United	Practice	TOTALS
Sample size:	N = 63	N = 41	N = 240	N = 39	N = 383
Abused as a child(%)					
Physical	66.7	61.0	48.3	41.0	52.0
Sexual	65.1	61.0	50.0	48.7	53.5
Use of force(%)					
Physical Aggression Against					
Family of origin:	28.3	48.6	22.7	2.7	24.2
If physically abused	42.5	70.8	32.7	6.3	37.3
If not physically abused	0.0	7.7	12.9	0.0	9.4
If sexually abused	32.5	56.5	27.5	0.0	29.2
If not sexually abused	11.8	25.7	17.4	5.0	16.9
Others outside of family	29.3	51.4	13.4	8.6	20.1
If physically abused	43.6	69.6	19.0	13.3	30.5
If not physically abused	0.0	16.7	7.0	5.0	6.6
If sexually abused	38.5	71.4	15.0	16.7	26.5
If not sexually abused:	16.7	21.4	11.3	0.0	11.5
Mean age at onset(x)	15.8	13.4	18.7	17.8	17.2
In a dating relationship	21.3	16.2	12.2	5.7	13.5
If physically abused	29.3	17.4	12.2	13.3	16.5
If not physically abused	5.0	14.3	12.3	0.0	10.1
If sexually abused	20.0	16.7	15.0	10.5	15.8
If not sexually abused	22.2	14.3	9.3	0.0	10.1
Sexual Agression Against					
Family of origin	27.9	46.2	18.3	16.2	22.6
If physically abused	31.0	52.0	23.4	12.5	27.8
If not physically abused	21.1	35.7	13.4	19.0	16.8
If sexually abused	36.6	56.0	26.5	26.3	32.2
If not sexually abused	5.9	26.7	9.8	15.0	11.6
Others outside of family	30.5	50.0	15.2	27.0	22.5
If physically abused	34.1	62.5	14.2	31.3	25.8
If not physically abused	22.2	28.5	16.1	23.8	18.7
If sexually abused	41.0	54.2	20.2	36.8	29.9
If not sexually abused	16.7	40.0	9.9	25.0	15.2
Mean age at onset(x)	15.8	14.1	26.9	25.8	24.2
Witnessed abuse(%)					
Spouse	46.0	53.7	42.1	33.3	43.1
Sibling	44.4	56.1	35.4	25.6	38.1
Reported incest					
Between others	19.0	36.6	25.0	17.9	24.1
Family members	34.9	63.4	30.8	41.0	36.0

(continued)

Table 3.2 (Continued)

VARIABLE	INSTITUTIONAL		COMMUNITY-BASED		
	Prison	Mental Health	Parents United	Private Practice	TOTALS
Age when first engaged as incest perpetrator					
If physically abused	22.85	21.52	30.37	31.36	28.07
If not physically abused	31.90	30.0	35.21	33.75	33.37
If sexually abused	23.12	24.4	28.37	30.64	28.03
If not sexually abused	32.12	26.2	37.78	34.38	33.74
Number of incest relationships since first					
If physically abused	3.71	4.12	4.12	2.33	3.43
If not physically abused	4.125	3.33	3.46	2.52	3.14
If sexually abused	4.30	4.21	4.55	2.66	3.73
If not sexually abused	2.62	3.36	2.64	2.0	2.59
Had a homosexual relationship(%)	34.9	31.7	12.5	20.5	19.1
Number who have had extra-marital affairs(%)	49.2	48.8	N/A	46.2	48.3
Have visited prostitutes(%)	46.0	43.9	N/A	51.3	46.9
Bestiality(%)					
Physically abusive	22.2	31.7	N/A	20.5	24.5
Sexually abusive	22.2	19.5	N/A	12.8	18.9
Use of pornography(%)	84.4	85.1	N/A	69.3	80.4
Number of incest relationships after the first (% having)					
None	41.3	39.0	80.8	43.6	66.1
One	15.9	17.1	10.4	17.9	12.8
Two	15.9	9.8	3.7	10.3	7.0
Three	4.8	9.8	1.2	10.3	3.7
Four	4.8	2.4	1.2	2.6	2.1
Five +	17.5	22.0	2.5	15.5	8.4

As predicted, there were some significant differences in beliefs and behavior between the victimized and the nonvictimized offenders, as well as those in the various settings. The victimized group did engage in offending at a consistently younger average age, 31 as opposed to 35. Statistical significance was also established for the average age at the time of the first incest act. With respect to the overall number of victims, again the victimized perpetrator was more likely to engage more victims.

Of interest also are the figures for the institutionalized groups versus the noninstitutionalized. Use of force was more common in those offenders who were victims and institutionalized. It is assumed that these settings were selected as this group appeared more threatening to society.

Overall, the abusers in all categories show families of origin that are relatively unstable. While those offenders in less restricted settings show lower rates of abuse—the private practice group showing the least involvement—both physical and sexual abuse were common. Of particular importance is the incidence of physical and sexual aggression. Those offenders in mental health settings were the most inappropriate in the amount of force used with victims and their demonstrations of violence outside the family. Characterological differences and multiple emotional problems tended to cluster in the mental health, institutionalized population, so that even the prisons appear to shunt these offenders into another setting.

These settings appear correctly chosen in response to the anti-social character of their behaviors and the need to protect others. The prison population was also less functional and demonstrated more forms of deviant sexual acting out than the community-based programs. Sexual behavior was engaged in earlier and more frequently among the institutionalized samples. Inpatients were generally more attracted to less socially sanctioned forms of behavior: various forms of pornography, drugs, homosexuality, extramarital affairs, and bestiality. These qualities indicate that, at least for the most versatile offenders, excitement and addiction are evident whereas the specific age of the victim is not important. From a treatment perspective, certainly the more violent and aggressive offender needs to be differentiated from the experimental perpetrator. Although treatment on a regular basis was not always available to these institutionalized perpetrators, the placement seemed appropriate from a social standpoint.

Social Skills

Considering the rising number of offenders who are diverted from institutional settings into the community and the economics involved, the area of social skills deficits is of increasing diagnostic importance.

Our research demonstrated that the greater the social skills, the more likely the perpetrator will be in a less restrictive setting. It is the comprehensive nature of these variables that makes assessment so difficult and that has confused the average clinician in making an accurate determination of the dangerousness and deviance of these perpetrators.

The following considerations were used in combination to examine the holistic concept of "social skills," and will provide a more inclusive and operational diagnostic repertoire for the clinician.

Social Diagnostic Variables

Because social skills are often used to manipulate the therapist and the criminal justice system, there is a concern that by improving these skills the system prepares certain offenders to more effectively manipulate, thus rendering them more dangerous. Yet, these skills must be recognized by clinicians who make informed assessment and treatment plans. Each area will be discussed to illustrate the importance of its inclusion.

1. Social appropriateness and awareness (psycho-sexual characteristics— unnaturalness of incest feelings, ability to change, use of physical and sexual behavior with others, as well as physical force. Concern with community awareness and use of secrecy). (See Tables 3.1, 3.2 and 3.3 for related social characteristics.)

2. Physical and mental health—past and present physical health, use of drugs and alcohol. Psychiatric history. Emotional satisfaction. (See Table 3.1.) Feelings of self-esteem. (See Table 3.4.)

3. Education and occupational history—amount of formal schooling or training, job skills, history of employment, income. (See Table 3.1.)

4. Social and familial relationships—number of friends and level of sociability, marital status and quality of that relationship (overall), number of marriages, problems with the law and social rules. Feelings of social isolation. (See Tables 3.1, 3.2 and 3.4.)

5. Ability to operationalize resources—use of Community services, seeking help, sources used, total use of resources, range of services. (See Table 3.5.)

6. Qualities of incestuous relationship—behaviors, termination, choice of partner, and reason for offending. (See Table 3.6.)

The degree and details of these variables determine the overall assessment of offenders and their treatment needs and placement. At this point, the criminal justice system and mental health (forensic) facilities appear to have evaluated many of these factors, and current placement appears to reflect this awareness in some areas. The average clinician must be able to connect these factors in an effort to better advise and treat those clients seeking their counsel.

Social appropriateness and awareness are specifically noted in Table 3.3. Certainly, those expressing the belief that incest was acceptable and those using physical force were more deviant than the others and should be considered more dangerous. A lack of awareness concerning community response also indicates that their perceptions are faulty. The inappropriate use of sexual behavior is common to all offenders and the use of physical force is not unusual, yet these are expressed in varying degrees and levels of acceptability. These factors combine to describe a perceptual profile exhibiting more social distortions and lack of reality testing as well as a more advanced psychological diagnosis.

Physical and mental health is a broad category designed to de-

Table 3.3 Social Diagnostic Variables

| VARIABLE | INSTITUTIONAL | | COMMUNITY-BASED | | |
	Prison	Mental Health	Parents United	Private Practice	TOTALS
Responses to psycho-sexual characteristics					
Did you discuss these feelings with anyone at that time, or get help before it happened? (%)					
Yes	3.3	4.9	12.1	7.9	9.4
No	96.7	95.1	87.9	92.1	90.6
Did you think that anything could have been done prior to the incest to prevent it? (%)					
Yes	74.6	80.5	74.4	89.5	76.7
No	25.4	19.5	25.6	10.5	23.3
In general, how would you describe yourself? (%)					
Very Social	6.3	7.3	N/A	20.5	10.5
Moderate Social	52.4	51.2	N/A	41.0	49.0
Minimal Social	27.0	26.8	N/A	33.3	28.7
Social Isolate	14.3	14.6	N/A	5.1	11.9
Did you think your feelings were improper, unnatural, or wrong?					
Yes	72.6	75.6	74.6	83.8	75.3
No	27.4	24.4	25.4	16.2	24.7

termine how well these physiological and psychological aspects are measured. Overall, general health is equated with better mental health. There is a critical link between these variables in the social science literature, indicating this area as another important variable in the holistic assessment package. The necessity of evaluating these physiological and psychological variables is indicated in the lower levels of general health, use of drugs and alcohol, and satisfaction between institutionalized offenders and those in the community. A poor self-image or poor health color anyone's ability to use coping skills.

Education and employment status are important indicators of social management skills. They also predict the ability to operationalize resources and support, particularly at an economic level. The quality of social relationships also directly defines a person's ability to get along and manage effectively the interpersonal contacts in his/her life. These measures directly describe the social skills used in direct contact with others, as well as reflect the perception of normative rules and regulations in society.

The use of community services again addresses the social variable of coping skills. They are discussed in more detail in Chapter 10, which describes the connection between personal identification of deviant behavior and the need to prevent public disclosure. The appropriate use of resources and the desire to change are generally interpreted as critical areas with respect to coping mechanisms and social awareness. The earlier and more appropriately resources are used, the more functional and socially compliant the offender.

The qualities of the incestuous relationship connect the limits of social acceptability and the degree of deviance from these social rules. The nature of the offense describes this range of behaviors with respect to social allowances.

Completing the analysis of perpetrators' social skills are the final two questions on the survey, which ask: Why did they become involved in an incestuous relationship, and what is the reason for their selection of the victim? The categories for their involvement in an incestuous relationship were (1) loneliness, (2) poor self-esteem, (3) poor spousal relationship, (4) I don't know, (5) family history of incest, (6) power and control, (7) excitement, (8) unmet needs, (9) expression of love to victim, (10) confusing sex with love, (11) no control over emotions, (12) revenge and anger, and (13) poor sex education.

For the prison group, poor self-esteem was listed as the most prominent explanation for involvement in an incestuous relationship, with 26.8% responding in this category. The greatest percentage (25.7%) of the private practice group involved in an incestuous relationship listed the explanation of excitement. The next highest percentage (17.1%) of the private practice group listed power and control as an explanation.

The final question asked the perpetrators their reasons for selecting the victim. They were categorized as follows: (1) available or convenient, (2) vulnerable, (3) confused sex and love, (4) sexually attractive victim, (5) I don't know, (6) victim seduced perpetrator, and (7) revenge or anger. The two highest categories for all four populations were that victims were available and that they were vulnerable.

CONCLUSION

The social demographic description and abuse history are important in diagnosing and treating offenders. The notable differences indicate a need for a broader typology of offenders, while the similarities support the treatment of all sex offenders as a group. Specific concerns (i.e., alcohol, sexual addiction, and so on), however, indicate that additional treatment components need to be part of a more individualized treatment package.

With the emergence of DSM-III-R, social inadequacy, social skills deficits and poor social performance are finally being acknowledged and allowed some diagnostic significance. Currently, a standardized definition of social skills is lacking.

Given the fact that individuals perform various social skills at different levels, evidence from our findings support our belief that social skills impact treatment choices. A major problem that arises when comparing the existing literature with our study is the limited number of specific studies available for an accurate comparison. The perpetrators in the community-based group were found to have greater social skills than those found in the institutional group.

If the incestuous behavior could have been prevented, what stands in its way? Are the resources for perpetrators known to them? Does society provide enough public awareness for individuals to know where to turn to when they need help? In assessing the perpetrators' social skills, the question needs to be asked as to whether or not the perpetrator has the skills to pursue (assertiveness) programs, social skills development and facilities that are available to them, unless forced to do so!

Conceptually, social skills deficits of the perpetrator are displayed by the general inability to find resources available to them. The notion of inadequacy and social perception appears to play a major role in the functioning level of the perpetrator. Findings of this study support the literature alluding to the poor social skills of the perpetrator.

Strong confirmation of incest perpetrators lacking essential social skills was found. Also found was an even more distinct social skills deficit in institutionalized perpetrators, as opposed to perpetrators found in community-based treatment settings. Some of the most notable results are that (a) perpetrators often think that the incestuous behavior is improper and unnatural prior to involvement in incest; (b) perpetrators are not able to assert themselves and discuss the incest with anyone, but close to 90% think something could have been done to prevent it before it happened; (c) these groups of perpetrators reported improvement in self-esteem, adult relationships, social skills, and empathy; (d) they have few close friends and generally describe themselves as moderately sociable; (e) marital satisfaction is rated as poor and used as a main reason for becoming involved in incest; and (f) the perpetrators reported availability and vulnerability of the victim as the main reason for selecting their victim.

As the perpetrator population becomes more available to researchers, greater general information about the incest perpetrator will emerge. Assessment tools need more testing and refinement. Knowing the incest perpetrator's characteristics, abuse history, and poor social skills will further aid the development of new strategies and treatment interventions for this population. As this takes place, professionals will be better informed and able to treat this social problem and family dilemma.

Table 3.4 Social Diagnostic Variables

VARIABLE	Prison	Mental Health	Parents United	Private Practice	TOTALS
Feelings concerning self-esteem					
Did you need help with self-esteem? (%)	44.4	53.7	N/A	30.8	43.4
Social and familial relationships					
How many close friends do you have? (mean)	3.9	4.5	N/A	3.9	4.1
Did you need help with relationships with adults? (%)	39.7	53.7	N/A	23.1	39.2
Did you need help with isolation and poor social skills? (%)	50.8	61.0	N/A	23.1	46.2
Did you need help understanding victim's feelings? (%)	63.5	80.5	N/A	59.0	67.1

Table 3.5 Social Diagnostic Variables

Resources Used by Perpetrators

	INSTITUTIONAL		COMMUNITY-BASED		
VARIABLE	Prison	Mental Health	Parents United	Private Practice	TOTALS
Sample size:	N = 63	N = 41	N = 240	N = 39	N = 383
Percent (%) who have discussed their incest behaviors with					
Therapist/counselor	71.4	68.3	84.6	82.1	80.4
Spouse	58.7	51.2	72.5	66.7	67.4
Other family member	52.4	61.0	47.1	74.4	52.2
Parents United/self-help group	1.6	7.3	77.1	2.6	49.6
Law enforcement	28.6	36.6	46.7	33.3	41.3
Treatment facility	46.0	43.9	36.7	48.7	40.2
Friend	49.2	46.3	31.7	43.6	37.3
Clergy	33.3	31.7	35.0	28.2	33.7
AA/drug rehabilitation	14.3	9.8	16.7	15.4	15.4
Crisis line	6.3	2.4	9.6	7.7	8.1

(*continued*)

Table 3.5 (Continued)

Resources Used by Perpetrators

| VARIABLE | INSTITUTIONAL | | COMMUNITY-BASED | | |
	Prison	Mental Health	Parents United	Private Practice	TOTALS
Resources listed as most helpful (%)					
None listed	52.4	26.8	38.3	30.8	38.6
Therapist/counselor	30.2	56.1	18.3	35.9	26.1
Parents United/self-help group	0.0	0.0	32.1	10.3	21.1
Law enforcement	4.8	9.8	2.1	5.1	3.7
Clergy	3.2	0.0	2.9	5.1	2.9
AA/drug rehabilitation	1.6	2.4	2.1	0.0	1.8
Spouse	3.2	2.4	.4	5.1	1.6
Other family member	1.6	2.4	.8	5.1	1.6
Crisis line	1.6	0.0	1.7	0.0	1.3
Friend	1.6	0.0	.8	2.6	1.0
Resources listed as least helpful (%)					
None listed	52.4	48.8	63.3	84.6	62.1
Law enforcement	22.2	14.6	21.2	2.6	18.8
Clergy	4.8	12.2	2.1	7.7	4.2
Therapist/counselor	6.3	9.8	2.9	2.6	4.2
Spouse	9.5	4.9	1.7	0.0	3.1
Other family member	3.2	4.9	3.3	0.0	3.1
Parents United/self-help group	0.0	4.9	2.9	0.0	2.3
Friend	0.0	0.0	.8	2.6	.8
AA/drug rehabilitation	1.6	0.0	.8	0.0	.8
Crisis line	0.0	0.0	.8	0.0	.5
Child Protective Services has contacted them (%)	73.0	68.3	77.9	79.5	76.2
Use of law enforcement resources (%)					
Arrested for incest	54.0	63.4	50.4	48.7	52.2
Charged with a sex crime	60.3	61.0	46.7	51.3	50.9
Convicted of a sex crime	58.7	63.4	41.3	43.6	46.7

Table 3.6 Social Diagnostic Variables

Incest Perpetrator's Choice of Victim

Victim's age (N = 340)

	(Mean)
Prison	8.5
Mental health	8.2
Private practice	8.9
Parents United	10.0

Relationship of victim (%) (N = 351)

	Daughter	Step-daughter	Sister	Niece	Other
Prison	33.7	31.7	11.7	5.0	17.9
Mental health	20.0	17.5	25.0	12.5	25.0
Private practice	36.3	33.3	7.7	11.1	11.6
Parents United	39.1	37.7	13.0	10.2	0.0

Why became involved in incest (%) (N = 257)

	Prison	Mental Health	Private Practice	Parents United	TOTAL
Loneliness	3.6	2.7	8.6	NA	4.7
Poor self-esteem	26.8	13.5	8.6	NA	18.0
Poor spousal relations	12.5	8.1	0.0	NA	7.8
I don't know	7.1	13.5	14.3	NA	10.9
Family history	8.9	10.8	0.0	NA	7.0
Power/control	1.8	2.7	17.1	NA	6.3
Excitement	7.1	2.7	25.7	NA	10.9
Unmet Needs	5.4	13.5	2.9	NA	7.0
Confuse Love/Sex	3.6	10.8	2.9	NA	5.5
No Control of Emotions	3.6	13.5	17.1	NA	10.2
Revenge	10.7	2.7	2.9	NA	6.3
Poor sex education	3.6	2.7	0.0	NA	2.3
Other	3.6	2.7	0.0	NA	2.3

Why particular victim was chosen (%) (N = 252)

	Prison	Mental Health	Private Practice	Parents United	TOTAL
Available/convenient	33.3	27.0	48.6	NA	35.7
Vulnerable	35.2	35.1	22.9	NA	31.7
Confused sex/love	18.5	24.3	5.7	NA	16.7
Sexually attractive	3.7	2.7	2.4	NA	5.6
Seduced by victim	3.7	2.7	0.0	NA	2.4
Revenge/anger	5.6	5.4	5.7	NA	5.6

REFERENCES

Bandura, A. (1977). *Social learning theory*. Englewood Cliffs, NJ: Prentice-Hall.

Burgess, R. L. (1978). *Project Interact: A study of patterns of interactions in abusive, neglectful, and control families*. Final report to the National Center on Child Abuse and Neglect.

Finkelhor, D., & Williams, L. M. (1988). The characteristics of incestuous fathers: A review of recent studies. In W. L. Marshall, D. R. Laws, & H. E. Barbee (Eds.), *The handbook of sexual assault: Issues, theories and treatment of the offender*. New York: Plenum.

Groth, A. N. (1978). Guidelines for the assessment and management of the offender. In A. W. Burgess, A. N. Groth, L. L. Holmstrom, & S. M. Sgroi (Eds.), *Sexual assault of children and adolescents*. Lexington, MA: Lexington Books.

Groth, A. N. (1983). Treatment of the sexual offender in a correctional institution. In J. G. Greer & I. R. Stuart (Eds.), *The sexual aggressor: Current perspectives on treatment*. New York: Van Nostrand Reinhold.

Groth, A. N., Hobson, W., & Gary, T. (1982). The child molester: Clinical observations. In

J. R. Conte & D. A. Shore (Eds.), *Social work and child sexual abuse*. New York: Haworth.

Herman, J. C. (1981). *Father-daughter incest*. Cambridge, MA: Harvard University Press.

Holmes, R. M. (1983). *The sex offender and the criminal justice system*. Springfield, IL: Charles C Thomas.

Horton, A. L., & Williams, D. (1988). What perpetrators need (but are not getting) from the clergy and treatment community. In A. L. Horton & J. A. Williamson (Eds.), *Abuse and religion: When praying isn't enough*. Lexington, MA: Lexington Books.

Julian, V., Mohr, C., & Lapp, L. (1980). Father-daughter incest. In W. Holder (Ed.), *Sexual abuse of children: Implications for treatment*. Englewood, CO: American Human Association.

Kelly, J. A. (1982). *Social-skills training: A practical guide for interventions*. New York: Springer.

Knopp, F. H. (1984). *Retraining adult sex offenders: Methods and models*. Orwell, VT: Safer Society Press.

Langevin, R. (1983). *Sexual Strands: Understanding and treating sexual anomalies in men*. Hillsdale, NJ: Lawrence Erlbaum.

McBroom, E. (1979). Socialization and social casework. In R. F. Roberts & T. S. Nee (Eds.), *Theories of social casework* (pp. 204–213). New York: Holt, Rinehart & Winston.

McIvor, D. L., & Duthie, B. (1986). MMPI profiles of incest offenders: Men who molest younger children and men who molest older children. *Criminal Justice and Behavior, 13*, 450–452.

Muldoon, L. (Ed.) (1981). *Incest: Confronting the silent crime*. St. Paul: Minnesota Correctional Facility–Lino Lakes.

Parker, H., & Parker, S. (1986). Father-daughter sexual abuse: An emerging perspective. *American Journal of Orthopsychiatry, 56*, 531–549.

Pelto, V. L. (1981). Male incest offenders and non-offenders: A comparison of early sexual history. *Dissertation Abstracts International, 42*(3), 1154.

Wolpe, J., & Lazarus, A. (1966). *Behavior therapy techniques*. New York: Pergamon.

4

Sexual Abuse by Paternal Caretakers: *A Comparison of Abusers Who Are Biological Fathers in Intact Families, Stepfathers, and Noncustodial Fathers*

Kathleen Coulborn Faller

INTRODUCTION

Changes in family life and family forms have resulted in changes in the configurations of incestuous abuse of children. The clinical exploration of intrafamilial sexual abuse has focused primarily on incest by biological fathers in intact families. With the dramatic increase in the number of divorces in the United States—close to one marriage in two ending in divorce and about half of divorces involving minor children (Jacobson, 1987)—two additional forms of incest have been increasingly recognized, sexual abuse by stepfathers and sexual abuse by noncustodial fathers.

This chapter will be based on the author's clinical experience and research with a sample of 196 paternal caretakers who were identified as having sexually abused children, with reference to the clinical writing and research of others. Although the findings are felt to be very informative for both clinicians and researchers, the reader needs to appreciate the limitations of the sample. It consists of cases of sexual abuse referred to a single agency, the Interdisciplinary Project on Child Abuse and Neglect, based at the University of Michigan.

A COMPARISON OF THE DYNAMICS OF INCEST BY BIO-FATHERS, STEPFATHERS, AND NONCUSTODIAL FATHERS

The author assumes that there are prerequisite and contributing factors that lead a person to sexually abuse a child (Faller, 1988). The

65

prerequisite factors are (a) sexual arousal to children and (b) the willingness to act on the sexual arousal. These factors are present in almost all cases of sexual victimization, and it is assumed that they will be present regardless of the type of paternal caretaker involved in sexual maltreatment. While some contributing factors, such as substance abuse and social isolation, appear equally likely to be found in all types of intrafamilial sexual abuse, others seem to vary depending on the role relationship between offender and victim. The variations in contributing factors leading bio-fathers, stepfathers, and noncustodial fathers to sexual abuse will be discussed in this chapter.

Cases Involving Biological Fathers in Intact Families

A gross synthesis of the explanations in the clinical literature for sexual abuse by bio-fathers in intact families (classical incest) is that the dysfunctional family structure and process that lead to sexual victimization are in fact functional for the incestuous family. Some writers describe this structure and process as an adaptation that allows the family to remain intact (Gutheil & Avery, 1977; Lustig, Dresser, Spellman, & Murray, 1966). That is, without the incest, the father would have to go outside the family to get his sexual needs met, and both the family and he prefer the incest to destruction of the family, which would result from an extramarital affair.

Mothers are seen as playing a central role in the incest as they overtly or covertly condone the behavior (e.g., Brant & Tisza, 1977; Lustig et al., 1966; Matchotka, Pittman, & Flomenhaft, 1967; Sarles, 1975; Walters, 1975; Weiner, 1964). The mother may support this arrangement, because she does not wish a sexual relationship with her husband. This classical "typology" may be because the marriage is very conflictual and, therefore, she does not desire intimate contact with her spouse. Alternatively, she may fear pregnancy, may have been sexually victimized herself and therefore phobic about sex, or she may even be overwhelmed by other responsibilities and not have the time or the inclination to engage in coitus. She may sometimes be described as undesirable to her partner. She may be physically incapacitated or ill, mentally deranged, or physically unattractive, causing her spouse to avoid a sexual relationship with her and to prefer one with their daughter. Mothers of victims are also designated as inadequate women who neglect maternal role responsibilities, such as household chores and child care. The vacuum created by the mother's failure to perform is filled by the oldest female child, who takes on the mother's sexual role as well. Because this pattern is adaptive, it is likely to persist for years.

This explanation of classical incest implies that the perpetrator is at the mercy of family dynamics. Such an explanation is inconsistent with the author's research findings and clinical experience. An examination of 65 cases of classical incest suggests a fair amount of variability in factors that contribute to sexual abuse by bio-fathers. However, it was determined that only three mothers knew about the sexual abuse prior to its report. They did not appear to desire or benefit from it, but felt powerless to stop it.

In-depth interviews with mothers and offenders uncovered that in only 6 cases were there significant sexual difficulties and in only 11 reports was the relationship a hostile one. When there were sexual difficulties, they were as likely to be the consequence of the husband's sexual preference for children as to be the wife's lack of desire or lack of desirability. About four-fifths of these men sexually molested more than one child, and in a third of the cases there were victims outside of the home. Thus, an explanation that implies that incestuous fathers are merely redirecting their sexual interest to their daughters, when relationships with their wives are thwarted, is not supported by the author's experience.

The most consistent finding that might explain this type of incest is that of male dominance in the marital relationship, noted in 29 out of 60 cases. In addition, mothers in these incestuous families were rated "more dependent" than were those in the two other types of incest. Therefore, the explanation for sexual abuse that applies to the largest number of these cases appears to be that the will of the father prevailed. He wished to have a sexual relationship with his child(ren), and the mother and the victim(s) felt they were powerless to stop him.

Cases Involving Stepfathers and Mothers' Boyfriends

Stepfather cases appear to be a little more homogenous in their dynamics than the bio-father cases. Clinicians generally regard the attenuation or absence of the incest taboo as an important contributing factor to sexual abuse by father surrogates (Perlmutter, Engel, & Sager, 1982), and researchers have found stepfather status increases risk for sexual abuse (Finkelhor & Baron, 1986; Russell, 1983, 1986). Furthermore, vulnerability to sexually abusing children may be exacerbated by the role confusion experienced by the stepfather. He often enters the family as a boyfriend and subsequently becomes a stepfather. There may be uncertainty regarding role expectations because of his changing and fairly undefined status in the family.

An additional factor, found in the author's sample of 62 stepfather cases, arguably added to the stepfather's role confusion. This key factor was that in more than a third of the cases he was younger than the mother. Some instances were dramatic. In one case, the stepfather was 19, the mother 32, and the victims 7- and 11-year-old girls. In another, the mother was 34, the offender 24, and the victims 17-, 13-, and 12-year-old girls. Moreover, many mothers, in describing their experiences with these partners, would say it was like having another child in the family. This sort of description was sometimes given by mothers in classical incest, but was more frequent in the stepfather cases. Furthermore, while blurring of generational boundaries is designated as characteristic of classical incest, it appears to be more pronounced in cases of stepfather incest.

Another important characteristic that may explain why sexual abuse happened in these families is that close to one-third of the children had been previously sexually maltreated by their biological fathers. Such experiences are likely to increase the vulnerability of children to additional sexual abuse because they have been socialized to expect sexual behavior from adult males. They may also engage in behaviors, because of this socialization, that are perceived as seductive by their stepfathers. Furthermore, the fact that the child has already had sex with an adult may encourage sexual abuse by a man who has not previously had this problem. He may be titillated by the child's prior victimization, or knowledge of her past maltreatment may make him consider having sex with a child when, in the past, he has had no such thoughts. Moreover, he may rationalize his maltreatment, using the excuse that he is not the first adult with whom the child has had a sexual encounter.

In addition, there were six instances of stepfathers with a past history of sexually abusing, who entered these families apparently with the intent of developing sexual relationships with the children. Finally, although more than two-thirds of the stepfathers sexually abused more than one child in the home, there were only three reports of additional concurrent victims outside the home.

Cases Involving Noncustodial Fathers

When noncustodial fathers sexually abused their children, this generally occurred when they had them for visitation. Of the 69 validated cases of sexual abuse by noncustodial fathers seen by the author, in only 7 was there evidence the abuse started before the marital demise. However, in about two-thirds of the cases there were signs of the offender's sexual attraction to children during the marriage. Examples of this are the offender experiencing an erection while bathing with the child or while the child was sitting on his lap, French-kissing with the child, excessive caressing of the victim, and sleeping with the child.

The dynamics of sexual abuse by noncustodial fathers can be understood by examining the circumstances surrounding the marital dissolution. First, a common result of divorce is the loss of structure in the life of the father. His wife and children are no longer there; thus, daily routines are often absent. For example, regular meals, set bedtimes, and prescriptions regarding sleeping arrangements are missing. No longer is there anyone there to monitor his behavior. He has unsupervised access to his children on visits, and there may be no rules. Therefore, there may be increased opportunity for sexual abuse. Further, the absence of rules about household functioning may encourage the offender to violate other rules, for example, the incest taboo.

There are additional dynamics that may facilitate sexual abuse by noncustodial fathers. In three-fourths of the cases in the author's sample, the mother was the initiator of the marital breakup. The father often was bewildered and emotionally devastated by her action and blamed her for the problems in the marriage and its demise. Feelings of desolation because of the loss of his wife and/or anger at her resulted. These feelings appear to have been transferred to the child, who became an avenue for their expression and a substitute for the mother.

Thus, the father may seek affection and comfort from the child, and appropriate interaction becomes sexualized. The father may also regress under the stress of the marital demise, and therefore feel more comfortable with an immature sex object. Similarly, his desire to retaliate against his wife leads him to harm the child by sexually abusing her/him. When anger is the dominant underlying dynamic, the child is more likely to be physically injured during the sexual encounter.

CHARACTERISTICS OF VICTIMS

Interesting differences were found in the age and sex of victims abused by the three types of paternal caretakers. Victims of noncustodial fathers were the youngest, their mean age being 3.6 at onset. The mean age, at onset, of victims of bio-fathers in intact families, was 5.2 years, and that of victims of stepfathers was 7.5 years. The older age of victims of stepfathers is quite understandable, as there would need to have been a marital breakup and a reconstitution of the child's family during the child's lifetime before victimization by a stepfather. The very young age of the victims of noncustodial fathers is not so easily understood.

Noncustodial fathers were also significantly more likely to sexually abuse boys than were bio-fathers in intact families and stepfathers. Twenty-eight percent of victims of noncustodial fathers were male, while the percentage for bio-fathers was 5% and for stepfathers, 11%. The relatively larger percentage of male victims might be explained by the fact that noncustodial fathers were significantly more likely to have sexually abused all their children. In 92% of cases, noncustodial fathers were documented as having victimized all the children who came for visits, while a little more than half of bio-fathers in intact families and less than half of stepfathers were identified as having abused all of the children in their households.

Finally, the fact that noncustodial fathers victimized very young children, often males, when, for most of them, their primary sexual orientation appeared to be to adult females, is possibly an index of their regressed and disorganized state at the time of divorce.

CHARACTERISTICS OF THE OFFENDERS

The three types of paternal caretakers were fairly similar in a number of areas that were explored, for example, in their education, employment histories, and substance use. However, there were some differences that may be helpful to clinicians trying to understand and treat these three types of offenders. Differences related to perpetrator's experiences of sexual abuse as children and admission to sexual abuse will be discussed.

Data were collected on sexual abuse in both the paternal caretakers' and the mothers' backgrounds. In about a fourth of the cases in all three groups, no sexual abuse was reported for either parent, and in 10% to 15% of cases in each group both parents reported having been victimized. For bio-father cases, either father or mother was about equally likely to have had a traumatic sexual experience in childhood. For stepfather cases, the mother was much more likely to have been victimized, with about 70% reporting such an experience. In contrast, for noncustodial father cases, the father was the one with sexual mal-treatment in his past, this being noted in 68% of cases.

An interpretation of these findings might be as follows: Recalling the high rate of incest behavior by bio-fathers in stepfather cases dis-cussed earlier, perhaps the mother's choice of partners is crucial in stepfather abuse cases. Her past victimization may lead her to repeat-edly choose partners who do not make adult sexual demands upon her because these men are immature and/or prefer immature sexual ob-jects. In contrast, when noncustodial fathers sexually abuse their chil-dren, men who are vulnerable because of their childhood sexual ex-periences become active abusers under the stress and anomie of marital dissolution. It is also possible that their exposure to sexual abuse as children leads to sexual and other problems in their marriages that increase the risk of divorce.

Finally, important in terms of case planning, differences were found in rates of admission to the sexual abuse in the three groups. In most cases, data on admission were gathered when the initial mental health assessment was undertaken. Rates might have been higher if this in-formation had been collected later—after some treatment or after lit-igation. At the time of the initial assessment, approximately half of fathers in the bio-father and stepfather groups made some level of ad-mission to the sexual abuse. In contrast, only 20% of noncustodial fa-thers did.

This finding may be due to the fact that the offender was a member of the child's household, and his wish to stay with the mother and the family impelled him to acknowledge his problem so that he could re-ceive help. This interpretation is reinforced by the observation that more than a third of the noncustodial fathers merely withdrew from their relationships with their children after the allegations were made. The withdrawal usually consisted not only of failure to attempt or maintain contact but failure to pay child support.

IMPLICATIONS FOR CASE MANAGEMENT

The findings from this examination of three different kinds of incest perpetrators, although tentative, provide some helpful guidance for clinicians. Three issues will be explored. First, different types of chil-dren may be vulnerable when fathers have varying role relationships. When the biological father is the alleged abuser, his daughters may be more vulnerable, as well as children outside the family. Stepfathers appear to be more likely to target female children, and there seems to be less risk of them molesting outside the home. Noncustodial fathers are prone to victimize all their children, boys as well as girls, and children who are very young.

Second, quite different strategies may be necessary for protecting a victim from future sexual abuse from perpetrators with different role relationships. Because of the dominance of the father and the dependency of the mother in bio-father cases, victims in these situations are likely to be at greatest risk. Although removal of the offender may be the protective intervention of choice, the mother may be unable or unwilling to enforce this. Moreover, the victim in these families may be at greater risk for being blamed for the exit of the offender and the disruption caused by intervention than in the other groups. Therefore, in this situation, removal of the victim may be the least damaging alternative for the bio-father and his family, although it may prove detrimental for the victim.

Removal of the offender may be a more feasible alternative in stepfather cases. The mothers will have in the past separated from a problematic spouse and are likely to be more able to do so than mothers in bio-father cases.

Mothers in noncustodial offender cases are very different. In most cases, protection does not require major upheaval and mothers are very cooperative. In fact, just the opposite problem may be present. They may refuse their ex-spouses even supervised access, despite the fact that this may be in the child's best interest and is court ordered.

Finally, assuming the perpetrator is found to be treatable, emphasis in therapy will vary based on the role relationship between victim and abuser. (However, for all of the men, work will be done on helping them control their sexual feelings toward children.) For bio-fathers, an important focus of therapy is likely to be on issues of power and dominance. For stepfathers, there will be greater emphasis on role definition and the establishment of intergenerational boundaries. Noncustodial fathers will need support in coping with the stress of marital breakup, resolving their anger toward their former spouse, and often, gaining a realistic view of the marriage and their role in its problems.

REFERENCES

Brant, R. S. T., & Tisza, V. B. (1977). The sexually misused child. *American Journal of Orthopsychiatry, 47*, 80–90.

Faller, K. (1988). *Child sexual abuse: An interdisciplinary manual for diagnosis, case management, and treatment.* New York: Columbia University Press.

Finkelhor, D., & Baron, L. (1986). High risk children. In D. Finkelhor and Associates (Eds.), *A sourcebook on child sexual abuse* (pp. 60–88). Newbury Park, CA: Sage.

Gutheil, T., & Avery, N. (1977). Multiple overt incest as family defense against loss. *Family Process, 16*, 105–116.

Jacobson, D. (1987). Divorce and separation. In *The Encyclopedia of Social Work* (18th ed., pp. 449–453). Silver Spring, MD: National Association of Social Workers.

Lustig, N., Dresser, J., Spellman, S., & Murray, T. (1966). Incest: A family group survival pattern. *Archives of General Psychology, 14*, 13–40.

Matchotka, P., Pittman, F., & Flomenhaft, S. (1967). Incest as a family affair. *Family Process, 6*, 98–116.

Perlmutter, L., Engel, T., & Sager, C. (1982). The incest taboo: Loosened sexual boundaries in remarried families. *Journal of Sex and Marital Therapy, 8*, 83–96.

Russell, D. (1983). The prevalence and seriousness of incestuous abuse: Stepfathers vs. biological fathers. *Child Abuse and Neglect: The International Journal, 8*(1), 15–22.

Russell, D. (1986). *The secret trauma: Incest in the lives of girls and women.* New York: Basic Books.

Sarles, R. (1975). Incest. *Pediatric Clinics of North America, 22* (3), 633–642.

Walters, D. (1975). *Sexual and physical abuse of children.* Bloomington: Indiana University Press.

Weiner, I. B. (1964). On incest: A survey. *Excerpta Criminologica, 4*, 131–155.

5

Isolation and the Adult Male Perpetrator of Child Sexual Abuse: *Clinical Concerns*

Jane F. Gilgun
Teresa M. Connor

INTRODUCTION

Isolation plays an important part in the perpetration of child sexual abuse. Types of isolation examined in this chapter are intrapersonal or psychic, interpersonal or social, and existential. The concept for this chapter was developed from in-depth interviews that the first author had with 14 perpetrators of child sexual abuse, and from consultation with 30 clinicians who work with perpetrators. A discussion of definitions of isolation and excerpts from the interviews that illustrate how these men experienced isolation throughout their lives will be presented.

Isolation has been used to describe both the perpetrator and the perpetrator's family of procreation. The isolation of the perpetrator's family is viewed as (a) a factor contributing to sexual abuse (Finkelhor, 1984), (b) a result of the incest (Larson & Maddock, 1986), and (c) a condition imposed on the family by a controlling incestuous father. Herman and Hirschman (1981, p. 71) described incestuous fathers as controlling to the degree that they became "the arbiters of the family's social life and frequently succeeded in virtually secluding the women in the family." Larson and Maddock (1986) wrote that the incest is a secret that family members protect by isolating themselves from persons outside of the family.

AUTHORS' NOTE: Support for this research was through the Minnesota Agricultural Experiment Station, the Saint Paul Foundation, the F. R. Bigelow Foundation, Edwards Memorial Trust, First Banks Saint Paul, the Mardag Foundation, the St. Paul Companies, and the Minneapolis Star Tribune/Cowles Media Company.

When the focus is on the perpetrator himself, isolation is viewed as a quality of the inner life and as a social-psychological characteristic. Psychoanalytically-oriented clinicians view isolation as a symptom of psychopathology, where the perpetrator is viewed as being a divided self, schizoid, and having tendencies to become isolated and withdrawn under stress (Apfelberg, Sugra, & Pfeffer, 1944; Peters, 1976). Psychosocially-oriented clinicians characterize the perpetrator's isolation in terms of difficulty in establishing social relationships. Groth (1983, p. 164) described the perpetrator as a loner, who is detached, self-centered, wary of others, and tending to have "superficial and transitory" relationships. Groth said the perpetrators' adjustment was a consequence of such experiences as abuse, neglect, exploitation and/ or abandonment, which blocked the capacity for trusting and reciprocal relationships. Justice and Justice (1979) found incestuous fathers to be isolated within themselves and in relationship to others. They wrote:

> Because of the way he was brought up and the kind of parents he had as a child, he hungers for a closeness, a sense of belonging and intimacy that he seldom can verbalize and never has experienced. . . . Most men who commit incest are completely out of touch with their needs and have no experience in meeting them in healthy ways. (p.63)

These qualities of being out of touch with the self and of being isolated from others develop in a social context. The family is the most influential single context for human development. Both Groth (1983) and Justice and Justice (1979) suggested that the family-of-origin experiences of perpetrators set the stage for later sexual abuse of children. Davis and Leitenberg (1987) reviewed research on the adolescent sex offender and found in study after study that these young people were socially isolated and often came from abusive and neglectful backgrounds. Isolation, then, is a key factor in understanding perpetrators of child sexual abuse.

DEFINITIONS OF ISOLATION

The term isolation was not explicitly defined in the literature that was reviewed for this study. Authors probably considered the term sufficiently understood not to require a formal definition. Isolation, however, can be defined in more than one way, and it is an important term

in three major theories related to human development: Freudian psychodynamics, existentialism, and Erikson's theory of psychosocial development. Each of these three schools has unique perspectives on
isolation.

Isolation as a Defense

In the Freudian school, isolation has been identified as one of the
defenses of the ego (Goldstein, 1984). Freudian isolation refers to a
separation of affect from intellect so that a situation that, from outward
appearances, would be emotionally laden is experienced by the person
as devoid of emotion. A parent who has no feeling attached to the
death of a beloved child is an example. Often these feelings are expressed in another situation, such as a death in another family.

Intimacy and Isolation

Isolation in the Eriksonian framework is one side of the intimacy
versus isolation conflict characteristic of young adulthood, or the sixth
of eight stages of psychosocial development (Erikson, 1959). A person
considered stuck at this stage—unable to establish intimate relationships, characterized as nurturing, interdependent, and reciprocal, experiencing isolation—feels left out and may endure lifelong loneliness.
As with the other stages, the successful resolution of this developmental conflict depends a great deal on the degree of resolution the person
has attained of previous developmental tasks. Through the first five
stages, the person has dealt with issues of trust, autonomy, initiation,
mastery, and identity. According to the principle of vertical compen-
sation, deficits stemming from earlier points of development can be
overcome in later stages when the environment is sufficiently rich (Erikson, 1959).

Isolation and Existentialism

Yalom (1980) has termed psychosocial isolation as interpersonal, resulting from factors such as geographic location, poor social skills, and
inner conflict about intimacy. According to the existential view, failure
to develop a capacity for intimacy places the person at risk to use others sexually.

Existentialists further developed the Freudian idea of inner isolation and they gave it a new name: intrapersonal isolation. This term
refers to a process by which parts of the self are partitioned off (Yalom,

1980). People become fragmented when they stifle parts of themselves, accept the judgments of others rather than their own, and allow their own potential to be stymied. Thus, people become cut off from their own feelings, wants, and desires. Identifying the feelings, wants, and desires of others becomes problematic when the person is cut off from his/her own inner life. These dynamics lay the groundwork for using others.

In existentialism, isolation is one of four ultimate concerns with which the human being contends. The other three are death, freedom, and meaninglessness. Existential isolation refers to the fundamental separation that exists between the person and others. This separation is unbridgeable and exists even when the person has achieved a high degree of intrapersonal and social integration. Existential isolation is an inescapable fact of existence.

Recognizing the separation of the self from others could be a condition of mental health. Well-functioning persons are characterized by respect for the interpersonal and intrapersonal boundaries of others. Less well-functioning persons are said to be enmeshed and have difficulty with separateness. They tend either to invade the personal boundaries or allow others to be invasive of them.

All three schools of thought posit that there are degrees of isolation, and each individual contends with all three. Resources within the developing person's environment set the stage for how individuals deal with isolation. A person who develops within a supportive environment is likely to be integrated intrapersonally, to have a capacity for developing intimate relationships, and can come to terms with the essential separation from others. Those persons whose environments are impoverished interpersonally are at risk for becoming isolated. The rest of this chapter describes themes of isolation in the lives of 14 adult male perpetrators of child sexual abuse. Ten of the men were married, two were divorced, and two had not married. Details of the method of this study are discussed elsewhere (Gilgun & Connor, in press). Isolation in three major areas will be discussed: in the family of origin; during adolescence in relationships with peers; and during adulthood, especially in marriage.

THE EXPERIENCE OF ISOLATION

Each subject described lifelong isolation, beginning in the family of origin, extending into adolescence, and continuing into adulthood.

The emotional resources in their environments were impoverished, which suggests support for the above theories about what leads to isolation.

Family of Origin

Parents' marriages were characterized by alcoholism, mental illness, physical disability, financial stress, wife beating, frequent separations, death, and divorce. Two men described no overt signs of strain between their parents, such as physical violence or verbal abuse, but they reported forms of pseudo-mutuality where differences were repressed and emotional pain not recognized. The men experienced their parents as isolated from each other, which was painful for them. One man described parental conflicts and their outcome:

> My mother and dad would fight, and they would have these blowups, and splits, and everything. Whenever they went back together, there was never anything ever said in front of us kids. Us kids were all thrown into complete chaos. I mean, they were killing each other, and my ma was throwing his clothes out, and he was running over them, but when it was into making up, and "I'm sorry's" or whatever took place, it was never done in front of us kids.

Another man recalled his parents coming home drunk:

> It was about 12:30, 1:00, when they come home. Drunker than a skunk. Mom said something and dad just got up and stumbled over and just started beating the crap out of her.

The men were hungry for signs of intimacy between their parents. One man described payday at his house:

> The only time my folks communicated was on payday. And that's the truth. It was so great. We didn't all get around the table to see how much money dad had made. We got around the table because, hey, mom and dad were getting along.

The men not only experienced their parents as isolated from each other, but they also felt a great gulf between themselves and their parents. Sometimes parent-child isolation was related to parental mental illness or physical disability. In other families, preoccupation with the stress of marriage compromised parental ability to be intimate with children. The result was that the men felt discounted, rejected, and unloved by their parents.

One man, whose father was brain-damaged through a work-related injury that occurred on the day he was born, felt isolated from his father. He described his conversations with his father:

> You could talk with him, but he had quite a bit of brain damage. Oh, sometimes we'd sit and talk about the past or something. I think all he ever really cared about all those years was his coffee and his cigarettes.

Feelings of rejection are evident here as they are in other statements made by subjects. The father's neurological impairment profoundly affected his son.

Isolation and Lovableness

From an early age, problems in parent-child relationships led subjects to doubt they were lovable. One man said about his relationship with his mother:

> I wasn't happy. I mean, when you love somebody, and you can't understand what in the world that you're doing wrong, and what you need more than anything else is to have your ma, you know, put her arms around you and say "I love you." And instead of that, I got the broom on my backside.

One man summed up the experience of all the others. He said, simply, "I can't remember being able to sit down and talk to my folks."

Nothing in the men's accounts of their relationships with their parents suggested that the parents deliberately sought to harm their sons. Their sons' experiences of being left out, ignored, and neglected may have been unintended consequences of parental preoccupation with their own struggles.

None of the men were able to confide in and feel close to siblings, either because of profound mistrust or because it did not occur to them. As one subject said, "As long as I can remember, even brothers and sisters, we never sat down and talked."

Modeling (or vicarious learning) and direct experience are two major socialization processes. Deficits in either area compromise the ability to form relationships. These men had limited opportunity to learn through the modeling provided by their parents. Unable to relate intimately to each other, the parents seem to have been unable to relate constructively to their children. Having neither modeling nor direct experience from parents, these men, then, did not develop relationships of trust and intimacy within the family.

Peer Relationships in Adolescence

The isolation that began in the family of origin continued to develop outside the family. All of the men described themselves as loners during childhood and adolescence or described this time of life in such a way that their emotional isolation was obvious. Some were avoidant of peer relationships, and when they did have relationships they either let themselves be used and/or were users of others. Even when they spent time with male peers, they reported feeling apart from them.

Care-giving responsibilities and frequent moves were two other factors that interfered with the formation of peer relationships. One man, whose family moved every two years and who had caretaking responsibilities, both of which kept him from peers, said, "I didn't have a chance in the social world." Another man recalled:

> I was afraid of being hurt or making close friendships to have them break up because of the life-style I led, being bounced from school to school. I never finished one year of high school in the same school. And it got to the point like I don't want to get real close to other guys because I know before the school year is out Dad's going to be moving somewhere.

This subject, like the others, was isolated from age-mates. His motivation for staying away from others was self-protection. He admitted only to being fearful of having to leave friends, but it is likely that he also did not know how to handle himself with peers. Another man who had care-giving responsibilities throughout adolescence clearly admitted his inability to deal with peer relationships. He said:

> For the most part I really didn't want anything to do with people. I stayed away from people. I didn't want to make myself vulnerable to their statements that I didn't want to hear. And I'd really keep to myself.

Lack of trust of others was a theme that appeared in the men's descriptions of their lives. As one man stated, "It's hard for me in any type of relationship to let people get close because I wonder what they want." He had felt that way from the time he was 10 or 11 years old. One man's observation sums up the men's thinking about closeness, "Maybe, as I look back at it, maybe I never really allowed anybody to get close to me."

The circumstances varied, but the outcomes were similar: These men were cut off from peers. Ironically, all but one of the men gave the outward appearance of being, at least partially, socially integrated. Seven were letter athletes in junior high and high school, several were also leaders in church and school activities, and all but one spent time with male peers. Their inner experience was not congruent with appearances.

Isolation and Sexuality in Adolescence

Without close friends to help them integrate the new demands adolescence placed upon them, some reported feeling ashamed and abnormal. Understanding and handling sexuality and establishing intimate relationships with members of the opposite sex are major tasks of adolescence. None of the men dealt well with these issues. Some were ashamed of their sexuality and avoided girls, while others sought and found relationships with girls that were based almost entirely on sexual activity. One man who was ashamed of his sexuality and did not find intimate female friends said:

> The sexual fantasies I had in high school, I was quite ashamed of them and I didn't want to talk to anybody about them. I thought it was me, that there was something wrong with me.

Shame about fantasies and poor social skills prevented some of the men from reaching out to girls. One man said:

> I found it real hard to talk with the girls. It was, like I had some kind of secret I was going to hide from them. I suppose it'd be how I felt about myself that I felt I was oversexed and there was something wrong with me having a sexual fantasy.

All of the men became preoccupied with sex. As one man said, the goal "was to have as much sex as I could." They all had orgasms on a regular basis. Eleven of the 14 sexually abused other children during their own adolescence, and many of them had exploitative relationships with age peers. Almost all of them masturbated several times a week, and some had been sexually exploited themselves. Some men were sexual with female relatives (aunts and sisters-in-law) more than 10 years older, and one man was a juvenile prostitute. Possibly, these men did not understand that they were being exploitative or being exploited.

Fearful of rejection by girls, two men who masturbated as often as once a day had fantasy relationships with girls they were attracted to. One man said:

> I had a real problem with rejection, and I would try not to get myself in a situation where you could get rejected. And rather than, like if you see a girl you like, ask her out or make a pass at her or something, rather than do that and maybe be rejected, it's easier just to fantasize about them and masturbate with it.

The second man got into "window peeking" and "having relationships with girls that way." He was afraid to talk to girls he liked in school, but at night he would peek in their bedrooms and watch them undress while he masturbated. The next day, in school, he would see the girls and fantasize about telling them that he had sex with them the night before whether they liked it or not. When asked why he did not try to have a relationship with these girls, he said, "I just felt inadequate."

Other men, as adolescents, had girlfriends or girls with whom they had sex several times a week. For these men, sex with their girlfriends was the focal point of their lives. One man worked two jobs so that he could afford to take his girlfriend to motels. Consequently, his school-work deteriorated. Although all of the men could be termed predatory, because they sexually abused children and/or same-age peers, one of the men identified himself as such. This man would seek out girls who had just broken up with boyfriends. He said:

> It was like cruising around like a shark for a victim. That one there just got dumped. I'll stay around her and a little hugging, a little hand hold-ing, a few words here and there, this one here, that one going to be a little bit of a challenge. Let's get the easy one out of the way first. Then, we'll go for the challenge.

This man had a "gift of gab" and could relate glibly to girls he saw as vulnerable. Feelings of connection and intimacy, however, were not present for him in these relationships.

Given their family background and their lack of interaction with peers, they appear not to have had a frame of reference to help them understand the difference between acceptable/nonacceptable behavior and that certain types of behavior are hurtful to themselves, to others, or to both. Their isolation in their families of origin probably led to being isolated from others.

Adolescence is a time of identity formation (Erikson, 1959). Cognitive, social, and biological change are in ascendancy, and young people depend a great deal on peers to help them learn to manage these major life tasks. Peer relationships provide adolescents with a frame of reference in which they test new behaviors, develop social skills, learn role-taking, which involves seeing the point of view of others, learn what is acceptable and *normal*, and discover their place in the social world. Socially isolated adolescents deal with these changes alone. The men in this sample gave information on what may happen when adolescents are socially isolated. They appeared to be filled with shame and self-doubt, as Erikson's (1959) theory predicts. They had few skills in taking the role of others. Instead of negotiating sexual relationships or accepting their fantasy life as simply part of being human, they became sexually exploitative of children and female peers and sometimes allowed themselves to be sexually exploited.

These men's description of their sexual behavior supports Yalom's (1980) statement that persons who have not developed the capacity for intimacy are at risk for using others sexually. That some of the men were also sexually exploited adds yet another dimension to Yalom's insight; that is, persons who have not developed the capacity for intimacy are themselves at risk for being sexually exploited.

Isolation and Marriage

These men's incapacity for relationships continued into adulthood, which they described as isolated and lacking in intimacy. As during adolescence, these men were preoccupied with sex. The married men described very active sexual lives with their wives as well as frequent sexual contact to orgasm with children. The window peeper, described above, was married throughout his adult life and also continued peeping until he was arrested for the sexual abuse of his stepdaughter. Regular sex with wives and the marital relationship itself, however, did not appear to help them overcome loneliness. As one man said:

I felt lonely even after I was married. We were together but I was still alone, which I guess the biggest part of that is my fault because I wouldn't open up.

In a variety of ways, these men walled themselves off from their wives. One man distanced himself from his wife by seeing himself as "king of my household." He said, "I am up here and my wife is down there, my kids are down there."

Frequently, the men used a "geographic" solution to maintain distance from their wives. One man went hunting or fishing "or something" almost every weekend:

I realized once I was there that it really wasn't there that I wanted to be. Golly, I'd be up there hunting three or four weekends in a row. Do I really want to be here? I'd sooner be home, but the situation at home, being what it was, maybe I didn't want to be there either. Where was I going to be, stuck in the middle somewhere.

This statement also illustrated the inner division that many of the men discussed. Sometimes the only inner conflict they were aware of was the conflict between being a sexual abuser of children and trying to hide this from themselves and/or others. Other times, they reported different types of inner division, such as the man quoted above. The only way he could manage conflict with his wife was to withdraw from her; his parents had also handled their conflict in this way. Another man graphically illustrated the conflicting feelings about themselves that many of the men experienced:

You still have those two voices talking to each other and there's a big battle going on inside you. I mean there's always a part of me that's telling me I'm OK and there's a part of me telling me you're a piece of crap.

A highly successful business executive—a three-letter high school athlete who had a public side and a hidden secretive side—thought of himself, alternately, as a "golden boy" and a "bastard." These men, then, exhibited signs of being divided selves, as suggested by psychoanalytic theory. These quotes are also examples of intrapersonal isolation.

For the subjects, sexual behavior with children often contributed to inner conflict. Some of the men managed to not think about their sexual behavior. For those who did think about their behavior, they typically felt as this man did:

> I was leading two lives. Life with my daughter and life with my wife. Battling it out before each episode and feeling really guilty about it after that.

The men said that for their wives the discovery that their husbands had sexually molested children was a shock. It would appear that the men had managed to hide their behavior. One man reported, "My wife said to me, 'We've been married for 20 years, and I thought I knew you.' There are parts of me that are so secretive." The social isolation that the men had felt was mirrored in the isolation they experienced within themselves. The man who considered himself a "golden boy" and a "bastard" had these inner images alternatively. It was only after treatment that he began to see that he had both of these self-images. Before treatment, he would either think of himself as one or the other, a classic example of splitting.

Existential Isolation

These men dealt with the existential isolation in one of two ways: either by withdrawing from the experience of it, or, possibly, by invading the boundaries of others so as to avoid the pain of separation. Their avoidance of others is discussed at length above. Some of the men provided descriptions that showed that sexual invasiveness was a solution to separation. One man said that "being sexual with my daughter" was his way of comforting himself and making himself feel good. A second man said, "As I seen it when I was fondling a little girl, I felt close. And that's it. I wanted to be close to somebody." Another man said having a child fellate him was the most wonderful feeling in the world. He felt accepted, and it made him feel like a man. Equating being fellated by a child with being a man suggests a profound problem with identity.

Most of the men, however, saw their sexual invasiveness as a fix, as a way of fixing their own feelings, of temporarily making themselves feel better through orgasm. These men explained their sexual behavior with children as "another way of getting my rocks off." Such statements suggest isolation not only from the spouse and other relationships, but from the child victim as well.

DISCUSSION

Isolation was a significant part of the experience of these male perpetrators of child sexual abuse. They were isolated in their families of origin, in their relationships with peers, and in marriages. Their parents' marriages were strife-ridden and/or distant. Parents, therefore, did not model patterns of interpersonal relationships that build and maintain intimacy, nor did they interact with their children in such a way that the children developed social skills and a capacity for intimacy. This led to their isolation from peers.

Being isolated in adolescence prevented these men from learning about and internalizing socially acceptable and normative behavior. Without peers in whom to confide they were unable to normalize their sexual interests, and often felt ashamed and guilty about sexual fantasy and masturbation. During adolescence when they were dealing with the identity versus shame and doubt conflict (Erikson, 1959), shame and doubt were predominant. Their marriages were characterized by isolation from spouses and the inability to share their inner thoughts and feelings; these men were out of touch with themselves and others.

Clinical intervention into these patterns of isolation is a major challenge. Children's groups, perpetrator groups, family therapy, multiple-family groups, and couples therapy could emphasize both social skill-building and the expression of inner thoughts, feelings, and fantasies. These strategies would help many isolated children and their families increase communication. The primary question guiding the therapist would be, "How can I devise treatments that would help perpetrators connect with other people in meaningful ways?"

In the assessment of perpetrators, attention needs to be paid to their relationship history. Commonly in treatment programs, the sexual history of perpetrators is done in minute detail. If isolation is an important factor in sexual abuse and if isolation results from an inability to form relationships, then a relationship history may be as important as a sexual history. The long-term goal in the treatment of perpetrators and their families could be the integration of parts of the self and social integration. As one perpetrator said, "I don't feel that I've ever really totally been able to love somebody." Therapy cannot teach people how to love, but it can help people to create conditions under which love has an opportunity to develop.

REFERENCES

Apfelberg, B., Sugra, C., & Pfeffer, A. Z. (1944). A psychiatric study of 250 sex offenders. *American Journal of Psychiatry, 100*, 762–770.

Davis, G. E., & Leitenberg, H. (1987). Adolescent sex offenders. *Psychological Bulletin, 101*, 417–427.

Erikson, E. (1959). Identity and the life cycle. *Psychological Issues, 1* (1).

Finkelhor, D. (1984). *Child sexual abuse.* New York: Free Press.

Finkelhor, D., & Associates (Eds.) (1986). *A sourcebook on child sexual abuse.* Beverly Hills, CA: Sage.

Gilgun, J. F., & Connor, T. M. (in press). Children as objects of sexual gratification. *Social Work.*

Goldstein, E. G. (1984). *Ego psychology and social work practice.* New York: Free Press.

Groth, A. N. (1983). Treatment of the sexual offender in a correctional institution. In J. G. Greer & I. R. Stuart (Eds.), *The sexual aggressor: Current perspectives in treatment* (pp. 160–176). New York: Van Nostrand Reinhold.

Herman, J. L., & Hirschman, L. (1981). *Father-daughter incest.* Cambridge, MA: Harvard University Press.

Justice, B., & Justice, R. (1979). *The broken taboo: Sex in the family.* New York: Human Sciences Press.

Larson, N. R., & Maddock, J. W. (1986). Structural and functional variables in incest family systems. *Journal of Psychotherapy and the Family, 2*, 27–44.

Peters, J. J. (1976). Children who are victims of sexual assault and the psychology of offenders. *American Jornal of Psychotherapy, 30*, 398–421.

Yalom, I. (1980). *Existential psychotherapy.* New York: Basic Books.

6

The Grooming Process in Father-Daughter Incest

John R. Christiansen
Reed H. Blake

INTRODUCTION

Considerable evidence indicates that father-daughter incest does not usually involve violence or severe force. Rather, it is a deliberately planned event. In her study of 80 victims of incest by their fathers or stepfathers, de Young (1982) found that only five (8%) were raped. Likewise, in her study of 930 women from the San Francisco area, Russell (1986) found that in 68% of the cases no physical force was involved. Indeed, in less than 29% of the cases of incest studied, only the mildest forms of physical force were used, and in only 1% was severe force used.

Most acts of incest perpetrated by fathers involve coercion without physical force. De Young described various aspects of such relations. These include "evolved incest," in which the father pays special attention to his daughter, while making increasingly intimate sexual advances as time passes, and "devious behavior" incest in which fathers molest their daughters while they are asleep. Fathers also use "courting behavior," patronizing and bribing their daughters to participate in incestuous acts. In addition, de Young indicated that secrecy is often used by incestuous fathers to perpetuate the "affair." Usually, all such interchanges between father and daughter initially tend to avoid physical violence and threats.

Perpetrating fathers generally adopt the role of a suitor with their daughters. Herman (1981) wrote that sexually abusive fathers "courted their daughters like jealous lovers, bringing them presents of flowers, expensive jewelry, or sexy underwear." According to Herman this "courting behavior" also involved talking about sex with their daughters, leaving pornographic materials for them to find, exhibiting themselves to their daughters, and spying on their daughters while they were undressing. These behaviors are designed to obligate and eroticize daughters, while exciting and gratifying fathers.

THE GROOMING PROCESS

Drawing on the research of de Young (evolved incest and courting behavior), Russell (persuasion), Herman (courting behavior), and others, a series of studies was begun in 1986 by a research team consisting of both faculty and graduate students (Christiansen, Blake, and Gibbons, 1988; Monson, 1988; Negron, 1988; Passey, 1987; Warner-Kearney, 1987) that illuminated the psycho-social process involved in father-daughter incest. We call this form of socialization, the "grooming process."

These studies support the view that perpetrators use trust, favoritism, alienation, secrecy, boundary violations, and evaluation in "grooming" their daughters to participate in sexual activities.

TRUST

The first process fathers use to initiate their daughters into incestuous activity is building trust. Ninety percent of father-perpetrators reported to Warner-Kearney (1987) that they took deliberate steps to establish a relationship of trust between themselves and their daughters before they began any type of sexual activity. Indeed, having the trust of their daughters was viewed by 73% of those perpetrators as an "important" factor in their sexual relationship as it reduced the risk of disclosure.

Father-perpetrators built trust between themselves and their daughters deliberately. They did this by (a) giving them presents of candy, food, money, and clothing; (b) spending time with them; (c) assuring them of the "rightness" of what they were doing; and (d) telling the child that the acts would not hurt them. These step-by-step efforts were carefully planned to cause their daughters to accept later demands.

Victims perceived that their fathers had indeed developed their trust. Interviews by Passey (1987) with victims of father-daughter incest participating in a Parents United program provided evidence that trusting their fathers resulted in their participation in incestuous behavior.

FAVORITISM

Another part of the grooming phase involves the process of placing the intended victim in a "favored" relationship. Reporting on this process, Warner-Kearney described one father who "bought gifts and extra treats, and nice clothes, and told her [potential victim] that she would have to be nice to me back." Fathers make it clear to potential victims that reciprocity is expected if favors are accepted.

Victims also report that their fathers began treating them as "special." This usually meant that the potential victims were treated differently than other siblings and their mothers. As this occurred, the daughters' legitimate and traditional role relationships are deliberately blurred. Daughters are made to believe they are unique friends of their fathers in addition to being daughters. Other fathers used the technique of telling their daughters of their loneliness and indicated that their daughters can eliminate the lonely feelings. Through these means, daughters' feelings of worth are enhanced relative to other persons in their lives and the lives of their fathers.

ALIENATION

Perpetrating fathers may also use alienation as a means of ensuring their exploitative successes with their daughters. The alienation process often begins as a consequence of the trust built by perpetrators. Moreover, alienation increases as favoritism is established. Potential victims become alienated from the mothers because these daughters are placed by their fathers in their mothers' traditional role of confidante, intimate friend, and sex partner. Alienation from siblings occurs because of the privileges and special favors potential victims receive. Such favorable treatment is often correctly seen by siblings as unfair and preferential. Finally, potential victims are often alienated from their friends because fathers often dominate the lives of their daughters so much that they are not able to interact normally with their peers. All such alienation serves to further isolate daughters from support groups and possible sources of help, and causes them to be even more dependent on their fathers.

SECRECY

A stifling environment of secrecy is usually built by perpetrators once trust has been established. Fathers often use persuasive, subtle, and confusing rationalizations with their potential victims in developing secrecy as part of their "special" relationship. In this regard, one victim reported that her father told her, "Mom wouldn't understand how special we are together. Ours is a special love that others wouldn't understand."

Secrecy, however, is not always achieved by subtle means. In fact, it is at this point that potential victims may first perceive that their fathers are capable of intense, possessive, threatening, and even frightening behavior regarding their budding relationship. Passey noted that 90% of the victims in her study reported their father used threatening looks, glares, or other body language whenever they felt their daughters were revealing undesirable information about what was going on. At this point daughters often begin to experience a "love-fear" relationship with their father.

BOUNDARY VIOLATIONS

Together with the building of trust, favoritism, alienation, and secrecy, violation of boundaries is another important element in the grooming process. Christiansen et al. (1988) confirmed that these violations occur in relationships between fathers and daughters as early as infancy and involve rejection of accepted norms of modesty and personal intimacy. These are most noticeable in bathing, dressing, bathroom behavior, and in conversations.

Bathing

Fathers frequently insist on being the person to bathe their daughters to the exclusion of others. Most often, such bathing of daughters involves all parts of the child's body, including the genitals.

Frequently the father bathes with the daughter, soaping and washing the daughter, and teaching the child to reciprocate. Such behavior involves inappropriate and sexually stimulating behavior. With younger victims, it sometimes continues during the entire course of the incestuous experience. This behavior is, in reality, a seemingly legitimate entree to child sexual abuse.

Dressing

Other oppressive and smothering—apparently innocent—involvement includes dressing the daughters, dressing together, or watching daughters dress.

Bathroom Behavior

Watching and participating with the child in bathroom behavior after the child is toilet trained is common with perpetrating fathers. This type of interaction lends itself to conversations dealing with body and sexual functions.

Sexually Explicit and Vulgar Conversation

Through language and conversations, sexual themes can be carried away from the bathroom. This type of boundary violation by fathers in the grooming process makes sex commonplace, accessible, and pervasive. Perpetrators speak to daughters using sexually explicit language. They frequently interpret daily experiences in a sexual context. The result of such communication is to increase the sexual content in daughters' psychosocial environment, provide easy movement from conversations to overt actions, and to eroticize the child.

EVALUATION OF THE
GROOMING PHASE'S RESULTS

During the grooming phase, fathers generally attempt to determine if, from their point of view, they may safely engage in more intimate and overt acts. If their daughters are evaluated as being receptive to further intimacies, fathers proceed with their demands. For example, one father proceeded with more intimate incestuous acts after he observed that his daughter "acted interested and did not show any fear." Another said of his victim, "She was careful to keep the whole affair secret." Only after such reassurances did most of these fathers begin specific sexual activities. In other words, the daughter has been "groomed" to desire and enjoy things sexual in nature.

GROOMING PROCESS CUES

In the grooming process, perpetrators engage in activities with their daughters that are designed to prepare their daughters for more intimate incestuous experiences. There are sufficient cues available in this stage to sufficiently alert observant family members, friends, professionals, and others to the fact that seriously inappropriate interactions are taking place.

Our research team has identified these cues, which include:

1. Efforts on the part of the father to build a unique kind of trust in the intended victim. The type of trust being built is that in which the father is to be trusted more than any other person. Such trust building is often accompanied by a bestowal of favors on the daughter.

2. Alienation of the daughter from family members, peers, and other significant persons in her life.

3. Demands of secrecy upon the daughter. Such demands might be exhibited in furtive conversations, being alone together frequently, cessation of speech or change of subject when others approach, and similar kinds of conspiratorial-like actions.

4. Boundary violations that involve intrusion of the father in what should be the daughter's private and intimate acts of bathing, dressing, and bathroom behavior, and actions by the father to have the daughter participate in his own similar intimate acts. Additionally, the father violates the daughter's personal environment by conversing with her in sexually-explicit language and speaking to her in sexually-suggestive ways.

THE ONGOING PHASE OF FATHER-DAUGHTER INCEST

If the grooming proceeds successfully from the perpetrators' point of view, they generally attempt with even more exploitative sexual acts. These acts result in their own physical as well as psychological gratification. This does not mean, however, that psychological gratification does not come to perpetrators in the earlier grooming activities. Our research suggests that perpetrators use careful planning, scheming, and execution of strategies, which, if not stopped, result in increasingly intimate acts.

The ongoing phase in father-daughter incest consists of other definable processes. These are (a) a stepwise progression of sexual acts, (b) checking of risks, (c) finding places where incest may occur, (d) determining the most propitious time for it, and (e) using bribes, threats, and punishment.

A STEPWISE PROGRESSION OF SEXUAL ACTS

Incestuous relationships among fathers and daughters follow a pattern similar to that seen in most heterosexual relations. They begin with acts that are least intimate and progress to more intimate acts.

With prepubescent daughters, perpetrators tend to begin by touching. This is followed by kissing, fondling, breast stimulation, reciprocal fondling, masturbation, oral stimulation of breast and genitals, reciprocal masturbations, oral sex, and finally coitus. If daughters have reached puberty, Negron (1988) reported that fathers are more hesitant to engage in coitus owing to fears of pregnancy. Thus, with pubescent victims they engage in acts that bring physical gratification, but that do not have a high risk of impregnating the daughter.

REPEATED CHECKING OF RISKS

This progression toward greater intimacy in sexual acts is usually stopped if fathers feel their incestuous activity might be made known to others. Consequently, fathers are careful to ascertain their victims' willingness to continue being exploited without exposing the relationship by constantly checking their daughters' psychosocial state. For example, one father reported to Warner-Kearney that he felt he could proceed with further intimacies because the victim "remained quiet when I put my hands on her." Another father felt he could safely proceed when his daughter "would talk nasty to me and grab me in my crotch." About 40% of the perpetrators in the study reported that their daughters became eroticized to the point that receptivity to further exploitation was observable. According to fathers, receptivity was shown by daughters' caressing their fathers' bodies, cuddling up to their fathers, or presenting themselves in revealing ways. (It must be recognized, however, that these observations may involve rationalizations.)

SELECTING A PLACE WHERE INCEST MAY OCCUR

In the ongoing phase of incest, a particular place is usually selected by the perpetrator where incestuous acts occur. Most of the time the place used is the family home. Within the home, the child's bedroom is most often used for these acts. The room used next often is the living room. Only occasionally do fathers take their daughters away from the home for sexual activities. When they do, they generally take them on rides in vehicles, on camping trips, or into buildings adjacent to their homes. Part of the betrayal that children feel results from the fact that their homes, and particularly their own bedrooms, are not the places of security and safety they wish them to be.

SELECTING A TIME WHEN INCEST MAY OCCUR

As with the place, fathers carefully select the time when incestuous exploitation will occur. The time selected is intended to minimize risk of exposure, but also to maintain the appearance of normality. Consequently, most fathers choose the late evening hours. This time corresponds to the time the victims are undressing for bed, perhaps bathing, watching late TV, and going to bed. The routine, relaxed nature of these activities provide perpetrators with an opportunity for initiating and completing sexual exploitation.

Rather than finding a time when they are entirely alone—when mothers are away working, or siblings are at school, for instance—perpetrators frequently abuse their children when other family members are in the house.

BRIBES, THREATS, AND PUNISHMENT

Bribes and other kinds of rewards are used not only to initiate child sexual abuse, but also to perpetuate it. In the ongoing phase of father-daughter incest, threats and punishment are also apt to be used by fathers to perpetuate the relationship and to deal with threats of exposure.

While material gifts continue to be given to daughters during this time, nonmaterial rewards are more apt to be bestowed. These take the form of extra privileges, lowered demands for housework, and being treated more like an "adult" than the other children. The effectiveness of these rewards is reflected in the comment of one victim who said that she could get "anything she wanted" if she agreed to her father's sexual demands. Similarly, another victim stated, "he never punished me like my mother did."

Another type of bribe used by fathers with their victims is alcohol. In interviews with victims, Monson (1988) found that nearly one-fifth (18%) of the victims of father-daughter incest reported they were given alcohol by their fathers prior to engaging in incestuous acts. Likewise, their fathers also used alcohol.

The effects of using alcohol as a bribe or "conditioner" for sexual relations varied among victims. Some victims welcomed the effects of alcohol to deaden their apprehensions and guilt. One victim, for example, said, "When my father gave me alcohol, I felt better and more relaxed before he touched me sexually. I also felt less guilty about betraying my mother when I had sex with my father." Another daughter reported, "My dad was drinking alcohol when he abused me and he was only interested in having an orgasm. I needed alcohol to help me block out the incest."

In this phase of the incestuous relationship, fathers seem to be anxious to perpetuate the relationship as long as possible, and at the same time prevent exposure from occurring. Consequently, if the earlier grooming has failed somewhat, fathers often begin to use forceful means of subjecting their victims. In our study, less than one-fourth of the perpetrators reported using threats or actual physical punishment, yet almost half (45%) of the victims said that perpetrators did. The following quotations illustrate the kinds of threats and punishment used:

> "He shot my dog—and I knew he would do the same to me."
> "He would beat me up and feel my breasts at the same time."
> "My father would hit me hard and throw me up against a wall. He dislocated my jaw once, and put me in the hospital."
> "He told me I was his property until I was 18, and there was nothing I could do."

Other kinds of threats are also made by fathers. These threats deal with the consequences of having others know of the relationship. Perpetrators frequently mentioned the likelihood that they will lose their job, that the mother will get a divorce and siblings be put in foster placement, that economic suffering will follow and possible legal entanglements. Ironically, these statements are more apt to be true than most others made by fathers. When one or more of these events occur, victims find it difficult to realize that they are the consequence of fateful decisions made by perpetrating fathers—and not by themselves.

ONGOING INCEST CUES

Our research observed additional cues for family members, professionals, and others, which help identify ongoing sexual abuse. These include:

1. Social and psychological characteristics of victims that are described quite fully in available literature. These include low self-esteem, antisocial behavior, withdrawal, sexual acting out, sudden lack of interest or motivation in school, and mood changes.

2. Interaction by the father with his daughter in which the father places unusual demands on his daughter's time—for her company, attention, and loyalty—and peers tend not to be made welcome at the family home.

3. The perpetrator being with his daughter on a regular basis in her bedroom. This might follow attending her while she undresses and bathes.

4. The father being with the daughter alone late at night in the living room or in her bedroom.

5. Evidence of increased apprehension and tension on the part of the daughter, resulting from threats and intimidation; evidence of actual physical assaults.

6. Use of alcohol and drugs by perpetrators and victims.

AMELIORATION PHASE

The last stage of the usual father-daughter sexual abuse scenario, which our research identified, is the amelioration phase. In this period, the daughter ends the exploitation through such means as leaving home, confiding in and obtaining help from others, or through other measures. Or, others in the family may intervene to end the abuse. It is at this time that the father usually attempts to shift as much of the responsibility for his own guilt to the daughter.

Daughters are often verbally denigrated by their fathers at this time as well. Daughters report that fathers angrily label them "sluts," "whores," "bitches," and "no good." Such labeling adds to the guilt and worthlessness that these victims may feel. These feelings may account for some victims' long-lasting guilt and shame.

In some instances, daughters' sexual awakenings are used as a weapon against them, and as a means of ridding fathers of some of their guilt. Perpetrators freely point to the daughters' behaviors, which they perceived and interpreted as inviting and seductive. These perceptions and accusations are confusing and difficult for daughter-victims to deal with, as they are half-truths, shameful, and guilt-inducing.

In attempting to lessen the effects of father-daughter incest, it may be helpful to recognize the following:

1. Perpetrators deliberately make victims feel that they (the victims) are largely responsible for what has happened. This guilt results from the fathers' projections of their own guilt, from the negative labeling of victims for responsive actions, and from the confusion victims feel that sometimes occurs through erotization.

2. Any negative actions that befall the father, the family, or others connected with exposure of the incest is likely to be viewed by the girl as her fault, and must be dealt with therapeutically.

3. Obtaining a complete and responsible confession. Edmonds and Christiansen (1988) indicated that the father's confession of his guilt for wrongs done, coupled with a full apology to the daughter, is highly desirable for reducing guilt in both the short term and the long term.

CONCLUSION

Rather than being a sudden, initially traumatic occurrence, most father-daughter incest involves a gradual, deliberate, and predictable entanglement planned and carried out by the father, whereby the daughter is "groomed" to participate in sexual intimacies. When the incestuous relationships end, victims are left by their perpetrators to feel at least partially responsible for their own victimization and for other traumatic events that occur within, and to, the family. By identifying the processes and phases of father-daughter incest, however, it is more likely that prevention and education can occur, and then incest can be stopped. The means of reducing the traumatic consequences of incest may be enhanced through more informed intervention.

REFERENCES

Christiansen, J. R., Blake, R. H., Gibbons, W. G. (1988, April). *The nature of grooming behavior used in father-daughter incest.* Paper presented at the Western Social Science Association, Denver, CO.

de Young, M. (1982). *The sexual victimization of children.* Jefferson, NC: McFarland.

Edmonds, R., & Christiansen, J. R. (1988, April). *Fathers' apologies in father-daughter incest.* Paper presented at the Western Social Science Association, Denver, CO.

Herman, J. L. (1981). *Father-daughter incest.* Cambridge, MA: Harvard University Press.

Monson, O. (1988, April). *Alcohol and drug usage among perpetrators and victims in father-daughter incest.* Paper presented at the Western Social Science Association, Denver, CO.

Negron, C. (1988, April). *Methods of birth control used in father-daughter incest.* Paper presented at the Western Social Science Association, Denver, CO.

Passey, L. S. (1987). *Behavior leading to father-daughter incest: A further test of the Warner-Kearney hypothesis.* Paper presented at the Western Social Science Association, El Paso, TX.

Russell, D. H. (1986). *The secret trauma.* New York: Basic Books.

Warner-Kearney, D. (1987, February). *The nature of grooming behavior used by sexual offenders in father-daughter incest.* Paper presented at the Western Criminology Association, Las Vegas, NV.

7

Adolescent/Sibling Incest Perpetrators

Lois H. Pierce
Robert L. Pierce

INTRODUCTION

Although sexual offending is typically thought of as an adult crime, early studies determined that juvenile offending is also a problem (Doshay, 1943; Groth, Hobson, Lucey, & Pierre, 1981; Shoor, Speed, & Bartlet, 1966). Recent studies also support a need to study this population. In fact, Thomas and Rogers (1983) suggested that even though evidence strongly supports the view that intrafamilial sexual abuse occurs most often among persons of roughly the same generation, most literature and theory still focuses on father-daughter incest.

This chapter attempts to narrow this gap in the literature. The authors did a survey of juvenile offenders, which included 43 incest offenders who had been reported to the Illinois Department of Child and Family Services during 1986. Because protective service agencies typically focus on abuse by family members or care givers, the majority of these cases involved siblings or other youth in the home. This chapter reviews pertinent clinical findings and information relevant to the treatment of incestuous adolescents as well as pertinent observations made by the child protective service worker during the investigation.

DEFINITIONS OF JUVENILE OFFENDING

Juvenile sexual offenders are youths under 18 who engage in sexual activities including exposure, genital fondling, oral, anal, and vaginal intercourse. The juvenile offender uses some type of manipulation or coercion—either threats or implied power—to engage the victim. Although many studies assume that the offender is older than the victim, some studies have shown that juvenile offenders are sometimes younger than their victims (Pierce & Pierce, 1987).

It is difficult to determine how many juvenile offenses actually occur because, unless a rape is committed, the offense is classified under the general category of assault. One-fifth to one-quarter of the rapes reported in the Uniform Crime Report are committed by individuals under 18 (Knopp, 1982). Twenty-three percent of these are committed by youths 14 and under. Thomas and Rogers (1983) found that of all sexual abuse cases reported to the staff of their unit at Children's Hospital National Medical Center in Washington, D.C., 54% involved a juvenile offender, with over 40% of those offenses involving a family member.

It is even more difficult to determine the number of sibling offenses that occur since these acts are often assumed to be experimentation or exploration and are not reported. Studies on reported sexual abuse cases suggest sibling abuse ranges from 6% (Pierce & Pierce, 1985) to 33% (Thomas & Rogers, 1983) of the cases investigated. De Young (1982) documented 5 cases of sibling incest in her sample of 80 incest victims; Meiselman (1978) found 11 cases of sibling incest compared to 38 of father-daughter incest; and Finkelhor (1980) discovered that 13% of his sample were sexually involved with siblings, although he feels this is an underestimate.

Sibling offenses appear to fall into two categories. One category generally begins early as a mutual exploration and may end as the children realize their behavior is not appropriate. If the relationship continues into adolescence, the siblings frequently have difficulty in subsequent sexual relationships, although Finkelhor (1980) did not find this to be true.

The second category involves one sibling forcing another to engage in sexual activities (de Young, 1982). Sometimes the offender is being sexually abused by a parent or relative and is participating in a promiscuous family life-style (Pierce, 1987). In other cases the offender may be copying the sexually precocious behavior of abused siblings (de Young, 1982) or may be acting out other family problems.

Due to cultural, ethnic, geographic, and individual differences among offenders, the notion of a typical offender becomes a relative issue. Loredo (1982) warned that, before a label of offending is attached, the clinician should determine if the incest involves some aspect of victimization, or two or more willing participants exhibiting some type of pathology.

Longo and Groth (1983) categorized offenders into two groups: passive and aggressive. The behavioral dynamics of the passive offender (Shoor et al., 1966) are likely to be more subtle (i.e., touching or rubbing, exhibitionism, and compulsive masturbation). In contrast, the aggressive adolescent offender's behaviors are interwoven in the complex relationship between violence and sex. These are the offenders who commit rape, engage in forced, same sex intercourse, or act out violent threats toward family members or friends.

DESCRIPTION OF JUVENILE OFFENDERS

The offenders, in this study, ranged in age from 4 to 16 years of age with an average age of 13.1 years. Twenty percent of the victims were either sisters, stepsisters, or adoptive sisters. Nineteen percent were foster sisters, 16% were foster brothers, and 5% were brothers. The rest were other relatives, friends, or children the juvenile was babysitting (caretakers). Determination concerning family members and home conditions were taken from home study reports performed by child protective service workers during the assessment process.

Eighty-one percent of the offenders in this survey were male and 67% were white. The offender was usually the oldest child of his/her sex in the family (46% of the males and 13% of the females) or an only child.

Several patterns of offending appeared: Only 30% were involved in one known offense while 16% were involved in multiple, frequently occurring incidents. In 30% of the cases, the offenses occurred infrequently over a long period of time, and, in the final group, several offenses occurred over a short period of time. When there were multiple reports, the adolescents were older and described as more dysfunctional than in other categories. These offenders were also more likely to be classified as delinquents by their protective service worker.

The most frequent type of offense in which the juveniles in our study engaged was fondling (51%), with oral intercourse next (30%). Other frequently occurring acts were vaginal intercourse (22%), attempted intercourse (19%), anal intercourse (19%), and exposure (19%). Most often the offender used verbal threats to coerce the victim, but in many cases no specific type of force was mentioned, suggesting that perceived power is sufficient.

Juveniles generally perpetrated against people who were younger.

In 46% of the cases the victim was at least 5 years younger. In 13% of the cases the offender was 10 years older. In 13% of the cases the offender and victim were close in age, but, in 22% of the cases, the offender was younger than the victim.

Caseworkers described juveniles involved in this study as exhibiting many problems in their families and at school. In fact, it is difficult to determine if the problems are the result of the offending or if the juvenile offenses are in response to dysfunctional families. In all probability, both play a role. Fifty-four percent of the juvenile offenders studied were described as aggressive toward family members, half had been involved in delinquent acts, and half had academic problems. Thirty-eight percent had other behavior problems at home, such as running away, stealing from family members, or withdrawing. Thirty-eight percent had been placed in special classes in school, 30% had behavioral problems at school, and 14% were diagnosed as mentally retarded.

Groth and Loredo (1981) described similar findings. The offenders in their study were typically loners with little skill in "negotiating emotionally intimate peer relationships" (p. 38). Moreover, low self-esteem, coupled with deep-seated feelings of inadequacy and emptiness, contribute to the juvenile's inability to handle life's demands. Shoor et al. (1966) discovered that, aside from being a loner, the juvenile offender prefers playing with younger children, tends to have a limited work history, and is generally immature in all areas of functioning.

Many of the offenders in our study, as has been the pattern in some other studies, were sexually victimized themselves—an indication of learned violence. Only three of the juveniles in our study were not reported as abused. Forty-three percent had been sexually abused by family members, 5% by others. Eleven percent were exposed to inappropriate sexual behavior, 63% were physically abused, and 70% were neglected. Longo's (1982) study shows that 47% of his subjects had been sexually assaulted in their childhood.

Not only have these children been abused, family problems predominate. Fifty-four percent of the juveniles' parents were judged to be mentally ill by their caseworker during the initial intake in our study. Twenty-four percent of the parents were involved in substance abuse, and 14% were in prison. Over half of the parents had financial problems, and almost half needed better housing. In two families, children had died because of neglect.

The researchers returned to the protective service agency approximately one year later to initiate a follow-up study that would determine whether or not the juveniles continued to offend, what services were being used, and what services were lacking. Six cases were closed by the agency and further information was unavailable. Eight of the remaining 37 juveniles had reoffended, all of whom were male. Females continued to be involved sexually, but were no longer seen as the aggressor. For example, a 13 year old was involved in prostitution. Sexual offending was suspected but not substantiated in several other cases.

At this point, it was possible to identify a pattern of reoffending among these eight juveniles. One-fourth of them continued to be involved with younger girls, and one-fourth engaged in contact with same-sex peers. Others exposed themselves, attempted rape, or were involved in several kinds of sexual activity. None of the reoffenders remained at home, although 38% were in foster care. The rest were in residential care centers or detention. Hopefully, caretakers in these settings are alerted and providing protection for other residents. Half of the reoffenders had parents with mental problems, and 25% had parents in prison. The caseworkers assessed that the reoffender's mentally ill parents were more disturbed than those in the total sample.

At the time of the follow-up, protective service workers felt the prognosis was fair or poor for almost 75% of the original juvenile offenders reported from their caseloads. Many offenders continued to have problems and appeared to lack the social skills needed to make friends. Workers frequently described these children as unlikable, which makes it even more difficult for them to receive help. On the other hand, one of the most likable adolescents in the study was judged recovered by his therapist and immediately began offending again.

TREATMENT

Although adolescents appear to be exploring and talking more openly about their sexuality today than in past decades (Parry-Jones, 1985), this seems to have had only minimal effect on how they are responded to within the treatment arena. Perhaps treatment providers are not as accepting nor as open concerning these behaviors; in other words, this is where the communication stops. Since many parents and clinicians are themselves struggling with the issue of identifying what is typical or normal sexual behavior and exploration among youth, the issue is frequently avoided. Thus, the juveniles who seem overly anxious, frightened, and confused about their sexual development, thoughts, and activities find little or no help upon confiding in adults about sexual matters. When this is compounded by the knowledge that the child has indeed sexually abused another, confronting the issue may be even more difficult. Juvenile offenders may threaten to abuse female therapists or may try to use seduction within the clinical setting. They are often frightening and difficult to work with unless the therapist is comfortable with his/her sexuality and with discussing sexual matters.

To juvenile offenders, sex represents the vehicle through which they give and receive attention. In this sense sex, in and of itself, appears to be secondary to what it supposedly brings: closeness, perceived caring, or importance. Waggoner and Boyd (1941) pointed out that juvenile offenders are insecure children who engage in aberrant sexual behaviors to gain approval and to release tension and anxiety. Helping the adolescent offender redirect his/her strong sexual drives into socially acceptable and desirable channels is one of several treatment issues facing clinicians. They also pointed out that offenders frequently reside in homes that are characterized as rejecting, tense, and unstable.

When clinicians examine the multiplicity of problems facing juvenile offenders and their families, it becomes obvious that treatment must focus on several issues. The family and the juvenile must be involved in treatment if the juvenile is to return home, especially if the victim is still in the home. Involvement of the family may be difficult because of the tendency to deny the abuse, but it is an integral component of most treatment programs.

Treatment begins with individual and group sessions for the offender. During this time, the victim and family members are also seen, but this discussion will examine areas of concern in treatment of the juvenile. Most programs ask that the offender be removed from the home, at least during the initial phases of treatment (Thomas & Rogers, 1983). Care must be taken to ensure that the youth is not placed with other vulnerable children, who, themselves, will perpetrate the abuse. If the offender is placed in a foster home, the foster parents should be well-trained concerning the behaviors they may expect and the appropriate responses to those behaviors.

When working with the juvenile offender in a treatment setting, five interrelated areas that must be addressed are:

1. the low feelings of self-esteem experienced by the offender;
2. the offender's own victimization; this can help the offender gain some empathy for the victim;
3. the social isolation experienced by offenders; they often have few social skills and few friends;
4. that offenders need sex education; they must learn acceptable ways of acting out their sexual feelings; and
5. that offenders need to learn their pattern of response and offending.

Low self-esteem. As has been noted, juvenile offenders frequently come from dysfunctional families. They have received little warmth or support from parents and are functioning at a much younger age developmentally than their chronological age would imply. Therapy must supply or replace much of the structure and consistency missing in the youth's life. As the therapist supports the youth and encourages the youth to explore issues and change behavior, the therapist can also point out those areas in which the youth is successful.

The offender's own victimization. A large number of juvenile offenders have been sexually victimized. Others have been physically abused and neglected. The offender should be helped to acknowledge his/her feelings of anger, shame, and worthlessness. The offender may also feel some responsibility for his/her abuse and may be attempting to overcome these feelings by abusing others. Once offenders can accept their own victimization, they can be helped to empathize with victims, and they are more likely to feel remorse for their acts. Groth (1982) cautioned that some offenders may become depressed when they reach this point.

Social isolation. As noted earlier, many juvenile offenders have few social skills. They often need assertiveness training, as well as social skills training. Many report difficulty in forming relationships and feel uncomfortable around the opposite sex. In addition, they feel put down and ignored when trying to express their needs and often respond by being aggressive or passive (Longo, 1983). Group sessions are particularly helpful in this respect.

Sex education. Because most juvenile offenders come from families in which sex is either presented as something dirty or in which there are few sexual boundaries, most have little idea of what a loving sexual relationship involves. They are used to taking what they want and have little concept that decisions can be made around sexual matters. Adolescents who have been involved in same-sex abuse may wonder about their sexual orientation and will need help resolving this issue. Most have minimal knowledge of anatomy and sexual response. Sex education should start with basics and assume nothing.

Patterns of response. Each offender has a pattern of behavior antecedent to incestuous activity. It is important for him/her to recognize the behaviors that lead to the sexual offense and to find other ways to respond. Many adolescents can be helped to understand the situations that result in sexual arousal and can develop alternative responses.

After the juvenile offender has been in treatment for a while, usually longer than with other kinds of problems, the family can be seen together. Thomas and Rogers (1983) described how this occurs in their program. Because the family faces many situational/environmental problems as well, clinicians must also have access to community resources or must be willing to advocate for changes in the services available.

SUMMARY

Although juvenile sexual offending, particularly sibling abuse, appears to be the most common type of incest, the research and literature in this area have not yet caught up to that on father-daughter incest. It does appear that juvenile offenders frequently reside in families where they receive minimal warmth and care. Many offenders have been victimized themselves and, thus, have few social skills. Findings also suggest that many offenders begin to have problems at an early age, but families and communities refuse to regard this behavior as serious.

To be successful in treating adolescent offenders, interventions must occur on several levels: with the offender, the offender's family, and the offender's community. With a greater understanding of the offender's problems, the clinical community will be better prepared to effectively intervene. Suggestions for treatment will be developed as more juvenile offenders are being reported and mandated to receive treatment. The classification and identification of these young offenders should be a high priority for treatment providers and researchers, eventually leading to more adequate treatment diagnosis with this population.

REFERENCES

de Young, M. (1982). *The sexual victimization of children*. Jefferson, NC: McFarland.
Doshay, L. (1943). *The boy sex offender and his later career*. New York: Grove and Stratton.

Finkelhor, D. (1980). Sex among siblings: A survey of the prevalence, variety and effects. *Archives of Sexual Behavior, 9,* 171–194.

Groth, N. (1982). The incest offender. In S. Sgroi (Ed.), *Handbook of clinical intervention in child sexual abuse* (pp. 215–240). Lexington, MA: Lexington Books.

Groth, N., Hobson, W., Lucey, K., & Pierre, J. (1981). Juvenile sexual offenders: Guidelines for treatment. *International Journal of Offender Therapy and Comparative Criminology, 25,* 265–272.

Groth, N., & Loredo, C. (1981). Juvenile sexual offenders: Guidelines for assessment. *International Journal of Offender Therapy and Comparative Criminology, 25,* 31–39.

Knopp, F. (1982). *Remedial intervention in adolescent sex offenses: Nine program descriptions.* New York: New York State Council of Churches, Safer Society Press.

Longo, R. (1982). Sexual learning and experiences among adolescent sexual offenders. *International Journal of Offender Therapy and Comparative Criminology, 26,* 2335–2340.

Longo, R. (1983). Administering a comprehensive sexually aggressive treatment program in a maximum security setting. In J. Greer & I. Stuart (Eds.), *The sexual aggressor: Current perspectives on treatment* (pp. 177–197). New York: Van Nostrand Reinhold.

Longo, R., & Groth, N. (1983). Juvenile sexual offenses in the histories of adult rapists and child molesters. *International Journal of Offender Therapy and Comparative Criminology, 27,* 150–155.

Loredo, C. (1982). Sibling incest. In S. Sgroi (Ed.), *Handbook of clinical intervention in child sexual abuse* (pp. 177–190). Lexington, MA: Lexington Books.

Meiselman, K. (1978). *Incest: A psychological study of causes and effects with treatment recommendations.* San Francisco: Jossey-Bass.

Parry-Jones, W. (1985). Adolescent disturbance. In M. Rutter & L. Hersov (Eds.), *Child and adolescent psychiatry: Modern approaches* (pp. 584–598). London: Blackwell Scientific.

Pierce, L. (1987). Father-son incest: Using the literature to guide practice. *Social Casework, 68,* 67–74.

Pierce, L., & Pierce, R. (1987). Incestuous victimization by juvenile sex offenders. *Journal of Family Violence, 2,* 351–364.

Pierce, R., & Pierce, L. (1985). Analysis of sexual abuse hotline reports. *Child Abuse and Neglect, 9,* 37–45.

Thomas, J., & Rogers, C. (1983). A treatment program for intrafamily juvenile sexual offenders. In J. Greer & I. Stuart (Eds.), *The sexual aggressor: Current perspectives on treatment* (pp. 127–143). New York: Van Nostrand Reinhold.

Shoor, M., Speed, M., & Bartlet, C. (1966). Syndrome of the adolescent child molester. *The American Journal of Psychiatry, 122,* 783–789.

Waggoner, R., & Boyd, D. (1941). Juvenile aberrant sexual behavior. *American Journal of Orthopsychiatry, 11,* 275–291.

8

Women as Perpetrators of Child Sexual Abuse: *Recognition Barriers*

Craig M. Allen

INTRODUCTION

The beginning of the eighties was marked by an "explosion" of literature on child sexual abuse (Conte, 1982), and the pace has continued throughout the decade that has followed. Contributing to this explosion were results from major research efforts conducted during the latter half of the seventies (e.g., Finkelhor, 1979) that broke through deep-seated cultural denial about the scope of the occurrence of intrafamilial sexual abuse. Few beliefs about the family had been held so universally as the belief that parents did not commit sexual acts with their children.

This belief is now recognized, of course, to be a myth for many families. Unfortunately, some of the secondary beliefs associated with the incest myth have continued on into the eighties. The most powerful of these has been the assumption that only males are the perpetrators of child sexual abuse. Only recently has this belief begun to be seriously questioned (Alford, Grey, & Kasper, 1988; Condy, Templer, Brown, & Veaco, 1987; Faller, 1987; Fehrenbach & Monastersky, 1988; Johnson & Shrier, 1987; Knopp & Lackey, 1989; Masters, 1986; Mathews, Matthews, & Speltz, 1989; McCarty, 1986; National Adolescent Perpetrator Network, 1988; Scavo, 1989; Vander May, 1988).

Why has recognition of the sexual abuse of children by women developed so slowly? Part of the answer is that it has seldomly been reported. But perhaps an even more important part of the answer is

AUTHOR'S NOTE: Preparation of this chapter was made possible by a grant from the National Center on Child Abuse and Neglect. Special thanks need to be extended to Diane Baldrige and Hui Mei Huang for their help in researching this project.

reflected in the unacceptability of such behavior, for few actions deviate as far from cultural norms and deep-seated beliefs as do those committed by female child sexual abusers. These observations and beliefs may intertwine to produce barriers that prevent the recognition of female child sexual abuse. The discussion that follows will focus on three barriers: (1) overestimation of the strength of the incest taboo, (2) overextension of feminist explanations of child sexual abuse, and (3) overgeneralization of the observation that female child sexual abuse is rare.

OVERESTIMATION OF THE STRENGTH OF THE INCEST TABOO

A major barrier to the recognition of female child sexual abuse has been overestimation of the strength of the incest taboo, considered by anthropologists "to be the foundation of all kinship structures," its purpose "the preservation of the human social order" (Herman & Hirschman, 1977). Freud incorporated these beliefs about the incest taboo into his own works, but not before a fascinating reversal of his position. As Kendrick (1988) noted, in an earlier lecture on the development of his theory of hysteria, Freud had reported what he considered unequivocal findings: When they were younger, all 18 of his patients had been sexually abused by an adult or an older sibling.

However, by the time his monumentally influential work on psychoanalysis was published a year later, Freud had completely altered his position (Kendrick, 1988, pp. 178–179). He then denied the possibility that the reports of incest by his patients could have been correct. In what became one of the most critical decisions ever made about incest, Freud decided instead to consider these reports as mere sexual fantasies, and to use sexual fantasy and the incest taboo as cornerstones of his psychoanalytic theory (Arkin, 1984).

As psychoanalytic theory continued to develop, men's and women's roles were differentiated substantially. Men were considered to be sexual predators and women docile recipients, qualities inherent in the psychogenetic makeup of each sex. As Arkin (1984) noted:

> Freud's hypothesis considers the taboo against incest as originating solely from the strife between the males of the family in the course of their competition for the sexual favors of the females. The role of the

females is depicted as essentially passive. They stand by and merely
grant themselves to the victors. (pp. 375–376)

A breach of the incest taboo by a female, consequently, is viewed as a
far greater deviation than incest committed by males (Barry & Johnson, 1958; Lieske, 1981; Messer, 1969; Nakashima & Zakus, 1979;
Raphling, Carpenter, & Davis, 1967).

These theories, and the beliefs about incest upon which they were
built, profoundly influenced professional attitudes in the decades that
followed Freud's original formulations (Arkin, 1984; Herman, 1981;
Herman & Hirschman, 1977). As a first consequence, the sexual abuse
of children by women was essentially ignored. Its occurrence, expected to be an extremely rare aberration, was taken only as bona fide
evidence of the severity of the psychotic disturbance, mental retarda-
tion, and/or organic brain damage that impaired the woman's impulse
control and her ability to comply with social norms (e.g., Mathis, 1972,
p. 135).

Second, these beliefs have contributed to substantial bias on the
part of professionals against the possibility that females could sexually
abuse children. For example, Mathis (1972) dismissed female child
sexual abuse because it was "of little significance," commenting that
our society "never becomes very excited" about female sexual deviations. He noted that females were considered sexually harmless, and
that it was difficult to accept the idea that a woman could have active
sexual impulses and drives. To him, the idea that a woman could sexually abuse a child seemed to be an affront to common sense: "That
she might seduce a helpless child into sexplay is unthinkable, and even
if she did so, what harm can be done without a penis?" (p. 54). The
possibility that sexual abuse may not require a penis is not considered.
Unfortunately, this line of thinking still continues to exert a powerful
influence. For example, West (1987) recently commented "sexual deviations are much commoner in men than in women, arguably because
men are more imaginative and venturesome!" (p. 30).

Such presumptions of psychogenetically inherent differences in the
sexuality of men and women, especially when coupled with absolutist
beliefs about the incest taboo, may continue to lead professionals to
make unwarranted assumptions about female child sexual abuse.
Friedman (1988, p. 346) stated that generalizations about incestuous
behavior or its absence tend to be slanted toward gender-specific perspectives, and that professionals may look with greater scrutiny for the

potential sexual misbehavior of fathers while discounting or ignoring that of mothers. He suggested that these factors and the theoretical perspectives underlying them may contribute to underreporting of female sexual abuse.

OVEREXTENSION OF FEMINIST EXPLANATIONS OF CHILD SEXUAL ABUSE

A second barrier to the recognition of sexual abuse of children by women has been the overextension of feminist explanations of child sexual abuse. In these perspectives (e.g., Finkelhor & Russell, 1984; Herman, 1981; Russell & Finkelhor, 1984) child sexual abuse is considered to be a direct result of culturally-based socialization processes, which lead to male dominance and promote the sexual exploitation of women and children. Briefly stated, males are socialized to be sexually aggressive and to seek younger, more innocent and powerless sex partners, while women are socialized to be recipients of sexual encounters, at least initially, and to be attracted to older, more powerful companions. These patterns, condoned and even encouraged by the male subculture, foster the sexual abuse of children by males while inhibiting such behavior by females. Women are socialized to be the victims of child sexual abuse, not the perpetrators.

The barriers to the recognition of female sexual abuse do not stem directly from the basic theoretical premises of these perspectives. Male dominance, differential socialization, and sexual exploitation in fact may help to explain a substantial portion of child sexual abuse. Rather, barriers to the recognition of female perpetration develop when feminist perspectives are presented as the only viable explanations for child sexual abuse, and female sexual abuse is consequently considered nonsignificant.

The influence of these barriers in turning attention away from the recognition of female perpetrators is subtle, but powerful. Explaining child sexual abuse solely in terms of male dominance and aggression makes it difficult to explain the behavior of female perpetrators, especially those who sexually abuse children without the involvement of a male partner. However, no explanations are required if the perspectives also portray instances of female child sexual abuse as unusual, isolated, and insignificant events. And if instances of female sexual abuse are insignificant, professionals need not concern themselves much about them.

These barriers to the recognition of female child sexual abuse developed as a strong and surprising reaction to a straightforward empirical generalization that began to appear in the literature near the beginning of the eighties, a generalization formed as a logical extension of the "discovery" of incest:

> If child sexual abuse occurs much more frequently than psychoanalytic theories and their derivatives have indicated, then female-perpetrated child sexual abuse might also occur much more frequently as well.

Several researchers, accepting the generalization as plausible, began to do some theory building. Perhaps it was not the incest taboo that was explaining the scarcity of female offenders. Rather, professionals simply may not have been seeing the female-perpetrated child sexual abuse that was "out there" because of their biases against its occurrence; and they offered several alternative hypotheses to explain why it had not been seen.

One possibility was that female abuse might be easier to hide and/or mask as role-appropriate behavior (Goodwin & DiVasto, 1979; Gordon, 1976; Groth & Birnbaum, 1979; Justice & Justice, 1979; Plummer 1981). Another explanation was that females might be more likely to abuse boys, but boys might be less likely to report the abuse (Groth & Birnbaum, 1979; Nasjleti, 1980). Still another suggestion was that female sexual abuse of children might occur more often as incest, and thus was less likely be reported (Groth, 1982; Groth & Birnhaum, 1979).

Almost immediately these views were challenged by two prominent sociologists, Diana Russell and David Finkelhor. Both took issue with these alternative theories because they seemed to underemphasize or diminish the importance of the "traditional view of child molestation as a primarily male deviation" (Russell & Finkelhor, 1984). After presenting powerful theoretical arguments in support of their contention that women rarely sexually abuse children, Russell and Finkelhor insisted that:

> The explanation of male preponderance is significant to virtually every theory of child sexual abuse. . . . Every theory of child molestation must explain not just why adults become sexually interested in children, but why that explanation applies primarily to males and not females. (p. 228)

Thus, no other explanations were to be considered. Surprisingly, the need for comparative studies of female and male abusers to test the validity of the male dominance theory was not suggested. Rather, available data on female and male child sexual abuse was reviewed by Russell and Finkelhor solely to demonstrate that "child sexual abuse is primarily perpetrated by males," and to hint at their surprise that "so many experts in the field [were] arguing that the number of female perpetrators ha[d] been seriously underestimated." In their conclusion, the possibility that female child sexual abuse had been underreported was dismissed as a "wave of speculation," resulting from increased awareness of all types of sexual abuse cases and from "defensiveness in those who oppose feminist thinking" (Finkelhor & Russell, 1984; Russell & Finkelhor, 1984).

Thus, professionals were being misled and defensive if they focused on female sexual abuse. Such attention would only distract them from the real issue: the sexual exploitation of children by *males*. However, in a more recent publication one of the proponents of this perspective appears to have modified his position somewhat. In their *Sourcebook on Child Sexual Abuse*, Araji and Finkelhor (1986) stated:

> Theories of why adults become sexually interested in and involved with children have come primarily from psychoanalytic theory and, more recently, from sources such as social learning theory and feminism. What most of these sources tend to share is that they are "single-factor theories." They identify one or, at the most, a couple of mechanisms to explain sexual interest in children. Not surprisingly, they have been inadequate to explain the full range and diversity of pedophilic behavior. (pp. 91–92)

Finkelhor (1986) noted further that attempts "to explain all child molesting with single-factor theories" are "a serious problem" in child abuse studies. Research instead "has shown that no single factor can begin to explain fully all sexual abuse" (p. 119).

These statements seem to indicate that Finkelhor has shifted his theoretical stance considerably from the strong feminist position he espoused a few years earlier. He now argues that multi-factor models developed from a variety of perspectives are the most effective strategies to explain child sexual abuse. He summed up his new perspective by stating:

> . . . researchers need to caution against all single-factor theories and
> quick explanations in general, because they can lead easily to misin-
> formed public attitudes and short-sighted public policy. (p. 124)

Unfortunately, theories about the occurrence of female child sexual
abuse do not seem to be included in this cautionary statement. Although Finkelhor softened his position about the approach to be used
in explaining child sexual abuse, he did not soften his position about
what they were to explain.

> . . . every theory of pedophilia [still] needs to explain not just why
> adults become sexually interested in children, but why that explanation
> applies primarily to males and not to females. (p. 126)

Although a multi-factor model now replaces the single-factor feminist perspective, the purpose is still the same: to validate a "men-do-
and-women-don't" gender-dichotomy theory of child sexual abuse.
Finkelhor (1986) continued to insist that "practically no evidence" supports the notion that sexual abuse of children by women might be
underreported. A review of the research shows that female child sexual abuse comprises "a distinct minority of child sexual abuse cases,"
occurring in only "some fraction of child abuse cases." Women rarely
sexually abuse children (Finkelhor & Russell, 1984; Russell & Finkelhor, 1984).

Thus, underneath the arguments about which theoretical explanation of child sexual abuse is or is not appropriate lies a deeper issue.
The empirical generalization discussed previously, which suggests that
if male-perpetrated abuse of children occurs much more frequently
than psychoanalytic theory has predicted then so might female-perpetrated abuse, is simply not acceptable. The core issue is empirical,
not theoretical. Although theoretical perspective may replace theoretical perspective, the empirical "fact" on which they are all based remains the same: The sexual abuse of children by women occurs infrequently. Unfortunately, conclusions drawn from this "fact" may form a
third barrier to the recognition of female sexual abuse.

OVERGENERALIZATION OF THE EMPIRICAL
OBSERVATION THAT FEMALE CHILD
SEXUAL ABUSE IS RARE

The third barrier is overgeneralization of the empirical observation
that female sexual abuse of children is rare. This barrier develops

when observations of the low relative frequency of female child sexual abuse become entangled with distorted or mistaken interpretations and lead professionals to conclude that female sexual abuse is a much greater rarity than it actually may be. Two types of misinterpretations leading to such conclusions about female sexual abuse of children are (1) assuming that reports in the literature accurately reflect rates of female perpetration and (2) assuming that low rates of occurrence means low absolute numbers of instances.

Assuming That Reports Accurately Reflect Rates

With respect to the first type of misinterpretation, until recently reports of female-perpetrated child sexual abuse were seldom encountered in the literature. Most that appeared were psychoanalytic case studies of one or two instances of mother-son incest, and invariably the psychopathology of the female offender and/or the victim were highlighted (e.g., Barry & Johnson, 1958; Forward & Buck, 1979; Hammer, 1968; Lidz & Lidz, 1969; Lukianowicz, 1972; Margolis, 1977; Mathis, 1972; Raphling et al., 1967; Yorukoglu & Kemph, 1980; Wahl, 1960; Weinberg, 1955). Authors wrote in isolation from one another, and few were aware of any other reports of maternal incest besides their own.

These few case studies conveyed the impression that female sexual abuse of children was so rare that it was almost unique in its occurrence. Because of the widespread acceptance of this empirically based conclusion, female child sexual abuse was virtually ignored or totally discounted in the literature, as these statements demonstrate:

> Since pedophilia either does not exist at all in women, or is extremely rare, only men were included in the study. (Freund, Heasman, Racansky, & Glancy, 1984, p. 193)
>
> Mother-son incest . . . is so rare and the taboo so great that when it occurs one or both of the partners may be assumed to be severely disturbed or psychotic. (Sarles, 1975, p. 634)
>
> reported cases of female pedophilia are so uncommon as to be of little significance. (Mathis, 1972, p. 54)

However, there is another possibility that the beliefs and attitudes these professionals held against the occurrence of female child sexual abuse may have actually prepared them to *not* see it.

Edwards (1986) noted that the treatment of female offenders is greatly dependent on the degree to which (1) traditional sex role and gender behavior attributions are imposed on them by professionals, and (2) the degree to which these women are perceived as conforming to these attributions. Women "are generally regarded as being 'out of place' in the criminal justice system," a factor that helps them "nego-tiate the various escape routes within it." Men, aggressive and domi-nant, are expected to be criminals. Women, stereotyped to be gentle, passive, and domestic, are anomalies in the system.

Various processes work, Edwards (1988) continued, to bring anom-alous female behavior into congruence with the traditional sex role and gender expectations professionals may hold about women. If these processes are successful, that is, if professionals can perceptually "re-frame" the deviant behavior of women and bring their behavior into congruence with the professionals' traditional expectations about them, women may be given special consideration and more lenient treatment than men. As an example, Edwards noted that women con-victed of shoplifting or petty fraud who are poor and conform to the "appropriate domestic stereotype of good wife and mother" may be treated more sympathetically so that they can continue to care for the family. On the other hand, if congruence between female offender's behavior and the attributions of professionals is not achieved, female offenders may be given harsher, more severe treatment than men even when behaviors are the same, and labeled more often as "sick" or "disturbed."

Edwards (1988) narrowed the context of her discussion to profes-sionals in the criminal justice system who work with violent female offenders. However, her arguments about the attributions of female behavior by professionals may apply equally well to professionals in the child abuse "system." Theoretical, cultural, or idiosyncratic beliefs, which state that female sexual abuse does not occur, may, in fact, pre-vent professionals from observing it. As Kempe and Helfer (1980) observed:

> Society tends to be more concerned with fathers sleeping with or geni-tally manipulating daughters or sons than mothers doing the same things to sons, or very rarely, daughters. This double standard is most likely based on the belief that the sheltering mother is simply prolonging, perhaps unusually but not criminally, her previous nurturing role. . . . Intervention is very difficult because mothers are given an enormous leeway in their actions, while fathers and brothers are not. (p. 207)

For instance, a district judge recently dropped charges brought against a mother for sexually abusing her children, a case carefully prepared by a child protective services worker, a police detective, and the county attorney. The district judge reportedly gave the following justification for his decision: "Women don't do those kinds of things, especially in this community. Besides, the children need their mother." One wonders if the judge would have come to similar conclusions if the defendent had been the victim's father. In any event, the judge's attribution processes, fueled by the strength of his traditional beliefs about women, were strong enough to help him perceptually reframe this woman's behavior to be congruent with his expectations. If attribution processes fail, however, and the deviant behavior cannot be denied or minimized in spite of traditional expectations, female child sexual abusers may be treated quite harshly. As a local investigative social worker noted while reflecting on her experience in the "system" women who sexually abuse children "are either let off the hook or have the book thrown at them."

The impact of attribution processes that deny female child sexual abuse would be greatly magnified if they were jointly held by professionals at multiple points along the child abuse "system" continuum. For instance, if their beliefs and expectations are that women do not sexually abuse children, informants may be less likely to report occurrences of female sexual abuse of children, investigators less diligent in conducting inquiries, county attorneys less likely to prosecute, and judges more likely to dismiss or reduce charges. Even if they made it past some of the initial "gates" women could still be dropped out of the system at any of the successive "gates" that follow. In the case mentioned above, the mother charged with child sexual abuse had made it past the informant, the investigative social worker, the police detective, and the county attorney before being dropped out of the system by the district judge. Perhaps only those women whose behaviors were so deviant that their actions could not be brought into congruence with the expectations of any one of the gatekeepers in turn would be incarcerated or even referred to the therapist in the end.

The effectiveness of such "gatekeeping" attribution processes in winnowing female child sexual abusers out of the system would depend on the strength of the traditional beliefs about women that drove them. Among the most powerful beliefs and expectations against the sexual abuse of children by women have been those espoused and imposed by followers of Freud and his psychoanalytic tradition. Yet rather than being suspicious of possible "gatekeeping" processes, processes that may have winnowed out all but the most deviant of female child sexual abusers, most professionals have assumed that the few reported case studies appearing in the psychoanalytic literature accurately reflect the extent of female child sexual abuse.

For instance, Herman (1981), one of Freud's arch-antagonists, argued with great eloquence that psychoanalysts have enormously deceived themselves, their clients, and the public about the reality and extent of incest. However, this deception by psychoanalysts is apparently limited to male-perpetrated incest only. Herman seemed to accept without question the representativeness of the isolated cases of female-perpetrated child sexual abuse that have been reported by psychoanalysts, in spite of their even stronger preconceptions against its existence:

> Incest between mother and son is so extraordinary that a single case is considered worthy of publication, and we have been able to find a grand total of only twenty-two documented cases in the entire literature. (p. 18)
>
> Almost all the cases involve marked social deviance and severe psychopathology in either the son, the mother, or both. . . . Apparently the taboo against mother-son incest is breached only in bizarre instances. (p. 20)

However, the cases of maternal incest reported in these studies appeared in spite of theoretically shaped attitudes and expectations that precluded their existence. They did not seem to be anticipated or sought out, but were considered almost a novelty to those describing them. And almost invariably mother and/or son were described as pathologically disturbed.

To assume without question that the frequency with which case reports of female child sexual abuse have appeared in the literature is a good indication of the frequency of its actual occurrence may be a questionable strategy. This is particularly so when the possibility exists that attributions of traditional sex role and gender behaviors may have prevented all but the most deviant, pathological cases to surface to the attention of professionals.

As Finkelhor and Russell (1984) stated, although it is "extremely implausible" for children not to notice the sexual activities of women, it is possible for such behavior to go unnoticed by others. Marvasti

(1986) observed that mothers he studied in five cases of maternal incest had not been involved in the criminal justice system, were not psychotic, nor was their abuse centered around themes of "power" and "authority," patterns attributed to father-daughter incest. Interestingly, he noted that it was the mothers themselves who had reported the sexual abuse, not their victims, and this disclosure occurred only after several months of individual and group therapy. Marvasti concluded by suggesting that unless mothers and sons are psychotic and lack the necessary resources to keep the incest secret, they may escape the attention of professionals. And processes that also work to keep professional belief structures intact, belief structures that are against the possibility that women sexually abuse children, will only make it more difficult for female sexual abuse to be recognized, regardless of its actual frequency of occurrence.

Assuming That Low Relative Rates Means Low Absolute Rates

The second type of misinterpretation that may lead professionals to conclude that female child sexual abuse happens even less frequently than it does in reality occurs when low relative rates of its occurrence are assumed to be equivalent to low absolute rates. For instance, as noted previously, Finkelhor (1986) stated rather emphatically that "practically no evidence" supports the idea that female child sexual abuse might be underreported. He concluded that at most, 10% of offenders among reported cases are women, and among general population surveys only 5% of adult sexual contact with girls and 20% of adult sexual contact with boys are made by women.

However, these percentages bear closer scrutiny. When Finkelhor's rates are coupled with percentages cited for rates of female and male victimization, and with percentages cited for rates of prevalence and incidence, they lead to surprising estimates about absolute rates of female child sexual abuse.

With respect to rates of female and male sexual victimization, Finkelhor and Baron (1986, pp. 61–62) presented two sex-of-victim ratios. One was derived from two national studies of reported cases of child sexual abuse. The other was computed as the mean ratio for eight random sample community studies in which both men and women were interviewed. The estimated ratio for the agency studies was five female victims for every male victim, and for the survey studies, a ratio of 2.5 female victims for each male victim.

Lack of consensus among professionals makes estimates of preva-

lence rates a little more difficult to find. In their review of the prevalence of child sexual abuse, Peters, Wyatt, and Finkelhor (1986)
simply list the prevalence rates obtained in each of the 19 prevalence
studies they reviewed. These range from 8% to 62% for females. The
mean prevalence rate for female victimization in these 19 studies is
23%, which will serve as a rough estimate of prevalence for discussion
purposes.

One additional set of figures is needed before estimates of the relative occurrence of female child sexual abuse can be converted into
absolute numbers. These are total population estimates. For the
United States as of July 1, 1988, these estimates are 126,000,000 females and 120,000,000 males (Spencer, 1989).

With total population figures, prevalence rate estimates, and estimates of the relative frequencies of female and male child sexual
abuse, estimates of absolute rates of female child sexual abuse can be
calculated. First, an estimate of the absolute number of females who
have been sexually abused will be determined. Taking 23% of the 126
million women in the United States, which is the percentage of women
prevalence studies suggest have been sexually abused as children, produces an estimate of 29 million female victims. And if this estimate is
multiplied by 5%, the proportion estimated by Russell and Finkelhor
(1984) to have been sexually abused as children by adult females, the
result is approximately 1.5 million females sexually abused by females.

Finkelhor and Baron's (1986) victimization ratio of five females for
every male, a figure they derived from agency studies, converts to a
prevalence rate of 4.5% for male sexual victimization. Multiplying the
120 million American males by a 4.5% victimization rate produces an
estimate of 5.4 million male victims of child sexual abuse. If this estimate in turn is multiplied by 20%, the proportion estimated by Russell
and Finkelhor to have been sexually abused by females, the result is
close to 1.1 million males abused by females. If Finkelhor and Baron's
(1986) survey-based victimization ratio of 2.5 females for each male is
used, which they consider a more accurate figure, the estimate of the
number of males sexually abused by females doubles to 2.2 million.
Combining estimates for female and male victims results in a figure of
3.7 million victims of female child sexual abuse!

These figures hardly seem to justify the conclusion that children are
seldom sexually abused by females. Even if relative rates of female
child sexual abuse were only a tenth as large as Russell and Finkelhor
(1984) suggested, they would still result in an estimate of 370,000 fe-

male child sexual abuse victims, a number vastly larger than reports scattered throughout the literature, and conclusions based on them, have seemed to suggest.

CONCLUSION

The purpose of the discussion in this chapter has not been to suggest that rates of female sexual abuse of children are equal to rates for male perpetrators, or that these rates are even close. Substantial evidence gathered from self-report studies in the last ten years indicates that rates are, in fact, quite disproportionate. Rather, the purpose of the discussion has been to suggest that barriers to the recognition of the sexual abuse of children by women may lead to distorted perceptions about the occurrence of such behavior and contribute to underreporting of even the relatively low levels of female sexual abuse that actually occur.

Currently, increasing recognition of female sexual abuse is coming from four areas: male victimization studies (e.g., Nielsen, 1983; Vander May, 1988), adolescent sex offender studies (e.g., Fehrenbach & Monastersky, 1988; National Adolescent Perpetrator Network, 1988), studies of adult sex offenders (e.g., Alford et al., 1988; Condy et al., 1987), and recent clinical studies (e.g., Faller, 1987; Marvasti, 1986, Mathews et al. 1989; McCarty, 1986). A clearinghouse on female child sexual abuse research and information has recently been established by Faye Honey Knopp and the Safer Society Program of Vermont. Anecdotal information about female child sexual abuse is being provided more frequently by therapists, social workers, police detectives, and others who work closely with families.

Theoretical perspectives should keep pace. Focusing only on the low relative rates of female child sexual abuse may lead to deceptive conclusions in terms of absolute numbers. Gender dichotomy theories which cast perpetration into "men do/women don't" categories, divert attention from women who do sexually abuse children. More helpful would be theories that incorporate gender and socialization patterns to explain the disproportionate rates of female- and male-perpetrated child sexual abuse and the behavior of *both* male-initiated and self-initiated female sexual abuse of children.

Processes that minimize female child sexual abuse when it appears also need to be avoided. Freeman-Longo (1987) noted that over 40% of rapists he has worked with reported having been sexually abused as children by females, and "none of them reported it to be a pleasant experience." Discounting samples in which unusually high rates of female child sexual abuse is reported, such as those obtained in Groth's male rapist sample (cited in Russell & Finkelhor, 1984), may draw attention away from critical patterns that might help explain relationships between female child sexual abuse and other factors, such as the role negative experiences, stemming from having been sexually abused as a child by a female, might play in the development and unfolding of rapists' behaviors.

Most importantly, it may not really matter to victims of female sexual abuse that their experience was a low probability event. It happened, and the traumas that victims suffer in the aftermath of sexual abuse may be theirs as well. Yet these victims of female sexual abuse may experience further stigmatization when even the professionals themselves are disbelieving. The needs of all victims of child sexual abuse should be considered, whether the abuser is female or male. In this respect, comments from the National Task Force on Juvenile Offending are pertinent:

> Gender expectations and socialization factors may account for differences in male/female perpetration but the potential for harm to the victim is the same. Mandated reporters and investigators must be educated to not minimize the seriousness of female offending and move toward accountability. (National Adolescent Perpetrator Network, 1988, p. 42)

As the causes, patterns, and consequences of female child sexual abuse become more clearly sorted out, information will be obtained to help answer other questions. For instance, should sexually abusing women be prosecuted the same or differently than men? How should treatment procedures be conducted? Should female offenders be mixed with male offenders in treatment groups, as some agencies suggest, or should they be separated, as other agencies mandate? And do victims of female abuse have needs that are similar to or different from those of male abuse victims?

Serious attempts to gather data about female child sexual abusers are just beginning. In the meantime, while controversies about female child sexual abuse are sorted out and facts obtained to replace fictions, more caution needs to be exercised with speculations about why, and under what conditions, and with whom, females sexually abuse children. The strategy suggested by Bolton and Bolton (1987) may be most appropriate:

> Awareness of female sexual abuse perpetration is increasing. . . . It seems wise to withhold judgment about such cases until more is known. (p. 146)

REFERENCES

Alford, J., Grey, M., & Kasper, C. J. (1988). Child molesters: Areas for further research. *Corrective and Social Psychiatry and Journal of Behavior Technology, 34*(1), 1–5.

Araji, S., & Finkelhor, D. (1986). Abusers: A review of the research. In D. Finkelhor & Associates (Eds.), *A sourcebook on child sexual abuse* (pp. 89–118). Beverly Hills, CA: Sage.

Arkin, A. M. (1984). A hypothesis concerning the incest taboo. *Psychoanalytic Review, 71*(3), 375–381.

Barry, J. J., Jr., & Johnson, A. M. (1958). The incest barrier. *Psychoanalysis Quarterly, 27,* 485–500.

Bolton, F. G., & Bolton, S. R. (1987). *Working with violent families: A guide for clinical and legal practitioners.* Newbury Park, CA: Sage.

Conte, J. (1982). Sexual abuse of children: Enduring issues for social work. *Journal of Social Work and Human Sexuality, 1*(1), 1–19.

Condy, S. R., Templer, D. I., Brown, R., & Veaco, L. (1987). Parameters of sexual contact of boys with women. *Archives of Sexual Behavior, 16*(5), 379–394.

Edwards, S. (1986). Neither bad nor mad: The female violent offender reassessed. *Women's Studies International Forum, 9*(1), 79–87.

Faller, K. (1987). Women who sexually abuse children. *Violence and Victims, 2*(4), 263–276.

Fehrenbach, P., & Monastersky, C. (1988). Characteristics of female adolescent sexual offenders. *American Journal of Orthopsychiatry, 58*(1), 148–151.

Finkelhor, D. (1979). *Sexually victimized children.* New York: Free Press.

Finkelhor, D. (1986). Abusers: Special topics. In D. Finkelhor & Associates (Eds.), *A sourcebook on child sexual abuse* (pp. 119–142).

Finkelhor, D., & Baron, L. (1986). High risk children. In D. Finkelhor & Associates (Eds.), *A sourcebook on child sexual abuse* (pp. 60–88). Beverly Hills, CA: Sage.

Finkelhor, D., & Russell, D. (1984). Women as perpetrators. In D. Finkelhor (Ed.), *Child sexual abuse: New theory and research.* New York: Free Press.

Forward, S. & Buck, C. (1979). *Betrayal of innocence: Incest and its devastation.* New York: Penguin.

Freeman-Longo, R. E. (1987). *Child Sexual Abuse.* Workshop held at Drake University, Des Moines, IA.

Freund, K., Heasman, G., Racansky, I. G., & Glancy, G. (1984). Pedophilia and heterosexuality vs. homosexuality. *Journal of Sex and Marital Therapy, 10*(3), 193–200.

Friedman, S. (1988). A family systems approach to treatment. In L. E. A. Walker (Ed.), *Handbook on sexual abuse of children.* New York: Springer.

124 PROFILES AND IDENTIFICATION

Goodwin, J., & DiVasto, P. (1979). Mother-daughter incest. *Child Abuse and Neglect,* 3, 953–957.

Gordon, R. (1976). Pedophilia: Normal and abnormal. In W. Kraemer (Ed.), *The forbidden love: The normal and abnormal love of children.* London: Sheldon.

Groth, N. (1982). The incest offender. In S. M. Sgroi (Ed.), *Handbook of clinical intervention in child sexual abuse.* Lexington, MA: Lexington Books.

Groth, N., & Birnbaum, H. (1979). *Men who rape: The psychology of the offender.* New York: Plenum.

Hammer, E. F. (1968). Symptoms of sexual deviation: Dynamics and etiology. *Psychoanalytic Review,* 55, 5–27.

Herman, J. (1981). *Father-daughter incest.* Cambridge, MA: Harvard University Press.

Herman, J., & Hirschman, L. (1977). Father-daughter incest. *Signs: Journal of Women in Culture and Society,* 2(4), 735–756.

Johnson, R., & Shrier, D. (1987). Past sexual victimization by females of male patients in an adolescent medicine clinic population. *American Journal of Psychiatry,* 144, 650–662.

Justice, B., & Justice, R. (1979). *The broken taboo.* New York: Human Sciences Press.

Kempe, C. K., & Helfer, R. E. (1980). *The battered child* (3rd ed.). Chicago: University of Chicago Press.

Kendrick, M. (1988). *Anatomy of a nightmare: The failure of society in dealing with child sexual abuse.* Toronto: MacMillan.

Knopp F., & Lackey, L. (1989). *Female sexual abusers: A summary of data from 44 treatment providers.* Orwell, VT: Safer Society Press.

Lidz, R. W., & Lidz, T. (1969). Homosexual tendencies in mothers of schizophrenic women. *Journal of Nervous and Mental Disease,* 149(2), 229–235.

Lieske, A. M. (1981). Incest: An overview. *Perspectives in Psychiatric Care,* 19(2), 59–63.

Lukianowicz, N. (1972). Incest. *British Journal of Psychiatry,* 120, 301–313.

Margolis, M. (1977). A preliminary report of a case of consummated mother-son incest. *Annual of Psychoanalysis* 5, 267–293.

Marvasti, J. (1986). Incestuous mothers. *American Journal of Forensic Psychiatry,* 7(4), 63–69.

Masters, W. H. (1986). Sexual dysfunction as an aftermath of sexual assault of men by women. *Journal of Sex and Marital Therapy,* 12(1), 35-45.

Mathews, R., Matthews, J., & Speltz, K. (1989). *Female sexual offenders: An exploratory study.* Orwell, VT: Safer Society Press.

Mathis, J. L. (1972). *Clear thinking about sexual deviation.* Chicago: Nelson-Hall.

McCarty, L. (1986). Mother-child incest: Characteristics of the offender. *Child Welfare,* 65(5), 457–458.

Messer, A. A. (1969). The "Phaedra complex." *Archives of General Psychiatry,* 21 (August), 213–218.

Nakashima, I. I., & Zakus, G. (1979). Incest and sexual abuse. *Pediatric annals,* 8(5), 300–308.

Nasjleti, M. (1980). Suffering in silence: The male incest victim. *Child Welfare,* 59, 269–275.

National Adolescent Perpetrator Network. (1988). Preliminary report from the National Task Force on Juvenile Sexual Offending, 1988. *Juvenile and Family Court Journal,* 39(2), 1–67.

Nielsen, T. A. (1983). Sexual abuse of boys: Current perspectives. *Personnel and Guidance Journal, 62*(Nov), 1983.

Peters, S. D., Wyatt, G. E., & Finkelhor, D. (1986). Prevalence. In D. Finkelhor & Associates (Eds.), *A sourcebook on child sexual abuse.* Beverly Hills, CA: Sage.

Plummer, K. (1981). Pedophilia: Constructing a sociological baseline. In M. Cook & K. Howells (Eds.), *Adult sexual interest in children.* New York: Academic Press.

Raphling, D. L., Carpenter, B. L., & Davis, A. (1967). Incest: A genealogical study. *Archives of General Psychiatry, 16*(April), 505–511.

Russell, D., & Finkelhor, D. (1984). The gender gap among perpetrators of child sexual abuse. In D. Russell (Ed.), *Sexual exploitation: Rape, child sexual abuse, and workplace harassment.* Beverly Hills, CA: Sage.

Sarles, R. M. (1975). Incest. *Pediatric Clinics of North America, 21*(3), 633–642.

Scavo, R. R. (1989). Female adolescent sex offenders: A neglected treatment group. *Social Casework, 70*(February), 114–117.

Spencer, G. (1989). *Projections of the population of the United States, by age, sex and race: 1988 to 2080* (Series P-25, No. 1018, Population Estimates and Projections. Current Population Reports). Washington, DC: Bureau of the Census, United States Department of Commerce.

Vander May, B. J. (1988). The sexual victimization of male children: A review of previous research. *Child Abuse and Neglect, 12*(1), 61.

Wahl, C. W. (1960). The psychodynamics of consummated maternal incest: A report of two cases. *Archives of General Psychiatry, 3*(August), 188–193.

Weinberg, S. K. (1955). *Incest behavior.* New York: Citadel.

West, D. J. (1987). *Sexual crimes and confrontations: A study of victims and offenders.* Brookfield, VT: Gower.

Yorukoglu, A., & Kemph, J. P. (1980). Children not severely damaged by incest with a parent. In G. J. Williams & J. Money (Eds.), *Traumatic abuse and neglect of children at home.* Baltimore, MD: Johns Hopkins University Press.

9

Sexual Addiction

Patrick J. Carnes

INTRODUCTION

Jim is a bright, articulate, 48-year-old family man. His life story presents a prototypical case of the incestuous father. Physically and sexually abused as a child, he inflicted this same abuse on his wife and daughters. In his own words:

> I knew I was sick and I made that quite apparent to my children that I was a sick person and that was part of my way of getting them to take care of me . . . I set them up so that they would not go out of the family to get help for me. They would help me themselves. They became my counselors. I could share all my problems with my daughters. I totally enmeshed myself into their lives. I set them up early in childhood to physically touch them by bathing them as a child and becoming mother to them. Being their doctor, their nurse, their friend, I was always over-involved with them. . . .
>
> As they got older and became aware of their differences and sexuality they would make a statement of disgust—they don't like that. I would put them down for it. I'm your dad, this isn't any big deal. I'm the dad. I minimized it.
>
> . . . thinking back on how my daughter was suffering. I vividly remember her screaming and crying that I was hurting her so much. Why did I hate her and why did I have to hurt her?

Jim displays many of the classic characteristics often attributed to incest fathers, as summarized by Green (1988) in a review of the literature.

AUTHOR'S NOTE: This chapter was in part funded by a grant from the Institute for Behavioral Medicine, Golden Valley Health Center, Golden Valley, Minnesota. Dr. Carnes serves as a Senior Fellow at the Institute and is a consultant to Golden Valley Health Center's Sexual Dependency Unit.

- He has been abusing alcohol since he was 14 years of age.
- He has an unstable employment history, changing jobs every two or three years.
- He is socially isolated. By choice, Jim has no outside activities, concentrating all of his needs on his family. In doing this he isolated his family from outside social interaction as well.

The problem appears to be quite clear-cut. Jim is an incest father whose treatment should concentrate on this behavior and its family dynamics. A more complex diagnosis exists, however. Jim's history reveals a pattern of out-of-control sexual behavior that supplies a significant context to his incest issues.

As a young boy he began to escape a life of abuse and emotional deprivation through masturbation and sexual fantasy. As his guilt and shame built up, his need for escape increased. He began sexually molesting friends and siblings. A dangerous cycle was established in his life. His feelings of pain, loneliness, and shame were numbed by a sexual "fix" or, when that was not available, by alcohol abuse. Although temporarily successful in blocking his inner feelings of emptiness, his behavior fed this same sense of shame and worthlessness. All aspects of his life became affected as he reached adulthood. At work, he could not control his fantasizing about female coworkers and clients, periodically changing jobs to stay out of trouble. His wife and children became objects used to satisfy his sexual obsession. He could not even read a magazine without turning it into pornographic material to use for his sexual fantasies. Jim's life was unmanageable. He was powerless to control his behavior, for his problem had become one of sexual addiction.

A growing understanding of sexual addiction is significant in the field of sexual abuse research and treatment from several perspectives. Many abusers are sex addicts and sexual addiction issues need to be considered in their treatment. Focusing treatment on the exploitative behavior without diagnosing the addictive process itself excludes significant options in the healing process. Jim's story is classic. As an incest father he resembles a profile well-known to clinicians. Jim's case also characterizes the larger population of sex addicts.

The purpose of this chapter is to outline the connections between incest behavior and sexual addiction. Our focus will be a national survey of recovering sex addicts, a portion of which were also incest perpetrators. By contrasting subpopulations with the larger population, critical questions emerge about the nature of incest behavior, its etiology, and the role of being an abuse victim as part of being a perpetrator. Further considerations will be explored about differential diagnosis and treatment in the context of the data.

BACKGROUND OF THE PROBLEM: SEXUAL ADDICTION

By the middle seventies, a growing awareness of sex as an addiction was expanding the newly developed concept of addictionology as a discipline. Twelve-step fellowships had started across the nation. Richard Solomon (1974) had introduced his "opponent-process" theory of addiction. Jim Orford's (1978) classic article had appeared in the British Journal of Addiction. The National Science Foundation had identified sex addiction as a national research priority in 1977. Since that time there has been much speculation about the nature of the illness (Carnes, 1986; Coleman, 1987) and its causes. Some like Milkman and Sunderwirth (1983-1984) have identified a neurochemical basis for the illness. Others emphasize personality and family factors (Diamond, 1988; Schneider, 1988) and some underline cultural components (Shaefe, 1988).

In 1983, the author developed a model building on a common definition of alcoholism or drug dependency that states that a chemically dependent person has a pathological relationship with a mood-altering chemical (MacAulifle & MacAulifle, 1975). In a similar manner, the sexual addict substitutes a sick relationship to sexual behavior for a healthy relationship with others and is no longer able to manage or control that relationship despite physical, occupational, and familial losses resulting from his/her behavior.

There can easily be confusion regarding what kind of behavior constitutes a sexual addiction. Individuals who have abused their sexuality, who have engaged in a sexual binge, or even who have episodes of compulsive sexual behavior are not necessarily sexual addicts. The important consideration is the level of manageability and control that the individual exerts over his/her behavior. In entering the world of the sex addict, the individual engages in an addictive system that is self-perpetuating and unmanageable. This system is depicted in Figure 9.1.

The addictive system starts with a faulty belief system, developed during a dysfunctional early family life. This belief system supports

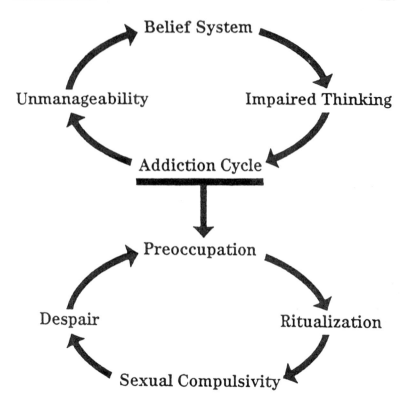

Figure 9.1 The Addictive System

impaired thinking which insulates the individual from reality. Denial and delusion are common methods of distorting reality for the sexual addict. The individual is then drawn into an addictive cycle of sexual preoccupation, ritualization, compulsiveness, and despair that is self-perpetuating and eventually takes over the person's life. The unmanageability of the addictive cycle confirms the faulty belief that he/she is a bad person incapable of being loved. The whole system is strengthened and the cycle begins once again. The sexual experience becomes the primary relationship for the addict.

Consider Jim, our case study. Jim's beliefs about himself were adopted from a brutal father and a passive yet sexually abusive mother. He learned from his father that he was worthless and that he could not trust intimate relationships. The sexually exploitative behavior of his mother taught him that it is only through sexual behavior that he could receive nurturance. He began to identify sex as his most important need. He applied his beliefs by relating to his friends and siblings in a sexually exploitative manner. Sexual gratification filled the void of his desperate need for nurturance, but only temporarily. When the fix was over, he was left with a greater sense of shame and worthlessness. More intense and frequent sexual fixes were required to numb the pain and block out his feelings. The cycle of addiction became self-perpetuating. He would eventually risk his job, his family, and even his physical freedom in service to this addiction.

By summarizing Jim's experience we can see that he developed a distorted belief system in four areas that ultimately became part of his sexual addiction. (See Figure 9.2.)

These four core beliefs are the foundation on which sexual addiction rests. As the individual reaches adulthood, each of these beliefs contributes to the disconnection and alienation between the addict's inner experience of pain and shame and the external image he is compelled to project to keep his secret. More and more barriers to true intimacy must be erected to keep the addictive secret from the world. The element of secrecy serves to intensify the whole addictive cycle.

Several characteristics appear to be common to most sexual addicts. Generally, the addictive cycle includes a variety of behaviors that form a pattern involving different levels of addiction. One level of behaviors is considered acceptable or tolerable by society, including masturbation, homosexuality, and prostitution. A second level of behaviors is clearly victimizing and illegal but is generally viewed as nuisance offenses, including exhibitionism and voyeurism. The third and the most serious degree of addictive behaviors has devastating consequences for the victim as well as serious legal consequences for the addict. This

Figure 9.2

	Self-image	— I am worthless.
Accurate	Relationship	— I cannot trust or rely on others to meet my needs.
core		
	Needs	— My needs can only be filled by sexual behavior.
beliefs		
	Sexuality	— Sex is my most important need.

includes incest, child molestation, and rape. Addicts can be compulsive at either one or at several levels. Generally, however, the addict engages in multiple forms of sexual compulsiveness.

A second common characteristic of sexual addicts is the existence of other addictions that become an intrinsic part of the sexual addiction. Overeating, shoplifting, gambling, and spending are all possible partners to the sexual addiction. But by far the most common concurrent addiction is dependence on alcohol or other drugs. When such addictions occur concurrently, they can be mutually reinforcing. Treatment of only one addiction, such as alcoholism, while ignoring the coexisting sexual addiction, is unlikely to lead to a successful outcome.

A third area relevant to the sexual addiction is the role of the family in the addictive cycle. As will be presented later within a discussion of our survey data, addicts frequently have experienced childhood sexual abuse. Both in the family of origin and current family dynamics, extremes of family dynamics such as extreme rigidity or chaos appear to be prevalent. Addictive patterns of other family members as well as coparticipation in the sexual addict's behavior may be important factors in the overall family system that supports the addictive cycle.

We have already seen, in Jim's case, the role of the family of origin in the development of a sexual addiction. The family dynamics of the adult addict often act to support his/her addictive world. Jim's wife was told by his daughters of the abuse that was occurring, but she denied the existence of the problem. In effect, she became a participant in her husband's addiction, a coaddict.

The coaddictive system parallels the process of the addictive system. There are similarly distorted core beliefs, which are reinforced by the behavior of the addict. There is distorted thinking such as denial and rationalization. Blame and judgmental thinking can be used to protect the coaddict from his/her own feelings of worthlessness. The addict can be blamed for all of the problems in the family. Coaddictive enabling behaviors, such as keeping the addiction secret, covering up, and protecting the addict from consequences, are important supports for the continuation of the sexual addiction. Treatment must be undertaken that deals with this family system as well as with the individual addict.

Many people suffering from compulsive disorders have translated the 12 steps of Alcoholics Anonymous for their own use, such as Overeaters Anonymous and Gamblers Anonymous. With titles like Sexaholics Anonymous, Sex Addicts Anonymous, Sex and Love Addicts

Anonymous, and Sexual Compulsives Anonymous, a nationwide network of support for sex addicts has emerged. Their fellowships, combined with treatment based on the 12 steps can be an effective way to interrupt the sexual addiction system. Addicts and coaddicts find new beliefs to replace the dysfunctional ones.

This strategy can help members restore and reclaim human relationships especially in the family. They start rebuilding by admitting that they are powerless over their sexual behavior and that their lives have become unmanageable. They find concrete strategies and support for behavior change. They see models of others with similar backgrounds whose lives have been transformed by the program. Plus, new, genuine relationships evolve within the environment of trust existing among the members. Clinicians need to consider the 12 steps as a viable option for their sexually addicted clients. For a more thorough discussion of the Twelve Step Program, as well as the dynamics of sexual addiction in general, see *Out of the Shadows: Understanding Sexual Addiction* (Carnes, 1985) and its companion volume for professionals in the field, *Contrary to Love, Helping the Sexual Addict* (Carnes, 1989).

THE SURVEY

A nationwide survey of recovering sex addicts was conducted using 12-step fellowships and cooperating therapists. One thousand surveys were sent out to be completed by individuals who were currently being treated for sexual addiction. The surveys included extensive questions regarding sexual behaviors, feelings, and thoughts, consequences of sexual addiction, a developmental history of the sexual addiction, past abuse history, a family profile, and treatment and recovery history.

Information regarding sexual behaviors, feelings, and thoughts was gathered by asking respondents to rate both the frequency and power of 101 items on a 5-point scale. Items were grouped by 10 major subject areas presented in Table 9.1. From the ratings of these items, a behavior saliency score was developed. The interaction of the power and frequency of a behavior can have different implications at different levels. That is to say, engaging in a behavior that has little power very frequently (power = 1, frequency = 5) is not the same as engaging in a behavior that has an extremely powerful effect very infrequently (power = 5, frequency = 1). Therefore, therapists with experience

Table 9.1 Categories of Sexual Behaviors, Feelings, and Thoughts

Major Subject Areas	No. of Items
Preoccupation, fantasy & ritualization	20
Masturbation	5
Pornography	10
Buying or selling sex	8
Sex partners	15
Exhibitionism	8
Voyeurism	6
Inappropriate liberties	7
Victimization	12
Other sexual behaviors	10

Table 9.2 Sexual Behavior Saliency Score

		Power				
		1	*2*	*3*	*4*	*5*
Not Part of Addiction		0	0	0	0	0
	1	1.0	1.0	2.0	4.5	5.5
	2	1.0	1.5	2.5	6.0	6.0
Frequency	3	1.5	2.0	3.5	7.0	7.0
	4	1.5	3.0	6.0	8.5	9.0
	5	3.5	3.5	7.5	9.0	9.0

treating sexual addiction were asked to rate each combination of power and frequency scores for the sexual behaviors. They were instructed to determine the overall saliency of the behavior based on their clinical experience. The ratings were averaged and rounded to the nearest half of a point. Table 9.2 displays the behavior saliency scores obtained.

The respondent's abuse history was gathered for three major types of abuse, sexual (15 items), physical (12 items), and emotional (16 items). Items were rated for frequency on a 5-point scale, the age of the respondent when the abuse began, and the abusing person. Abuse scores for individual items were taken to be the frequency ratings. Abuse scores for the three major types of abuse were calculated by summing individual item abuse scores.

There were also many open-ended questions within the survey, which provided the opportunity for individuals to give their unique perspective regarding various aspects of their addictive behavior, treatment, and recovery.

Surveys were completed and returned from 41 states, yielding a sample size of 412 sex addicts, 337 males and 75 females. Of this group, 15.3% (N = 63) indicated that they had forced sexual activity on a member of their family, an item within the section measuring sexual behaviors, feelings, and thoughts. This subgroup of 63, 54 male and 9 female, comprise the incest group for our study. The mean age for both the total sample and the incest subgroup was 38 years. For the total sample, 41.3% were currently married while this percentage for the incest group was 39.7%. Table 9.3 presents the distribution and percentages of the total sample and incest group by race. Table 9.4 presents the distribution and percentages of the total sample and incest group by sexual orientation. Table 9.5 presents the distribution and percentages of the total sample and incest group by level of education.

RESULTS

As Tables 9.3 through 9.5 depict them, our sample of 412 sexual addicts can be described as primarily white, male, heterosexual, and

Table 9.3 General Addict and Incest Addict Sample Frequencies and Percentages by Race

	(N = 412) Total Sample		(N = 62) Incest Sample	
Race	No.	Percentage	No.	Percentage
American Indian	7	1.7	2	3.2
Black	7	1.7	1	1.6
Hispanic	2	.5	1	1.6
White	387	94.6	57	91.9
Other	6	1.5	1	1.6
Missing	3		0	

Table 9.4 General Addict and Incest Addict Sample Frequencies and Percentages by Sexual Orientation

	(N = 412) Total Sample		(N = 62) Incest Sample	
Sexual Orientation	No.	Percentage	No.	Percentage
Bisexual	43	10.6	10	15.9
Gay/Lesbian	68	16.7	8	12.7
Heterosexual	262	64.4	40	63.5
Unsure	34	8.4	5	7.9
Missing	5		0	

Table 9.5 General Addict and Incest Addict Sample Frequencies and Percentages by Level of Education

Education Level	(N = 412) Total Sample		(N = 62) Incest Sample	
	No.	Percentage	No.	Percentage
Some High School	7	1.7	3	4.8
High School	30	7.4	8	12.9
Some College	92	22.7	13	21.0
Voc./Trade School	27	6.7	3	4.8
College Graduate	97	23.9	15	24.2
Post Graduate	153	37.7	20	32.3
Missing	6		0	

well-educated. Survey research always suffers the danger of response bias. This group may represent the sex addict who is willing to fill out a detailed and very personal survey. From the survey, as well as hospital admissions, we can say that people seeking help are better educated and have greater access to resources. This trend absolutely parallels the early demographics of alcoholism programs.

As we view the demographic characteristics of our sample as a whole and compare these characteristics to the incest addict group, they appear quite comparable in age, race distribution, income, and education level. There is a 4% greater percentage of men in the incest group, not an unexpected variation considering the differences in sample size. Examining sexual orientation from Table 9.4, there are differences in distributions, but not great differences. While heterosexuality is equally represented, the incest group shows a slightly greater percentage of bisexual as opposed to gay/lesbian orientation. Considering all the information, the differences are not striking. In fact, it is more striking to consider how easily the incest sample merges into the overall sample on these basic characteristics.

As a subgroup of sex addicts, the incest group is quite representative of the sex addict in many basic ways. They display a clear pattern of multiple compulsive sexual behaviors, which they describe as unmanageable. They have experienced abuse as a child and depict their families of origin as either extremely rigid or chaotic. The mean number of addictions endorsed by both groups is virtually identical, 3.29 versus 3.33 for incest addicts. Let us concentrate now on ways in which the two groups are different and what these differences tell us about sex addicts with incestuous behavior.

How is the sexual behavior of the incest subgroup different from the sample as a whole? Table 9.6 lists those items within the section of the survey measuring sexual behavior, thoughts, and feelings that appear different for the two samples. Preoccupation, delusional thinking, pornography, masturbation, and sexualizing others emerged as key areas of difference out of the 121 items in the survey. In addition,

Table 9.6 General Addict and Incest Addict Sample Mean Saliency Scores and Standard Deviations

Category Behavior	(N = 412) Total Sample		(N = 62) Incest Sample	
	Mean	SD	Mean	SD
SEXUAL BEHAVIORS				
Thinking that your special sexual needs make you different from others	4.6	3.78	5.7	3.74
Thinking deluded thoughts	4.7	3.69	5.8	3.69
Masturbating yourself	6.8	3.14	7.9	2.64
Looking at sexually explicit magazines	5.2	3.40	6.2	2.61
Sexualizing people or materials	4.1	3.59	5.7	3.48
Sexualizing others that you observe in public places	4.8	3.79	5.9	3.46
SEXUAL BOUNDARIES				
Touching or fondling other people inappropriately	2.0	2.96	3.5	3.46
Telling sexually explicit stories or using sexually explicit language at inappropriate times/places	1.5	2.59	2.6	3.10
Using flirtatious or seductive behavior to gain attention	3.5	3.72	4.6	3.62
Making inappropriate sexual advances or gestures toward others	2.1	2.98	3.6	3.39
SEXUAL VICTIMIZATION				
Forcing sexual activity on a child outside of family	.4	1.38	1.6	2.54
Forcing sexual activity on a member of your family	.6	1.79	4.0	2.70
Forcing sexual activity on a person whom you know	.8	2.00	1.9	2.60

categories of inappropriate liberties and victimization were particular
problems of the incestuous sex addict. As mentioned earlier, sexual
addicts generally display a wide variety of sexual compulsions that
span many general areas of sexual acting out.

The specific pattern of the incestuous addict, however, clusters
more heavily around victimization and indecent liberties. Based on
the direction of the differences across all items, this group of addicts
has more severe behavioral problems in these areas, in addition to
problems in other areas. While all sex addicts tend to sexualize their
relationships, this group suffered greater boundary lapses in general
and exploited family members in particular. The cluster of problem
behaviors within the area of victimization is important. There, sex addicts who forcefully exploited family members also tended to abuse
adults and children outside the family. The problem of perpetration for
this sample, then, was not restricted to the family.

A look at abuse history sheds additional light on the concept of inadequate boundaries for the incest subgroup. Table 9.7 summarizes
mean scores for the two groups across three types of abuse. Table 9.8
lists scores for those items within these types of abuse that appear
different for the two groups. The data shows more severe abuse experienced by the incestuous addict as a child. The most divergent
scores, in comparison to the general sample, are not sexual abuse, but
rather emotional, and to a lesser degree, physical abuse experience.
Fourteen out of the 16 items for emotional abuse were more often
indicated in the incest addict. For physical abuse, 8 out of the 12 items
were more often indicated. And for sexual abuse, 5 out of the possible
15 items were more often indicated.

Table 9.7 Comparison of Mean Abuse Scores for General Sexual Addicts Versus Incest Addicts

	(N=412) Total Sample		(N=62) Incest Sample	
Type of Abuse	Mean	SD	Mean	SD
Sexual abuse	11.50	13.37	10.22	9.93
Physical abuse	6.12	8.83	8.84	11.39
Emotional abuse	21.28	17.13	25.46	18.68
Total abuse	38.91	32.63	44.52	32.61

Table 9.8 Percent Indicating Item and Mean Scores for General Sexual
           Addicts and Incest Addict Samples

TYPE OF ABUSE	(N = 412) Total Sample		(N = 62) Incest Sample	
Abuse Item	Percentage	Mean	Percentage	Mean
SEXUAL ABUSE				
Inappropriate holding	24	3.0	33	2.6
Sexual fondling	36	2.9	43	2.7
Household voyeurism	21	3.4	27	3.6
Jokes about body	27	3.5	37	3.7
Criticism	26	3.5	31	3.5
PHYSICAL ABUSE				
Shoving	26	3.5	51	3.7
Slapping/hitting	38	3.4	53	4.0
Scratches/bruises	14	3.6	24	3.8
Cuts/wounds	6	2.8	12	2.7
Beatings/whippings	29	3.3	45	3.7
Inadequate medical	8	3.1	14	3.3
Pulling/grabbing	18	3.5	37	3.6
Inadequate food	6	4.2	12	4.0
EMOTIONAL ABUSE				
Neglect	56	4.3	73	4.4
Harassment	26	3.7	41	3.8
Shouting	46	3.9	67	4.0
Unfair punishment	30	3.5	45	3.6
Cruel confinement	16	3.2	25	3.2
Abandonment	35	3.8	47	3.8
Touch deprivation	38	4.5	51	4.2
Strict dress code	11	4.2	18	4.3
No privacy	24	4.1	31	4.3
Hide injury/wound	11	3.2	20	3.4
Forced to keep secrets	27	3.9	35	3.7
Adult resp. as child	36	4.2	55	4.2
Watching beating	19	3.4	35	3.8
Caught in parental fights	33	3.8	51	4.0

CRITICAL QUESTIONS

Sexual Addiction and Sexual Abuse

The data raises key questions about differential diagnosis and incest
behavior. First, we can suggest that there exists a group of incest perpetrators who are not addicts. As we have seen with the case of Jim,
some incest perpetrators are also sex addicts. Among sex addicts, the

data shows that a minority also are incest perpetrators. To further compound the issue, some of the sexually addicted incest perpetrators also committed other sex crimes. Some incest perpetrators who are not addicted probably commit other sex crimes as well.

An artist's drawing of a venn diagram illustrating the possible combinations clarifies the research questions (see Figure 9.3). Four special populations become identified:

1. the sexually addicted sex offender;
2. the sexually addicted incest perpetrator;
3. The incest perpetrator/sex offender;
4. the sexually addicted incest perpetrator/sex offender.

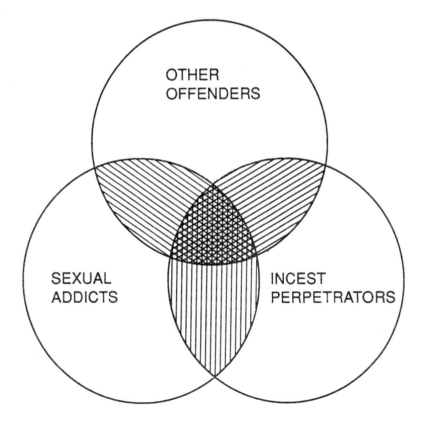

Figure 9.3 Possible Subpopulation Parameters

The contrast of each of the populations can teach much about addiction, abuse, and crime. The data clearly suggest, for example, that central to the division between sex addicts in general and sexually addicted perpetrators is the extent of physical and emotional abuse. In the model described earlier, the role of dysfunctional belief and thought patterns, the core beliefs of unworthiness and unlovability, the patterns of the use of force in sexual compulsivity, and the despair and shame about behavior are all components that would be severely impacted by physical and emotional abuse. Research detailing the connections between the addictive system of the sex addict and the role of physical and emotional abuse as contributors to incest behavior would clarify part of the larger puzzle of the intermingled subpopulations.

At this point, no one can say how significant each population is in relation to the others. The data does suggest that they exist, however. Understanding these populations becomes critical because each will require a different treatment process.

TREATMENT PLANNING

A primary task for treatment providers is to first assess if sex addiction is present. Usually, this involves an extensive sexual history that looks for patterns of out-of-control sexual behavior. Table 9.9 contains a 15-point code gaining wide acceptance for use in the diagnosis of sex addiction. If the patient meets code criteria, then the treatment plan needs to reflect strategies to arrest the addictive process. Usually this involves the integration of the 12 steps as adapted from Alcoholics Anonymous for sexual addiction into the therapy process. Consistently, treatment regimens also include family therapy with coaddicted family members, education about sex addiction and sexuality, relapse prevention plans, and stress reduction skills. Table 9.10 lists sample treatment goals for sex addiction.

On the basis of the data presented in this chapter, treating the addict/incest perpetrator as an adult survivor of abuse would also be appropriate. Treatment strategies for adult survivors as outlined by Maltz and Holman (1987) or Courtois (1988) would serve as good guidelines for therapists. In addition, special emphasis on relating family-of-origin work around physical and emotional abuse with current issues about boundary setting would be a significant integration strategy. The clinician must remember that abuse therapy and family-of-origin ther-

Table 9.9 Diagnostic Criteria for Sexual Addiction

PRESENCE OF FIVE OR MORE OF THE FOLLOWING:
1. Sexual obsession and fantasy is a primary coping strategy.
2. Sexual behavior is central organizing principle of daily life.
3. Inordinate amounts of time spent in obtaining sex, being sexual, or recovering from sexual experience.
4. Amount, extent, or duration of sexual behavior often exceeds what person intended.
5. Severe mood shifts around sexual acting out.
6. Escalating pattern of increasing amounts of sexual experience because current level of activity is no longer sufficient (exemplified by more of current sexual behavior, or addiction of new sexual behavior, or initiation of new high risk, illicit, or behavior considered to be immoral).
7. Persistent pursuit of self-destructive or high-risk sexual behavior.
8. Persistent desire or efforts to limit sexual behavior.
9. Inability to stop behavior despite adverse consequences.
10. Pattern of out-of-control (compulsive) sexual behavior for two years.
11. Pattern of alternating excessive control and out-of-control behavior over five years.
12. Severe consequence due to sexual behavior.
13. Presence of clear hierarchy of sexual acting out behaviors.
14. Important social, occupational, or recreational activities sacrificed or reduced because of sexual behavior.
15. Presence of any three of the following associated conditions:
    —extreme sexual shame
    —depression
    —other addictions
    —has been or is currently victim of sexual abuse
    —has been or is victim of emotional or physical abuse
    —secret or "double life" due to sexual behavior
    —sexualizing of nurturing
    —few or no nonsexual relationships
    —suicidal ideation or attempt
    —presence of sex-negative behavior
    —excessive reliance on denial
    —presence of codependent personality disorder

apy are long-term processes best begun after the addiction's development has been arrested. For a clear description of the family therapy process after addiction treatment by two therapists knowledgable about sex addiction, see Fossum and Mason's book *Facing Shame* (1987).

Several key ideas are developed in this chapter that ultimately impact treatment planning. First, by identifying typical characteristics of

Table 9.10 Sample Treatment Goals

To understand your own addiction or coaddiction cycle including the triggers for compulsive acting out and the underlying feelings that are medicated.

To accept personal powerlessness and unmanageability at both an emotional and an intellectual level.

To establish the foundation of a healthy sexual life based on emotional vitality and not self-destructive shame.

To initiate a life-style that minimizes vulnerability to addictive and coaddictive reactivity to life.

To confront gender shame and self-hatred.

To develop a capacity to feel and express a wide range of emotions including fear, anger, grief, shame, joy, and care.

To gain intimacy skills and the emotional capacity to sustain relationships both in the family and in support networks.

To accept personal needs beginning with ability to meet needs through nonaddictive means and allowing the nurturing of the little child within.

To set boundaries and reduce shame when in abusive family and cultural systems.

To work towards self-definition through taking responsibility for oneself in general, but especially sexually.

To prepare for the impact that recovery will have on other addictive disorders within oneself and/or in other family members.

To develop a clear aftercare plan including therapeutic tasks, support groups, relapse prevention strategies, and life-style commitments.

---

incest perpetrators and fundamental processes for sex addicts, we can see a merging of both populations. By contrasting subpopulations, special requirements for treatment become clear. From a clinical point of view, addiction as an illness and a history of abuse become vital areas of exploration in differential diagnosis among all possible subpopulations. The diagnostic process will then reflect the data trends that show the need for treating the victim in the victimizer.

REFERENCES

Carnes, P. (1985). *Out of the shadows: Understanding sexual addiction.* Minneapolis, MN: Compcare.

Carnes, P. (1986). A sex addict speaks. *SIECUS Report, XIV*(6).

Carnes, P. (1989). *Contrary to love, helping the sexual addict.* Minneapolis, MN: Compcare.

Coleman, E. (1987). Sexual compulsion vs. sexual addiction: The debate continues. *SIECUS Report, XIV*(6).

Courtois, C. A. (1988). *The incest wound: Adult survivors in therapy.* New York: W. W. Norton.

Diamond, J. (1988). *Looking for love in all the wrong places.* New York: Putman.

Fossum, M. A., & Mason, M. J. (1987). *Facing shame: Families in recovery*. New York: W. W. Norton.

Green, A. H. (1988). Overview of the literature on child sexual abuse. In D. Schetsky & A. H. Green (Eds.), *Child sexual abuse*. New York: Brunner/Mazel.

MacAulifle, M., & MacAulifle, R. (1975). *The essentials to chemical dependency*. Minneapolis, MN: American Chemical Dependency Society.

Maltz, W. & Holman, B. (1987). *Incest and sexuality*. Lexington, MA: Lexington Books.

Milkman, H., & Sunderwirth, S. (1983–1984). Advances in alcohol and substance abuse. *Journal of Alcohol Studies*, Fall/Winter.

Orford, J. (1978). Hypersexuality: Implications for a theory of dependence. *British Journal of Addiction*, 73, 299–310.

Schaef, A. W. (1989). *Escape from intimacy*. San Francisco: Harper & Row.

Schneider, J. P. (1988). *Back from betrayal: Recovering from his affairs*. Minneapolis, MN: Hazelden.

Solomon, R. (1974). The opponent-process theory of acquired motivation: The costs of pleasure and the benefits of pain. *American Psychologist*, 35, 691–712.

PART III

Treatment

Cindy's Poem

. . . a child's view of incest

I asked you for help and you told me you would
if I told you the things my Dad did to me.
It was really hard for me to say all those things,
but you told me to trust you—
then you made me repeat them to fourteen different strangers.

I asked you for privacy and you sent two policemen
to my school, in front of everyone,
to "go downtown" for a talk
in their black and white car—
like I was the one being busted.

I asked you to believe me,
and you said that you did
then you connected me to a lie detector,
and took me to court where lawyers
put me on trial like I was a liar.
I can't help it if I can't remember times or dates
or explain why I couldn't tell my Mom.
Your questions got me confused—
my confusion got you suspicious.
I asked you for help
and you gave me a doctor
with cold metal gadgets and cold hands
who spread my legs and stared, just like my father.
He said I looked fine—
good news for me, you said, bad news for my "case."

I asked you for confidentiality
and you let the newspapers get my story.
I asked for protection, you gave me a social worker
who patted my head and called me "Honey"
(mostly because she could never remember my name).
She sent me to live with strangers
in another place, with a different school.
I lost my part in the school play and the science fair
while he and the others all got to stay home.

Do you know what it's like to live
where there's a lock on the refrigerator,
where you have to ask permission to use the shampoo,
and where you can't use the phone to call your friends?
You get used to hearing, "Hi, I'm you're new social worker,
this is your new foster sister, dorm mother, group home."
You tiptoe around like a perpetual guest
and don't even get to see your own puppy grow up.
Do you know what it's like to have more social workers
than friends?

Do you know what it feels like
to be the one that everyone blames for all the trouble?
Even when they were speaking to me,
all they talked about was lawyers, shrinks, fees,
and whether or not they'll lose the mortgage.
Do you know what it is like when your sisters hate you
and your brother calls you a liar?
It's my word against my own father's.
I'm twelve years old
and he's the manager of a bank.
You say you believe me—
who cares, if nobody else does.

I asked you for help
and you forced my Mom to choose between us—
She chose him, of course.
She was scared and had a lot to lose.
I had a lot to lose too, the difference was,
you never told me how much.

I asked you to put an end to the abuse—
you put an end to my whole family.
You took away my nights of hell
and gave me days of hell instead.
You've exchanged my private nightmare
for a very public one.

—Feelings by Cindy, age 12
  Put into words by Kee MacFarlane, 1970.
  Reprinted with permission.

10

Offender Identification and Current Use Of Community Resources

David T. Ballard
Doran Williams
Anne L. Horton
Barry L. Johnson

INTRODUCTION

As a rule, male clients often feel a certain reluctance in approaching the mental health treatment community, but the incest offender recognizes that he has a dual concern. Any efforts to get help will not only involve him in a complex treatment process (prescribed to last anywhere from 18 months to 5 years), but will also identify his behavior as a criminal act carrying severe legal consequences. Clinicians, likewise, lack confidence and trust with perpetrators and tend to feel manipulated. Therapists also possess limited experience with these clients, yet are legally obligated to report them. Therefore, the initial issues of trust, confidentiality, and self-disclosure are often sadly compromised at the outset. Although not trusted by the research and treatment communities generally, from a clinical standpoint the offenders' ideas in respect to resources seem absolutely essential to good program development, efforts to satisfy unmet needs, and provision for helpful referrals.

This chapter discusses the offender's initial use of denial, his gradual recognition of a need for services, his various attempts to locate appropriate referrals, his level of satisfaction and dissatisfaction with his helpers, and his overall realization that many needed and desired support systems do not currently exist.

This chapter will also briefly describe the actual identification process beginning with the perpetrator, the victim, the family, and the community. This identification may take many years, but it is critical to beginning the recovery process, and it is important to clinicians during the intake process. Finally, it examines the intervention of many agencies and their function in the course of justice-making. The clients' use of social skills (Chapter 3) is positively correlated to an early involvement with community support.

While early intervention seems to involve fewer official intruders in the process, few clinicians are known to be available prior to the offense, and the availability of public resources before disclosure is very limited. Because there is often a considerable time gap between personal and public identification of offenders, the important role of interim support and counseling is a critical one.

ENTERING THE SYSTEM

All legal and mental health systems have gatekeepers—those who identify an individual as meeting the criteria for inclusion. Yet, with respect to incest perpetrators, certain reporting guidelines have already been established. While the clinical approach emphasizes safety for the victim and treatment of the family as the desired goal, the legal approach locates the perpetrator, establishes guilt, and punishes the offense. Thus, the new reporting procedure virtually empowers the entire community, ranging from trained mental health professionals to the untrained layman, as legally obligated reporting agents. Reporting is required of all professionals and semiprofessionals, regardless of whether they have or have not received training in the area of incest. The general public is also expected to report a large range of suspected crimes where child abuse is alleged.

Today, incestuous families comprise an increasingly large population in the treatment community—ranging from those in which members desire to change their own dysfunctional patterns and/or those in which court-ordered changes have been mandated. Some immediately attempt to link up with resources; others are more reluctant and find themselves more deeply involved with the legal system. While several options and combinations of programs may exist, it appears that timing is highly critical. Generally, the earlier these offenders and their families get involved in voluntary treatment, the more choices they will be allowed by the courts, and the less restrictive will be the correctional setting. Delayed recognition may result in institutional care rather than outpatient care.

PROBLEM IDENTIFICATION

Denial and Early Personal Awareness

Ideally, offenders would recognize a tendency toward inappropriate sexual feelings for other family members very early on—prior to acting out—and seek help accordingly. Yet, our research reports that this very rarely occurs. (See the Appendix, which details methodology, sample information, and specifics of the study.) Of the 374 incest perpetrators interviewed in depth for this study, 45% recognized an inclination to participate in an incestuous activity—a personal desire in themselves—prior to the actual act. But, fewer than 10% actually discussed the problem with anyone or sought help before the incest behavior took place. Interestingly enough, those offenders who recognized their need for early assistance make up the major portion of the group that eventually received out-patient treatment. Perhaps with an increased awareness and the ability to enforce change within "at-risk" populations, greater prevention might be a result of early identification.

Failing prior individual help, early intervention with the entire family would be very helpful for at-risk families at this early stage of awareness. However, this too is a rare occurrence. Depending on how and when identification takes place, as well as the attitudes of all the participants, the actual disclosure may range from severe crisis dimensions and total family upheaval to a more planned, responsible entry into the treatment process. Today, public disclosure and a mandated investigation usually precipitate the rapid intervention of a multitude of social service agencies (see Table 10.1), as many as five agencies and organizations are typical.

Interestingly, most offenders admit that they knew their behavior was improper at the time of the first act, but continued to conceal it rather than begin a reasonable course of treatment. More than 75% of the offenders in our sample admitted that they knew their behavior was "improper, unnatural, or wrong," but they continued to conceal it, some for as long as 30 years. Seventy-seven percent stated that they felt that intervention at that time—prior to the actual incest occurrence—would have been helpful and might have prevented it.

Currently, public admission or asking for help do not occur very often. Thus, most offenders may have a personal recognition of their problem, but do not acknowledge it publicly. It does illustrate that most offenders, at some level of awareness, are not deceiving themselves, but they do attempt deception with their victims and with the external system. Of course, once the incest occurs, many victims become unwilling silent partners. Because of the position and power of the offender—his status and role within the family—many victims are fearful of reporting.

This hesitation was misinterpreted by two-thirds of the perpetrators who saw the victim's silence as an affirmation of the behavior, because the victim "did not protest or express reluctance." However, those perpetrators whose victims did express unwillingness were more likely to be incarcerated—nearly half of those in prison and locked in forensic units as compared to one-third in outpatient settings.

Public Awareness

When public discovery occurs, many external changes follow. If knowledge of the incest has been limited to family members, more choices of services and legal remedies exist for the offender. At the point of public discovery, however, both the criminal justice and treatment communities must make some very serious, far-reaching, and more restrictive decisions, which may deeply affect these offenders and other family members.

Public disclosure almost always reduces the autonomy of the client and his family, thus, increasing the externally imposed restrictions of the system. Once community involvement occurs, offender autonomy diminishes, and public agencies assume accountability for these perpetrators. At present, both the legal and mental health systems are attempting a new partnership in which clinical treatment becomes an alternative to, and possible diversion from, incarceration. With the rising cost and growing numbers of sex offenders in prison, the legal system has turned more and more to community-based treatment, particularly when the risk to the public is believed to be low. Early self-detection and treatment (Rx) is more likely to allow the perpetrator a clinical approach, whereas the legal model may well emphasize punishment.

The following Chain of Discovery and Offender Identification model will describe the various points of potential intervention and indicate the increasing number of external systems that may become involved the longer treatment is avoided.

Intervention

In our study of offenders in four separate settings—prison, inpatient mental health, Parents United, and Private Practice—it ap-

Table 10.1 Chain of Discovery and Offender Identification

STAGE	Preincest behavior	Incest ideation	Initial incest act	Ongoing sexual behavior	Public identification	Legal intervention
AWARENESS	Perpetrator's earliest recognition	Perpetrator's desire acknowledged (no act)	Victim's initial involvement (act)	Familial awareness (at varied levels)	Community awareness	Formal charges/ adjudication
SYSTEM INVOLVED	Perpetrator only	Perpetrator only	Perpetrator & victim(s)	Perpetrator/ victim(s)/ spouse/siblings other/ relatives	Neighbors/ teachers/ school off./ friends/ clergy	Police/child protective services (CPS)/Prosecuting Attorney/offender's att./ community

peared that each offender, at some point in the incest scenario, identified himself as needing treatment. However, few actively pursued it before public identification took place. Offenders, as well as professionals, indicate a strong need for mandatory treatment because perpetrators have a tendency to avoid seeking help. This study tracked those offenders who ultimately became involved in a treatment facility as opposed to those who bypassed the system completely. Current statistics indicate that the latter group comprises the largest number of offenders: those who evade detection or treatment of any kind, those in the untreated prison population, and those who fail to locate resources.

PERPETRATORS' RECOGNITION OF THE NEED FOR TREATMENT

In retrospect, many offenders felt the problem could have been avoided if there had been help available, or if they had known how to get the appropriate treatment without fear of being punished. Yet, few perpetrators actually sought help or confided in anyone before the incest was made public. Figure 10.1 outlines the most utilized human service agencies and professionals that may intervene as the incest is reported and becomes public. It clearly indicates the potential points where interventions (Rx) might have been introduced.

Overall Use of Services

When the incest was made public, although reluctant to seek help previously, getting a team of helpers suddenly appeared more attractive to many offenders, particularly those with the better social skills and legal advice. It appears that those offenders who can figure out the system can manipulate it more to their advantage. Our sample reported involvement with one or more of the following individuals or agencies. (See Table 10.2.)

Response to Responses

By far, the mental health professional was selected by or forced upon the greatest number of perpetrators. Those in outpatient treatment were much more likely to seek early treatment, often before the community became involved, at the suggestion of other family members. Others gradually entered therapy during some point in the adjudication process, many as a condition of using community-based treatment rather than being incarcerated.

Communication between spouses was rated as a second preferred area of support (more than a form of treatment). As the reader will recall, the partners of community-based offenders were almost twice as likely to remain with their spouse as those of offenders in prison and of mental health (institutionalized) perpetrators. Family in general was particularly involved, and was evaluated as very helpful by some and very negatively by others. Yet, in respect to the overall number of resources, the outpatient community was much more likely to be involved in a multiplicity of services.

When asked which resources were *most helpful*, one-third of the Parents United group and 10% of the other outpatient community listed Parents United as most helpful. However, despite the significant number of offenders who did have contact with other resources, the level of satisfaction was surprising. For instance, although one-third consulted religious leaders, only 3% listed the clergy as most helpful.

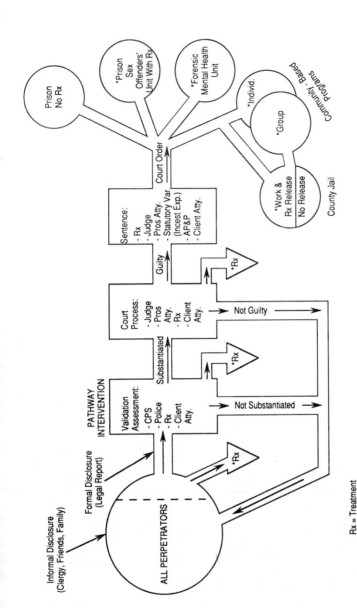

Rx = Treatment
* = Potential Treatment Intervention
AP&P = Adult Probation & Parole

Figure 10.1 Points of Potential Intervention with Perpetrators

Table 10.2 Resources Used by Incest Perpetrators

VARIABLE	Prison	Mental Health	Parents United	Private Practice	TOTALS
Sample Size	N = 63	N = 41	N = 240	N = 39	N = 383
Percent (%) who have discussed their incest behaviors with:					
Therapist/counselor	71.4	68.3	84.6	82.1	80.4
Spouse	58.7	51.2	72.5	66.7	67.4
Other family member	52.4	61.0	47.1	74.4	52.2
Parents United/self-help group	1.6	7.3	77.1	2.6	49.6
Law enforcement	28.6	36.6	46.7	33.3	41.3
Treatment facility	46.0	43.9	36.7	48.7	40.2
Friend	49.2	46.3	31.7	43.6	37.3
Clergy	33.3	31.7	35.0	28.2	33.7
AA/drug rehabilitation	14.3	9.8	16.7	15.4	15.4
Crisis line	6.3	2.4	9.6	7.7	8.1
Resources listed as most helpful (%):					
None listed	52.4	26.8	38.3	30.8	38.6
Therapist/counselor	30.2	56.1	18.3	35.9	26.1
Parents United/self-help group	0.0	0.0	32.1	10.3	21.1
Law enforcement	4.8	9.8	2.1	5.1	3.7
Clergy	3.2	0.0	2.9	5.1	2.9
AA/drug rehabilitation	1.6	2.4	2.1	0.0	1.8
Spouse	3.2	2.4	.4	5.1	1.6
Other family member	1.6	2.4	.8	5.1	1.6
Crisis line	1.6	0.0	1.7	0.0	1.3
Friend	1.6	0.0	.8	2.6	1.0
Resources listed as least helpful (%):					
None listed	52.4	48.8	63.3	84.6	62.1
Law enforcement	22.2	14.6	21.2	2.6	18.8
Clergy	4.8	12.2	2.1	7.7	4.2
Therapist/counselor	6.3	9.8	2.9	2.6	4.2
Spouse	9.5	4.9	1.7	0.0	3.1
Other family member	3.2	4.9	3.3	0.0	3.1
Parents United/self-help group	0.0	4.9	2.9	0.0	2.3
Friend	0.0	0.0	.8	2.6	.8
AA/drug rehabilitation	1.6	0.0	.8	0.0	.8
Crisis line	0.0	0.0	.8	0.0	.5

(continued)

Table 10.2 (Continued)

VARIABLE	Prison	Mental Health	Parents United	Private Practice	TOTALS
Child protective services has contacted them (%):	73.0	68.3	77.9	79.5	76.2
Use of law enforcement resources (%):					
Arrested for incest	54.0	63.4	50.4	48.7	52.2
Charged with a sex crime	60.3	61.0	46.7	51.3	50.9
Convicted of a sex crime	58.7	63.4	41.3	43.6	46.7

Four percent rated prison/jail/police and 2% selected A.A. and drug rehabilitation, with Parents United offenders significantly less supportive of individual therapy as compared to the other three groups. Parents United and individual counselors are often viewed as interchangeable. Most perpetrators were unaware of the professional training or background of the counselors, although the range of helpers went from uneducated lay leaders to Ph.D.'s and M.D.'s (see Chapter 13 on treatment providers). Those resources considered "least helpful" were police/jail, Child Protective Services/D.F.S., and hot lines. Hot lines were widely criticized primarily because of their inability and overall insensitivity to offenders' needs. It appears that while not all agencies met the needs of all perpetrators, those who were pro-police, pro-drug, pro-alcohol, and pro-church leaders responded either very positively or very negatively.

The observations and recommendations from the offenders will be offered as clinical considerations and guidelines in the remainder of this chapter. These conclusions have been taken from the in-depth questionnaire, with the perpetrator's discussion highlighting these therapeutic concerns and specific focused remarks aimed at "areas of improvement" for each resource.

Advice from Counselors to Offenders

The advice the perpetrators received from counselors that was regarded as most helpful by offenders basically fell into four categories.

1. "Get into treatment and stay with it." Counseling—individual, group, and family—was the most frequently recommended "advice" given by

professionals. Others suggested a combination of individual and group therapy. Many suggested group therapy and made direct referrals to different services. Concrete suggestions of whom to see, where to go, and how to pay for it were highly valued.

2. Professionals emphasized the necessity for the offenders to admit responsibility and take the consequences of their behavior. Many counselors urged perpetrators to turn themselves in and explained that they would have to report them. They advised them to get involved in treatment programs, be honest with the treatment providers, and advise the police or child protective services that they needed help. "Own up to what you have done and get involved in changing your life." Extensive treatment was recommended by most helping professionals although many did not see themselves as able to provide it. Honesty was a recurring theme. "Confront the problem." "Turn yourself in." Therapists who were easily deceived were not respected.

3. Counselors expressing empathy and concern (an openness and understanding) and support, but not condonation, were most appreciated. Those offering the opportunity for rebuilding self-esteem, self-worth, and personal dignity were also highly valued. Perpetrators need to have a belief that change is possible, that they can rebuild and recover, and that they can like themselves again. Perpetrators desire and hope for the future; they need reassurance that they are not crazy or evil beings. Informed, sensitive counselors are most desired, but perpetrators need to know that treatment will not be easy or short-term.

4. Many fears and losses face the perpetrator. Counselors who recognized relationship concerns and helped the perpetrators get in touch with their feelings were particularly helpful. Providing services to the perpetrator and his/her spouse as a couple, as well as to the entire family, was seen as extremely helpful. Many perpetrators wanted to know how to communicate effectively with other family members, but knew only dysfunctional ways of expressing themselves. Obtaining help for all family members is extremely important, but should not be allowed to interfere with or prevent the family from confronting the incest issues.

Counseling Improvements Suggested by Perpetrators

In addition to the broad suggestions given by counselors, perpetrators made the following suggestions on how the treatment community needs to improve their services.

1. Counselors and service agencies need to be more knowledgable about incest, attend workshops and training sessions, read material on incest, and talk with perpetrators. Until recently, material has been very

limited, but now there are resources. (See the Resource Directory at the end of this book.)

2. Build a list of trained counselors and service agencies, which you can refer to when a perpetrator needs additional assistance. All professionals should be encouraged to gain more knowledge and specialized training in the area of incest before counseling perpetrators. Therefore, take the time to screen these professionals carefully by discussing your interest in their areas of expertise over the phone or in person before suggesting them to an offender.

3. Counselors are encouraged to talk publicly about incest. Arrange to have speakers or lectures on the subject of incest offenders and their treatment with your professional colleagues and/or agency associates. Arrange for your own attendance at these professional meetings to update you and your associates about incest dynamics. Look for conferences or speakers that directly address perpetrators' treatment because, in the past, the major focus has been on the victims.

4. Provide therapy and support to the entire family. Let them know that change is possible, and how they can overcome their problems and rebuild their lives with help. If desired, encourage family therapy and preserve the family unit, but stress that it takes time. If necessary, form partnerships with other treatment providers to allow the family the fullest possible range of support services.

5. Provide a second list of supplementary community agencies in order to make additional appropriate referrals. Perpetrators will also need other services, such as Alcoholics Anonymous, Parent's hot line, drug rehabilitation, and child care services, in addition to individual, group, and family therapy.

6. Be clear in your own mind that reporting sexual abuse is mandatory, while also being sensitive in respecting the family's desire for privacy in their community.

7. Counselors are encouraged to create a "hot line" or emergency service for perpetrators on a 24-hour-a-day basis. Have crisis workers who are knowledgeable about incest, or offer them training. Many offenders' complaints about current crisis lines involve the listeners lack of understanding and knowledge about incest. Be available or see that someone else is.

8. Follow up on services for the incestuous families. Be sure that reports of abuse are attended to by the appropriate agencies, and that referrals to various sources are being carried out. The complexity of meeting all the family's needs requires case management skills.

9. Help arrange a network system to help these families and provide support for them.

10. Counselors are encouraged to ask the perpetrators direct and specific questions. Perpetrators preferred counselors to be confrontive and honest, rather than avoiding or minimizing what they had done.

Negative Responses to Professional Helpers

The major complaints launched by offenders included the following responses to all counseling professionals, regardless of their disciplines.

1. They did not know enough about incest, were untrained about its dynamics and causation, and did not understand the problem or the perpetrator.
2. They held many myths about incest, and some expressed open hostility toward the perpetrators.
3. They did not know what to suggest, or they denied or minimized the problem, assuming that recognition or expressed remorse constituted a cure.

Perpetrators, like all clients, want trained professionals who understand the problem and are in touch with appropriate referrals and interventions. Statements such as "you should be locked up," "leave your family," "many men have feelings like those you've expressed—it's normal," or "it sounds like you've learned your lesson" were defined as unsatisfactory. Offenders preferred to get a true evaluation of their offense and to deal with hard realities, rather than have it either lightly dismissed or overexaggerated.

New Services Perpetrators Suggest and Desire

The perpetrators gave the following suggestions for services that do not exist at present. The perpetrators felt that these new services would help prevent incest, help their families, and help themselves.

1. Train more qualified professionals to work with incest perpetrators and increase research efforts in this area.
2. Have more cooperation between services and professionals in the community.
3. Have individualized treatment plans—avoid stereotyping.
4. Provide more funding for all services to perpetrators and their families.
5. Locate sponsors or group services for perpetrators and their families immediately following arrest or involvement with the legal/child pro-

tection services. Group and/or individual therapy should also be offered to perpetrators and their families before they are convicted or
involved with the court process. Special groups should be set up for
teenaged perpetrators.

6. Educate the public at all levels—grade schools, adult education,
   churches, work places, the legislature, and public meetings through
   the media—regarding sex education, incest, and prevention techniques. Information about Parents United and other services that work
   with incest families should also be more publicized.

7. Participation in groups at a later date and trained group leaders should
   be available to help rebuild and reunite incestuous families.

8. Establish confidential hot lines for perpetrators. They should be maintained by well-informed listeners who understand incest and can discuss it comfortably. Many perpetrators desire someone to talk to about
   their feelings and thoughts before the sexual abuse occurs.

9. Have rehabilitated perpetrators work with the newly identified
   perpetrators.

10. Provide legal services for perpetrators at all points in the legal process.
    Perpetrators need to be advised of their rights, options, and legal
    responsibilities.

11. Establish halfway houses for perpetrators that would help with finan-
    cial assistance, housing, counseling services, future planning, and
    adjustments.

12. Arrange, with the legal system, a treatment program or alternative that
    can be used without the threat of jail. Incarceration deters from early
    intervention. Grant immunity to perpetrators who meet specified
    criteria.

13. Offer family counseling for perpetrators in jail, that could deal with
    incest issues.

14. Develop training materials and programs about the dynamics of incest
    for couples to study before marriage or remarriage.

15. Encourage churches to be more involved. Through charitable services,
    churches could offer support networks to perpetrators and their
    families.

CONCLUSION

Overall, perpetrators felt that services were extremely limited, inac-
cessible, and not well-known to the public. Their general concern
seems to be for more (qualitative) practical and more (quantitative)
direct services. Although they may come seeking reassurance and

peace, perpetrators urged professionals not to assume that cures come easily or without a great deal of treatment, effort, and time. Perpetrators wanted counselors to be informed, sensitive, understanding, and confrontive when working with sexual abuse. They also emphasized the need for cooperation and coordination between professionals and service agencies. Many services will be required for the incestuous family, and new treatment partnerships will be needed to fill these gaps.

Perpetrators particularly stressed the importance of the entire family receiving services, not just the victim or the perpetrator. Further research is needed to determine the success of incest treatment programs in preventive measures, rather than merely reactionary methods after incest occurs, but, first, preventive treatment programs need to be developed. Perhaps the suggestions offered in this book, by professionals and perpetrators alike, could serve as a point from which to begin.

REFERENCES

Conte, J. R. (1984). The justice system and sexual abuse of children. *Social Service Review*, Dec., 556–568.

Edelson, J. (1984). Working with men who batter. *Journal of Social Work*, 29, 237–242.

Finkelhor, D. (1984). *Child sexual abuse: New theory and research*. New York: Free Press.

Quinsey, V. L. (1977). The assessment and treatment of child molesters: A review. *Canadian Psychological Review*, 18(3).

Roberts, A. (1982). *Battered women and their families*. New York: Springer.

11

Professional and Treatment Issues for Clinicians Who Intervene with Incest Perpetrators

Lynn M. Roundy
Anne L. Horton

INTRODUCTION

Because of the complexity of treating incestuous families and the disparity in community services, the clinician today may be a primary-care provider to the perpetrator, a particular treatment component in the community, or a treatment coordinator relying heavily or entirely on referrals. At whatever level a clinician is involved, it is critical to focus on effective treatment for the perpetrator. While victims of sexual abuse may use a large repertoire of supportive agencies or individuals, the needs of the incest offender are often ignored. In order to bridge this gap in services, the therapist needs to become aware of several unique and clinically challenging treatment issues—those brought by the clinician and those brought by the client.

Incest, the well-kept family secret, has recently been moved out of the closet and has now become a serious public concern, with new laws and sanctions removing this form of inappropriate ownership from the family. Such behavior, traditionally, has had strong social taboos supposedly guarding against its occurrence, but now the public and various special interest groups have crossed the domestic threshold, involved the criminal justice system, and finally extended the right of personal safety to all family members. While legislation now exists in every state forbidding incestuous behavior (fulfilling the function of the judicial system to eliminate criminal behavior), the law does not address important familial and relationship concerns. Protection is the only public issue.

The dilemma comes from the interactional component of the family process. Who will protect the complex familial relationships and address the resulting hardships on this system? In general, victims and other members are accorded supportive forms of treatment; perpetrators, in contrast, receive punitive intervention. Certainly, clinical experience has taught us that these two methods by themselves do not produce a high rate of growth or change. Immediate safety needs may require initial family separation, but long-term treatment—and incestuous families all require an extended treatment period—is primarily concerned with behavior modification and education for families, rather than permanent dissolution. Ultimately, many of these families—two-thirds of the Parents United sample—prefer to reunite, and single perpetrators often seek new marital partners with children. Thus, these complex treatment issues and behavioral changes are left to mental health practitioners. At present, the success rate of treatment is unclear, but this does not eliminate the necessity of applying what clinical information we have. This chapter addresses those considerations and provides guidelines for the clinician.

ROLE OF THE THERAPIST

Basic Assumptions of Treatment

Examining the efficacy of treatment practices in regard to incest perpetrators poses many practical problems. Traditional treatment of any population presupposes three important conditions: (a) an identified client with a problem, (b) a developed strategy that will ameliorate the problem, and (c) a commitment to change. In addition, intervention with incest offenders demands that the therapist himself examines three additional conditions: (d) a willingness to treat, (e) an awareness of and attention to personal biases and issues that might negatively effect treatment, and (f) a commitment that treatment is an appropriate response to the problem.

From the outset, serious difficulties with all six conditions currently exist regarding the therapist's role in the treatment of incest offenders. Therefore, this chapter initially examines the emerging clinical role and outlines the treatment issues that must be resolved, both by the therapist personally, and by the offender himself.

The first critical issue is one of *client identification*. Who has the problem? Who is seeking relief? the victim? the perpetrator? the family? the community? the criminal justice system? the mental health community? All now become players in this complex scenario, yet each comes from a different perspective and set of expectations. Although the victim and the legal community may identify the offender as the person needing the treatment, this view is not generally held by the offender, and he may well have the support of others.

Because of an elaborate and well-established denial system, in addition to the intimate relationships and interdependencies of family members, offenders usually do not initially admit to any fault, much less regard themselves as criminals. They may, indeed, see themselves as victims of sorts and become angry at any external system that has invaded their privacy. Other family members may join them in this position as they see the threat of family dissolution or imprisonment resulting from the allegations of incestuous abuse. Entire communities have been known to support offenders, leaving a heavy burden of proof resting on the delicate shoulders of highly vulnerable and often reluctant victims and, at times, their therapists.

The second criterion introduces the problem of a *proven means of alleviating the problem* (i.e., incestuous abuse of children). This generic cure does not appear to exist currently, and certainly does not exist for all offenders. Although many treatment programs are presently in operation in a variety of settings—prisons, forensic-mental-health units, and the community—the nature of the offenders, their needs, and motivations appear to be more diverse than the present programs are able to address. These approaches often vary considerably. Also, agreement on measures of success shows great variance and leaves the careful clinician somewhat skeptical. While consensus currently appears to favor a combined strategy of treatment modalities and therapeutic approaches involving all family members and a team of coordinated treatment providers, such resources are costly and not in place in most settings at this time.

In addition, with the current emphasis on community-based treatment, many therapists are encountering this special population, which is unfamiliar to them and often undesired. To compound the problem, these clinicians—seldom specially trained regarding incest—do not possess a ready repertoire of treatment strategies, nor do they understand the expectations of the referring mental health or legal community regarding their roles and goals. Serious communication and philosophical gaps often exist. Given that the ideal treatment setting for incest perpetrators may not currently exist and is certainly not universally available, clinicians will often have limited resources and must make less than ideal referrals.

The third condition, *commitment to change*, is also sadly compromised, at least initially, in our current system. Resistant clients always pose special treatment challenges, and outright denial in the face of overwhelming evidence is not conducive to a positive treatment outcome. With a strong societal taboo and high social costs at risk, each actor in the family system often points the finger at someone else while clinicians and law enforcement officials often do their own version of finger pointing. In addition, the mental-health community often does not trust the veracity or motives of the offenders, tends to regard them as untreatable and characterological, is untrained and unprepared to absorb them into routine clinical practice, and lacks a conceptual treatment framework that defines their role. Nonetheless, mandatory treatment appears to be indicated, given the nature and seriousness of the offense. And, although many offenders initially resent being court ordered into treatment, as they begin making progress in overcoming the deep-seated issues that led them to sexually offend children, they often begin to value the therapeutic process. This is particularly true when the alternative to treatment is incarceration.

The three additional conditions for treating incest introduce or imply subjective elements for the therapist's consideration. Rogers (1951) urged clinicians to "start where the client is." However, in respect to incest perpetrators, it is most important to start where the therapist is. Careful self-examination is a must before undertaking this form of therapy.

The fourth condition, a *willingness to treat*, is a primary consideration for each therapist. Chapter 13 describes in detail the attitudes of professionals and graduate students regarding the treatment of perpetrators. A reluctance, or unwillingness to treat, is not uncommon, nor is it therapeutic. A searching self-examination must be done at the gut level rather than at an intellectual one. Do you really want to help one of those "baby rapers," those "perverts"? It is not unusual for the beginning clinician to have some mixed feelings about these offenders, but these are generally resolved by working in the field. However, many professionals find themselves uncomfortable or unwilling to treat perpetrators and need to develop a good resource file for making responsible referrals.

The fifth condition of treatment with this population suggests that *clinicians look carefully at themselves*, and at what they bring, personally, to the therapy session. Due to the perverse nature of incest, professionals who work with victims and with offenders are especially subject to a variety of preexisting biases and personal issues. These therapist biases and issues will undoubtedly have a counterproductive effect on the treatment process if they remain out of conscious awareness, and unresolved.

The final consideration in helping offenders involves the question of *how best to respond to incest.* Therapists who choose to treat incest offenders (and wish to treat them successfully) must be committed to treatment as the best course of remedial action. To maintain a therapeutic relationship with an offender, with the concurrent belief that incarceration or punishment is the best solution to the problem, is, at best, unethical. At worst, it may also sabotage the credibility of the treatment process, or constitute a charade, leaving all concerned parties (i.e., offender, family, courts, social services, and so on.) with the false impression that the offender is being successfully treated.

ISSUES FOR CLINICIANS

Biases Often Encountered in the Treatment of Incest Perpetrators

Cultural/Social Biases

Among the societal prejudices regarding incest that will likely be encountered by treating professionals are the following.

1. *An unwillingness, on society's part, to accept what the presence of incest among the normal population may suggest about that society.* If the incidence of incest victimization cited by Russell (1982) is accurate, then sexual abuse is common in families. The heinous and seemingly perverted nature of incest lends itself to a reluctance to acknowledge that incest is our problem (that we are a society of perpetrators), and that perpetrators are human beings, and in many ways, like us.

2. *"If you are not a part of the solution you are a part of the problem."* There is a significant percentage of the population that believes that the only just and effective response to incest is incarceration, preferably for life. Justice demands that perpetrators must be punished for their horrible offenses against society's most precious, helpless, and innocent citizens: children of tender years. If this constitutes a popular picture of the solution to incest, then "bleeding heart" therapists who attempt to thwart this process by diverting offenders into treatment may be perceived as another part of the problem.

3. *A lack of faith in the value of psychotherapy as a cure for perpetrators of incest.* If pedophiles are believed to be untreatable (a perception

shared by the public as well as many clinicians), then therapists who advocate for treatment in lieu of incarceration are jumping for the moon. "If we can't cure them, then let's at least keep them behind bars and away from our children."

4. *Biases based on the socioeconomic status of offenders and their families.* The intervention process often varies with families according to the perceived socioeconomic status of the offenders (Sege, 1989). Children from lower-class families are more likely to be removed than those from upper-class families, which are deemed less likely to constitute a continued risk to those children. Families of influence are likely to wield that influence in order to avoid traditional intervention processes (e.g., threats of lawsuit, appeals to powerful advocates, and so on.). The result of these biases is that upper-class families are less likely to be reported, and if reports are made therapists and social workers are more inclined to trust the judgment of upper-class offenders. This assumption of "privilege" that exists among upper-class offenders may, indeed, place their victims more at risk, as these perpetrators often regard themselves as "above the law."

Religious Value Biases

Conflicts may arise between clinicians and the clergy, between therapists and perpetrator clients—either of whom may or may not be affiliated with religious organizations—or between the clergy and perpetrators.

1. *It is not uncommon for the clergy to be unwilling to acknowledge the presence of incest perpetrators in the congregation.* A desire to view all adult church members as God-fearing may result in the child victim being called to repentance for fabricating vicious accusations of unspeakable evil about an active churchgoer. If clinicians treating offenders and their families believe the children's stories and attempt to treat perpetrators, they may be considered to be an obstruction to the work of God. In order to avoid this possible conflict between therapists and the clergy, it is recommended that a cooperative effort between the two sides be established and maintained.

2. *Conflict over what constitutes adequate and sufficient intervention.* Members of the clergy, in some cases, may believe that incest perpetrators who come forward, confess their transgression, and satisfy the prescribed requirements of repentance and forgiveness have completed the intervention process. Clinicians who expect perpetrators to address unresolved psychological issues, in addition to the spiritual steps described, may be perceived as interlopers into the religious realm, or

infidels who deny the power of God to forgive and heal penitent sinners. Treating incest offenders takes time and treatment that, if too quick, will not be respected by savvy offenders.

3. *"God and I have worked it out."* One area of potential disagreement is the inclination of perpetrators to seek and find absolution from God. Perhaps in an attempt to circumvent what promised to be a long and painful spiritual and psychological process, one perpetrator approached his therapist, six weeks into the relationship, with a request that he intervene with the client's clergyman. When questioned further, the client responded that he wanted the clinician to "get my priest off my back. I took the matter of my sexual abuse to God in prayer, asked for forgiveness, and I have been told by Him that I am forgiven, and cleansed of the problem. Oh, by the way, He also said I would have no further need of counseling. I am well now."

Clinicians, regardless of their level of religiosity, should find some difficulty with such a situation.

Professional Biases

Some traditionally accepted theories of psychotherapy may not accurately reflect the reality of effectively treating incestuous offenders.

1. *Dilemmas resulting from models of psychotherapy that are based on unconditional positive regard.* Incest perpetrators frequently use the defense mechanism of denial to avoid facing responsibility for the abusive behavior. Clinicians who espouse a therapeutic process emphasizing acceptance of the offender "as is" (e.g., Rogerian) might find it difficult to express unconditional positive regard if incestuous fathers will not acknowledge the degree of potential devastation they have inflicted on innocent children. Because empathy and unconditional positive regard are so important in allowing offenders to feel valued and able to begin dropping their defenses, resolution of this dilemma is critical (Ryan, 1986).

2. *Dilemmas regarding the development of trust in a therapeutic relationship.* Clinicians who offer services to offenders will frequently find themselves wrestling with questions relating to the issues of trust. "Should I believe my clients' statements?" "Can I provide treatment in an absence of trust?" A failure to adequately resolve these trust dilemmas might result, on the one hand, in a premature reunion of father and child, with the potential for remolesting. On the other hand, an absence of trust tends to be counter-therapeutic (Ryan, 1986). The setting of appropriate trust levels and clear limits seems to provide a healthy balance of structure and limited freedom.

3. *Professionals who treat incest are subjected to negative feedback from a segment of the clinical community.* Therapists who publicly discuss incest, accept the purported high incidence of the problem, and suggest that the level of public and professional awareness of incest should be raised will likely receive less than warm (sometimes bordering on openly hostile) support from a number of colleagues. This oppositional response may be especially prevalent among clinicians who come from the psychoanalytic model, which maintains that, as a natural process in resolving the Oedipal complex, most children will engage in incestuous fantasies involving the parent.

4. *Pedophiles (often perceived as all child sexual offenders, including incest perpetrators) are considered by many in the therapeutic field to be incurable.* Clinicians who hold to a belief that perpetrators are treatable are likely to encounter resistance from those professionals schooled in the previously prevailing notion of incurability. Attempts to provide therapy to this population might be viewed as unrealistic, idealistic, or even incompetent or unethical (e.g., promising hope for progress to clients and their significant others when such a goal is unattainable).

5. *Turf battles resulting from clinicians (e.g., individual vs. group therapists) competing for control of cases and from therapists' needs to be viewed as effective.* Therapists are professionals, earning income by providing therapy. As such, they compete for client resources and for funding from other sources (e.g., government agencies, and so on). Competition for clients may result in biased accounts favoring the efficacy of services provided by the therapist or disparaging remarks regarding services offered by others. A related issue that often surfaces is the question of who controls the direction of treatment. Is the group leader or the individual therapist in charge? Who decides when the perpetrator has completed the therapeutic process? Unless these issues are recognized and addressed they may prevent the cooperative effort that is critical to success with this population.

These battles may actually be encouraged by perpetrators as a means of diverting clinical effort from intervention (e.g., confrontation of denial or directly addressing painful client issues) to winning client approval (Ganzarian & Buchele, 1986). It is not uncommon, for example, to have perpetrators make negative comments in each clinical setting (e.g., individual and group) regarding the other therapist. "My other therapist is not very effective. He doesn't care about me at all! All he knows how to do is yell at me and get angry. I'm glad you understand me. I'm making much more progress here than I am with him."

Therapists who succumb to such manipulative attempts and rescue offenders from the oppressive other clinician are thereby drawn into the dysfunctional systems these perpetrators have created and carefully maintained in order to avoid facing the reality of, and responsibility for, the incestuous behavior.

Personal Biases

Dealing with incest effectively requires that therapists are willing to examine their own biases, many of which may create blind spots for clinicians unless they are faced and appropriately dealt with.

1. *Ambivalence regarding the responsibility of children who behave seductively or appear to have willingly participated in sexual contact with offenders.* Therapists with unresolved issues regarding sexuality and seductivity might be biased in favor of offenders if the victimized children's seductive nature becomes known. Rather than looking beyond this flirtatious behavior to the responsibility of perpetrators not to respond, they may affix part of the blame for the incest on the children.

2. *Gender biases regarding either children or the perpetrators* (James & Nasjleti, 1983). Clinicians of either sex will, inherently, bring any unresolved gender biases to the therapy session. Male therapists, finding themselves siding prejudicially with female victims, might attack offending "typical males" while presenting a nurturing or rescuing response to their helpless victims.

   Alternatively, if male clinicians are unwilling to accept that men could be guilty of such a terrible thing as incest (or if they have unresolved fears regarding their own sexual urges or behavior), they may side with perpetrators, displacing the blame for the sexual behavior onto seductive "typical females."

   In similar fashion, female therapists may respond favorably (albeit dysfunctionally) to the manipulative seductions (not necessarily sexual) of offenders and, as a result, react clinically in a manner biased against children.

   On the other hand, female therapists responding from a nurturing perspective might be inclined to support or rescue children, while reacting with hostility toward perpetrators.

3. *Biases suggesting that nonoffending spouses may be partially responsible as a result of their failure to perform their wifely duties to meet their spouse's sexual needs.* Some therapists (regardless of gender) may come to a clinical session with incest perpetrators with a belief that it is the duty of wives to meet their husbands' sexual needs. This point of view would lead them to excuse to some degree the natural reaction of offenders in turning to their daughters if their spouses were not providing them with adequate affection. "After all, a man has to have it, and if his wife is not there for him he will have to go elsewhere."

4. *Biases relating to the Oedipal complex theory* (Mrazek, 1981). Clinicians who operate from a psychoanalytic model may have to assess to what degree their beliefs regarding the incest fantasy may bias them and prevent them from accepting the accounts of incest by children. Other therapists may find themselves overreacting to Freud's position and accepting any incestuous account as fact. Either position is counterproductive.

PERSONAL ISSUES FOR CLINICIANS

Clinician Fear of or Discomfort with Incest

A number of factors related to the intense nature of incest may become obstacles to objective intervention by therapists.

1. *Pain associated with the incestuous behavior.* Victims of incest commonly experience intense pain and fear (Roundy, 1988). Lives that have been impacted by incestuous abuse are often shattered. Incest hurts. Therapists who have fear of addressing this pain may be unable to provide effective treatment.

2. *Emotional intensity.* Few issues have the capacity to elicit more emotional intensity than incest. Expressions of intense fear, anger, or hatred may be threatening to clinicians. One therapist, following a highly intense expression of affect, told his client, "We aren't going to talk about the incest anymore. It just upsets you."

3. *Specifics of the abusive behavior.* Incestuous behaviors may include bizarre or violent acts (e.g., satanic rituals, bestiality, or infliction of physically violent sexual behaviors), which could be perceived by treatment providers as beyond their tolerances, or as morbidly fascinating. Such reactions would obviously preclude objective therapy.

Clinicians' Need for Universal Success in Treating Clients

Helping professionals are inclined to hope for a successful treatment outcome with all of their clients. They may have some degree of ego investment in maintaining a high "batting average." This issue, if left unresolved, might bias therapists to accept unfounded client declarations of progress, or to terminate prematurely. Alternatively, unrealistic expectations for success in the face of the frequent treatment failures encountered in working with offenders could lead clinicians to experience frustration, self-doubt, or discouragement.

Therapists Who Need to be Liked by Clients

1. *Need to be "Mr. Nice Guy."* Clinicians who try too hard to be understanding or helpful may, in the process, become easy targets for manipulation by the clients and their families. For example, if offenders are highly cooperative and willing to get help, clinicians might erroneously choose to recommend that court-ordered treatment and separation from their families is not necessary. As suggested by Ryan (1986), this would likely result in a continuation of the dysfunctional influence and control previously exerted on victims and other family members. Additionally, when fathers determine that the problem is taken care of they will conclude treatment.

2. *Difficulty in confronting dysfunctional behaviors of clients.* Clinicians who have the need to be liked are less likely to appropriately confront incest offenders when they manifest dysfunctional behavior. To confront is to risk becoming the target of perpetrators' anger or rejection. Because confrontation is so necessary to treatment, therapists may wish to consider this aspect seriously. Being unable or unwilling to confront perpetrators constitutes a disservice to the client's recovery process.

3. *The more effective you are at therapeutic interventions the less well-liked you may be by offenders.* Successful treatment of incestuous offenders inherently involves inviting them to acknowledge and explore very painful issues. Such invitations are often strenuously resisted by clients. Clinicians with a need to be liked may be less likely to encourage offenders to overcome such resistance.

Unwillingness to Deal Directly with the Core Issues Associated with Incest

Helping professionals are human beings as well, and may feel varying degrees of discomfort in working with child sexual abuse. Rather than dealing directly with the pain, guilt, and so on, associated with the actual incest, they may choose to focus on the secondary effects (i.e., low self-esteem, and so on).

TRANSFERENCE AND COUNTERTRANSFERENCE ISSUES IN THE TREATMENT OF INCEST OFFENDERS

Attempts by perpetrators to seduce, imitate, intimidate, or invalidate their therapists. Incestuous fathers who are in treatment often view clinicians as just another group of authority figures to be controlled or manipulated. Transference issues may lead these offenders to use one or more of the methods previously employed with others. These might include acting seductively (sexually or nonsexually) toward therapists, mimicking clinicians' dress and manner (Ryan, 1986), use of anger or rejection to intimidate therapists, and invalidating treatment providers by negatively commenting on their skills or abilities.

Perpetrators' transference manifested by passivity, overcompliance, and immature behavior with clinicians. Offenders may transfer onto their therapists unresolved issues with either of their parents. Thus, clients may play "child" to "parental" therapists of either gender. This role of child may present in treatment in a number of ways. Perpetrators may passively agree with every observation made by the clinician. Overcompliance may occur in the form of absolutely-by-the-book behavior and immediate responses to every clinical directive or statement. The offender may also parentify the therapist and respond immaturely in interactions with the clinician.

Perpetrators' fear of being controlled by "another authority figure." Treatment providers may be cast into the role of controlling authorities by incest offenders. Unattended, such a transference could potentially inhibit therapy by creating resistance.

Abandonment or Betrayal Issues

Having been abandoned and betrayed often, both in childhood and in later years, offenders are likely to transfer these unresolved issues (with concomitant fear or anger) onto clinicians. Resolution of these feelings will be necessary in several common treatment situations, including the following therapist responses: reporting newly disclosed incestuous behavior (or remolest); insisting on a court-ordered therapeutic agreement; unwilling to side with offenders' efforts to blame victims or spouses for the abuse; confronting offenders' denial; or encouraging clients to work through painful emotions.

Of particular note is the likely emergence of abandonment issues as therapy nears termination (Ryan, 1986). Following a long—up to five years—and difficult process of treating incest, therapists and clients will have achieved significant relationships. Often this will constitute one of the only healthy interactions offenders have been able to develop and maintain. As the time for termination approaches, the impending loss of these healthy relationships may result in resentment or anger directed at clinicians. One means for preventing the development of such abandonment issues is to begin preparing clients well in advance—up to six months—for termination.

Addressing the countertransference issues of the abused child in the clinician. Miller (1986) maintained that everyone was, as a child, sexually, physically, or emotionally abused to some degree or another. Assuming that to be true, it follows that previously abused therapists would approach with ambivalence both the topic of incest—perhaps the most devastating form of child abuse—as well as clinical work with perpetrators.

1. *Hurt, fear, and anger directed at offenders with a desire to punish them* (Giarretto, 1981). Therapists who work with perpetrators may respond punitively to them as a result of their identification—from unresolved childhood abuse—with the pain of the children. The effect of this reaction might be for therapists to displace fear, anger, and so on, from their own childhoods onto offending clients. Confronting the offenders' behaviors might become more important than understanding the factors that led them to the incestuous activity (Ryan, 1986).

2. *Need to rescue offenders.* On the other hand, clinicians may recognize the abused children of the past (Groth, 1979; Miller, 1984; Williams & Finkelhor, 1988) within perpetrators. Responding to these hurting children, therapists might be drawn into protective or nurturing parent stances, which would preclude an appropriate focus on confrontation of denial or avoidance of responsibility for the acts of clients as adults.

   This need to rescue might also be manifest in therapists' willingness to respond positively to nonoffending spouses' requests for fathers to be allowed home for important holidays or family events (e.g., Christmas or birthdays). Rather than waiting until substantial behavioral change occurs, they are swayed by paternal promises of nonabuse and maternal promises of protection (Ryan, 1986).

3. *Potential for clinical abuse of perpetrators.* Clinicians who do not attend to their countertransference reactions toward offenders may be more likely to abuse therapeutic relationships as a weapon for administering justice. Such a position might be manifest as a "no holds barred" approach to fixing these perverts.

Issues of Displacement from Perpetrators and Their Families

Anger from perpetrators or family members that is displaced onto the intervening clinicians. Upon the disclosure of incest, there is a significant response from the various intervention agencies responsible for substantiating, investigating, and treating the problem. For families where privacy and secrecy have been a pattern of survival, these interventions are considered intrusive or even violative. It is common for offenders and other family members to displace anger, distrust, or hostility from the actual perpetrators of the incest onto child protective workers or therapists (Solin, 1986). As Ryan (1986) has noted, therapists and others who work with abusive families "have come to expect resistive, even hostile behavior."

Anger from perpetrators or family members that is displaced onto abused children. Some incestuous families perceive victims as villains. These children may be treated as the cause of the problems that these families are now experiencing. They may be socially and emotionally ostracized in their own families and may be emotionally or physically abused as punishment for telling. Concerted efforts by family members may be directed at persuading abused children to tell the authorities that they lied, reinstating the former stability that was disrupted.

Skills and Abilities—with a Willingness to Use Them—Needed by Clinicians Who Treat Incest Offenders

Willingness to invite perpetrators to relinquish long-held defense mechanisms. The development and maintenance of incestuous behavior is, to some extent, dependent on the existence of sufficient ego defense mechanisms to allow for overcoming personal and societal incest taboos. Once incest has emerged as an overt behavior, these defenses become particularly necessary to prevent direct contact with full comprehension of the nature and implications of the offending acts. In order to successfully treat perpetrators, therapists must be able and willing to facilitate the properly timed release of these defenses. Prematurely relinquished defenses leave the ego at risk for disintegration, whereas defenses that are maintained ultimately preclude therapeutic healing.

1. *Precipitation of plunge into despair, great emotional pain, and extreme self-hatred.* As ego defense mechanisms are faced and given up, offenders often experience (perhaps for the first time in their lives) the full impact of their behavior. Clinicians observing this plunge may be inclined to rescue offenders from their pain. This would be particularly likely for treatment providers with their own dysfunctional defenses in place. The ability for the therapist to offer appropriate support without rescuing is crucial.

2. *Perpetrators of incest will often have virtually no genuine external emotional support.* Once the incestuous acts have been disclosed, perpetrators are often left with extremely unstable emotional support from significant others. The firmly stated support of nonoffending spouses, other family members, and friends is often inconsistently punctuated with ambivalent bursts of love or concern and anger or resentment.

Ability to balance accepting perpetrators and rejecting their abusive behaviors. Therapeutically, a delicate balance must be established between offering appropriate "unconditional positive regard" to offenders and, at the same time, properly rejecting the incestuous acts. A failure to achieve and maintain this balance will likely leave offenders experiencing, in the reaction of the therapists, their own self-rejection, or an inability to distinguish between their worth and the unacceptability of their behaviors.

Ability to "get in touch with the pain they are in before dealing with the pain they have caused" (Broderick, 1983). Incest offenders, by virtue of their abusive behaviors, have created potentially significant pain in the lives of both abused children and other family members, friends, and so on. Therapists who provide treatment to this population are well advised to be open to hearing the client's expression of his pain before addressing the pain resulting from the abuse. Ryan (1986) suggested a process of initially "setting aside the factual information in favor of understanding" the offender, his fears, hopes, and feelings of loss and betrayal.

Comfort in addressing human sexuality, including the perversion of incestuous sexual behavior. In order to effectively assist incest offenders to resolve the sexual conflicts associated with child sexual abuse, clinicians must be clear in their own sexuality. If therapists have fears regarding sexual issues or the aberrant nature of incestuous behaviors, they are probably unable to objectively facilitate treatment of these issues in clients (James & Nasjleti, 1983).

Personal security sufficient to allow honest expression of affect (e.g., acceptance, caring, fear, anger, helplessness, vulnerability, and so on) toward perpetrators. In order to model self-awareness and healthy emotional expression, clinicians must be emotionally secure enough to observe and communicate their feelings to clients. Perpetrators will be unlikely to acknowledge and express their fear or vulnerability if therapists are unable or unwilling to accept and declare these issues in themselves (James & Nasjleti, 1983).

Personal commitment to be active participants in the effort to ameliorate and prevent incestuous sexual abuse. Any attempt on the part of treatment providers to assist in the prevention and amelioration of incest must be energized by a significant level of personal commitment. The task is too challenging, the clients are too resistent to therapy, the rewards are too small, and the successes are too infrequent for clinicians to remain involved with lukewarm intentions.

Ability to be healthy parent models to offenders and their families. Incestuous fathers and their families are likely to have experienced minimal healthy parenting. Clinicians working with this population must be clear regarding their own need to dysfunctionally parent clients. If these inappropriate needs do exist, they should be resolved. Healthy modeling of parenting principles within the therapeutic relationship (e.g., setting proper limits, allowing clients to assume responsibility for their own behavior and healing, and establishing and upholding appropriate expectations) is essential if offenders and their families are to learn appropriate parenting patterns (Ryan, 1986).

CAUTIONS, SUGGESTIONS, AND PRACTICAL GUIDELINES FOR MENTAL HEALTH PROFESSIONALS WHO TREAT INCEST OFFENDERS

Become aware of and resolve personal biases and issues that might negatively affect objective clinical work with perpetrators. As suggested by the focus of this chapter, it is essential that therapists who choose to treat incest offenders discover and clear up any unresolved biases or issues that would prevent them from being effective.

Accept the obligation to build and maintain clinical competence. This would include (a) establishing a solid theoretical base for affecting positive change in clients, (b) acknowledging the specialized nature of providing treatment to this population, (c) developing a thorough understanding of the etiology and present family dynamics of incest, and (d) accumulating—by way of special training or workshops—and refining a wide repertoire of skills and techniques that will enhance effective treatment.

Anticipate and work to reduce burnout. Burnout is an occupational hazard for therapeutic professionals, and it is especially common among those who treat incest. Clinicians who anticipate burnout and take active steps to prevent or reduce the problem are much less likely to become casualties of child sexual abuse. One of the most powerful efforts in this regard is a decision to accept the extensive incidence of incestuous abuse and its potential for devastating the family, and then to recognize and acknowledge the significance for society and especially for society's children of being a part of the effort to treat and prevent incest.

Establish a network of fellow clinicians in order to gain support and to process cases. Successful incest treatment providers virtually always have established and maintained their own support network. This allows them to frequently make "sanity checks," process issues, get second opinions on case management problems, and secure reinforcement that, despite appearances, they are generally on the right track.

Be open to observation and to feedback from fellow clinicians or supervisors. Essential in any attempt to provide treatment for incest offenders is a willingness to allow observation of clinical work by fellow professionals and to elicit honest and constructive criticism. This could be accomplished through the use of videotapes of sessions (audio tapes do not provide clues regarding nonverbal behaviors), one-way-mirror observation, or cotherapy. Feedback of particular value would include (a) observed therapist or client biases and issues, (b) transference and countertransference reactions, (c) comments regarding the treatment process itself (e.g., Does the treatment evolve from sound theoretical premises and solid understanding of likely treatment issues?), and (d) suggestions regarding the effective and timely application of appropriate techniques.

Be alert for the "quick cure" ploy. As perpetrators enter treatment and begin to realize the potential devastation they have inflicted on their victims, they may "flee into health" (Ryan, 1986). In order to lessen their guilt and to convince themselves and others they no longer constitute a risk to children, offenders may too quickly attempt to assure family members and clinicians that they will never reoffend, that they have changed their behaviors, and have taken care of their problems. Therapists who anticipate this early phase of treatment can assist clients to understand the underlying reasons for these premature claims. They can also avoid the temptation following such assurances, and at the request of mothers and children, to prematurely return fathers to their families.

Establish realistic clinical expectations regarding success with this population. Recidivism is a fact of life with this population. The dynamics that lead men to sexually abuse children are often deeply in-grained and constitute a formidable obstacle to effective treatment. Clinicians who have undue concerns about maintaining a glowing "track record" of positive treatment outcomes will likely find themselves facing discomfort over a significant proportion of treatment failures.

Measure success in smaller increments. Although the length of time required to provide effective treatment of incest offenders varies to some degree from client to client, the average length of treatment is approximately two years (Ryan, 1986), and it is not uncommon for clients to remain in therapy for up to five years. Considering this, it is imperative that clinicians develop the ability to perceive progress in increments smaller than those for shorter term and less dysfunctional clients.

Develop and implement a general response strategy to perpetrators' anticipated behaviors and defenses. Nowhere in the treatment of mental health problems does the adage, "Proper prior preparation prevents poor performance," have more significance. Providers will encounter typical and unusual circumstances in dealing with incest. Therapists will increase their effectiveness to the degree that these potentially challenging situations can be anticipated and therapeutic strategies planned. For example, clinicians might note personal characteristics in individual offenders that might trigger countertransference responses. With this awareness clearly in mind, healthy alternate reactions can be activated.

Do not bargain away court involvement in the treatment process. Clinicians who have worked extensively with incest offenders have long recognized the need for retaining the power of the courts as a motivation for serious therapeutic work (Ryan, 1986). The threat of what might be termed the "legal ax" seems to be essential to successful treatment outcomes. Offenders who are encouraged to visualize this ax waiting to fall (e.g., revocation of probation and subsequent incarceration) have a higher likelihood of seriously addressing their inappropriate behaviors and issues.

Be honest: Don't make promises you cannot keep. Therapists who treat offenders may be inclined to offer assurances of favorable court disposition in return for "coming clean." In fact, clinicians seldom have control of what will happen in the court process. Treatment providers may also be tempted to promise that "everybody will be better off" if the sexual abuse is fully disclosed. Perpetrators who spill their guts in response to such promises will likely feel betrayed, angry, resentful, and resistent to therapists and to treatment in general if these promises are unfulfilled (Ryan, 1986).

See the importance of dealing directly with perpetrator issues rather than avoiding them. As it is with therapy in general, so it is especially true with treating incest offenders: Avoiding difficult or unpleasant treatment issues is not conducive to successful therapy. Clinicians who are able to face and address even the "hard stuff" are effectively modeling the same essential behavior for clients. Therapists who can reframe challenging issues as "grist for the mill" (Yalom, 1985) will find that these feared issues can actually become friendly guides, leading therapists and clients to significant growth and awareness.

Use personal countertransference reactions as a tool to sensitize you to the anticipated reactions others may have toward offenders. One of the most effective methods of developing increased empathy and assisting perpetrators in dealing with their interpersonal experiences is to use countertransference responses to these clients as indicators of probable generalized reactions. With this knowledge, clinicians can prepare clients for the potential responses and assist these offenders in developing healthy methods for dealing with them.

PROFESSIONAL ISSUES

Mental health professionals who choose to treat incest offenders are confronted with numerous dilemmas. Perhaps the most difficult to resolve is the issue of duty to report vs. duty to maintain confidentiality. As Bolton and Bolton in Chapters 2 and Kelly in Chapter 16 have suggested, clinicians who treat perpetrators "must be able to balance a client's right to confidentiality with society's right to have its children protected."

Those who wish to explore this issue further are encouraged to read Chapters 2 and 16.

TREATMENT ISSUES OF INCEST OFFENDERS

The interpersonal dynamics that precede and are a result of incestuous behaviors are indicative of a variety of treatment issues. Therapists who work with incest perpetrators will do well to be prepared to recognize and address one or more of the following possible presenting symptoms.

1. *Confusion of sex and love.* Members of incestuous families very commonly believe the following equation: Sex = Love = Closeness (Intimacy). If perpetrators accept this statement as true, they may attempt to meet their love (closeness) needs through sexual contact with family members (Mayer, 1983).

2. *Sexual identity conflicts.* Conflicted sexual identity is common with offenders who may not perceive themselves as adequate in "masculinity" (Mayer, 1983; Williams & Finkelhor, 1988).

3. *Fear of adult females.* Perpetrators of incest may have been exposed to mothers or other significant adult females who were hostile toward, rejecting of, and superior to the males in their lives (i.e., their fathers, husbands, and so on), and, consequently, a generalized fear of all adult females may result (Finkelhor, 1984).

4. *Sexual addiction.* Incest offenders may exhibit symptoms of sexual addiction and have scores on sexual addiction scales that link them with such an addictive pattern (Benson, 1985; Carnes, 1983, Chapter 9 of this book).

5. *Previous history of abuse.* As in-depth histories are gathered with incest perpetrators, it is not uncommon to discover that offenders are also victims of prior physical or sexual abuse (Williams & Finkelhor, 1988). Groth (1979) found that 32% of offenders convicted of sexually abusing children had experienced sexual trauma in their youth (Steele & and Alexander, 1981). De Young (1982) found that 43% of incestuous fathers had been physically abused, and 37% reported sexual abuse in their childhood years (Mayer, 1983).

6. *Other forms of abuse.* Men who sexually abuse their own children may also exhibit other types of abusive behavior, that is, emotional abuse, physical child abuse, or spouse abuse (de Young, 1982; Dietz & Craft, 1980; Herman, 1981).

7. *Substance abuse.* Alcohol and drugs are often associated with incest offenders. These substances may serve to reduce normal inhibitions, allowing the tendency for abuse to emerge. Perpetrators may also attempt to excuse their sexual behavior by blaming it on the abused substance: "I didn't know what I was doing! I was drunk" (Deighton & McPeek, 1985; Herman, 1981; Mayer, 1983; Williams & Finkelhor, 1988).

8. *Sexual irresponsibility.* Many fathers who become sexual with children have failed to assume personal responsibility for their own sexual behavior. They seem to evidence an egocentric attitude, which might be expressed as: "I *must* have sex. If my wife won't give me what I have to have, then I'll have to go someplace else and get it" (Mayer, 1983).

9. *Poor stress management skills.* Men who sexually abuse their children often lack the ability to manage their lives and do not possess skills for

coping with and reducing the amount of stress or anxiety they encounter. They often seem to be in a chronic state of near overload (Justice & Justice, 1979; Mayer, 1983; Williams & Finkelhor, 1988).

10. *"Compartmentalization" (dissociation) of abusive episodes.* Abusers may employ "compartmentalization" as a defense against the unacceptable feelings that would be experienced if the incestuous episodes were allowed to enter their conscious awareness. They simply place the abuse in an unconscious compartment, and they are thereby not required to face the full weight of personal responsibility. They may also use this defense as a way of being honest in their denial of involvement in the abuse (Justice & Justice, 1979).

11. *Denial of involvement in or responsibility for abusive behavior, often with high degree of defensiveness.* Whether or not offenders have conscious awareness of their involvement in incestuous activities, they may vigorously deny any complicity. Their efforts may include attempts to depict accusing victims as habitual liars, as seductresses, as sexually promiscuous with their age-mates, or as children simply having "bad dreams" or fantasies (Mayer, 1983; Sanford, 1982). Defensiveness is not uncommon with incest offenders. Perhaps they have some realization of the magnitude of their offense and, fearing the consequences, they take a defensive posture, especially when confronted.

13. *"Mama's boy."* Because of unresolved issues related to their relationships with their mothers, incestuous fathers often present as "wimpy" or as "momma's boys," dependently tied to their mothers and lacking the normally developed masculine independence and strength usually associated with males (Mayer, 1983; Williams & Finkelhor, 1988).

14. *Isolation: Poor social skills with few significant relationships.* Some men who sexually abuse their own children exhibit varying degrees of social isolation. They may be uncomfortable in social settings, especially those where significant social interaction is normal. They may imitate a form of surface social skills; that is, they may be known as the friendliest member of their social or religious group due to their ability to shake hands with everyone, a social interaction requiring little or no real communication. This factor may influence where they live, as well as their choice of employment. Offenders may choose to live in small rural communities where social contacts would be minimal, or they may work as auto mechanics, carpenters, and so on, where their work requires little interaction with people (Justice & Justice, 1979; Williams & Finkelhor, 1988; see also Chapter 5 of this book).

15. *Egocentricity/narcissism.* This factor is best illustrated in the seeming lack of awareness of the significant pain and suffering incestuous fathers cause their child victims directly and the entire family indirectly. Fa-

thers often react with apparent genuine shock and dismay as they are brought to an awareness that their actions have been devastating to others. They seem to have been tuned in only to their own needs and concerns (Crewdson, 1988; de Young, 1982).

16. *Jealousy of daughter's association with boys.* Fathers in incestuous families frequently play the role of "jealous lover" to their daughters when they become involved with other age-mate males. They may discourage or restrict dating and may project their own sexual issues onto their daughters' boyfriends, accusing them of sexual intentions (Justice & Justice, 1979).

17. *Authoritarian parenting, often with submissive servitude outside of the home.* Incestuous fathers may present contrasting interactional patterns in and out of the home. In the home they may rule supreme, demanding absolute obedience and dealing out swift and harsh punishment for those who do not respond properly. Out of the home they may present as submissive and overly solicitous, eager to please, and anxious to avoid confrontations and conflict, especially in dealings with those who are perceived to be in power positions, that is, police, employers, religious leaders, therapists, and so on (Cormier, Kennedy, & Sangowicz, 1962; de Young, 1982; Herman, 1981).

18. *Low impulse control at home, with appropriately managed behavior elsewhere.* Offenders frequently claim to be unable to control themselves in their abusive behavior: As one perpetrator explained, "I feel like I'm in the St. Lawrence River, in an inner tube, headed toward Niagara Falls, and all I have to stop me from going over is my hands. No matter how fast I paddle I can't stop myself" (de Young, 1982; Mayer, 1983). By contrast, they often seem able to appropriately manage their behavior outside of the home, suggesting a voluntary (though perhaps unconscious) determination of what type of behavior is acceptable where.

19. *Highly manipulative manner.* Perhaps no single descriptive trait is used more often in describing incestuous offenders than "manipulative" or "slick." Perhaps in an effort to give appearances of being in control of their chaotic lives, they become master manipulators of their victims, wives, family members, and associates. In order to maintain the sexually abusive activity in the face of such powerful social taboos, they must be persuasive with respect to their innocence when suspicions arise, or when the secret is out. They may be very effective in their efforts to portray postures of circumspect character and may convince others and themselves (Mayer, 1983).

20. *Minimization of abusive behavior.* Perpetrators often attempt to minimize either the severity of their abusive acts or the number of such

contacts. "It was just a little simple messing around" might be the offenders' way of characterizing several incidents of oral, digital, and penile sexual contact with their daughters (Mayer, 1983; Sanford, 1982).

21. *Rationalization.* This common defense mechanism is frequently used by sexual offenders to justify their activities: "I couldn't help myself. She was dressed in a skimpy nightgown" (de Young, 1982; Mayer, 1983; Sanford, 1982).

22. *Self-deception.* Some perpetrators are so effective in their use of defense mechanisms that they successfully deceive even themselves into believing their distortions. For example, some offenders deceive themselves into assuming their daughters want the sexual contact and benefit by it in order to justify their continued involvement or reduce their own guilt (de Young, 1982; Sanford, 1982).

23. *Poor relationship with parents.* Incestuous fathers frequently describe histories of early childhood parental deprivations, which might have been economic, or more commonly, emotional or interpersonal in nature. These parental relationships were often negative or ambivalent in character (de Young, 1982). Common themes from childhood include abandonment, powerlessness, maternal seduction, and paternal rejection (Williams & Finkelhor, 1988).

24. *Possessiveness.* Incestuous fathers may believe that children are their "possessions" and therefore they have a right to do whatever they wish with them (de Young, 1982).

25. *Blurring of generational boundaries.* Incestuous fathers may, in interactions with their daughters, act impulsively or immaturely. They may act as if they were young suitors to their daughters (Justice & Justice, 1979).

26. *Low self-esteem.* Sexual offenders seldom have a high regard for themselves and often consider their behavior as indicative of the lowest form of life possible (Mayer, 1983; Williams & Finkelhor, 1988).

27. *Depression.* Upon disclosure of the sexual abuse, with the threat of potential disruption to the family system, court-ordered treatment, possible incarceration, and a beginning realization of the potential devastation resulting from the abusive behavior, it is not uncommon for incest offenders to experience periods of significant depression (Williams & Finkelhor, 1988).

28. *Paranoia.* Perhaps due to the virtually universal societal revulsion of incest, offenders commonly appear paranoid in their interactions with intervening individuals. Motives of helping professionals are often suspected by perpetrators to be negative. Claims of being persecuted are frequent (Williams & Finkelhor, 1988).

29. *Irrational reasoning or behavior.* Sexually abusive men may evidence "quick fix" mentalities. They may expect complete forgiveness from their spouses and victims in response to simplistic apologies, such as, "I'm sorry. Please forgive me" (Williams & Finkelhor, 1988).

Issues Clinically Observed but Not Documented in the Literature

30. *Sexual validation.* Offenders often see their value as persons corresponding to their sexual involvement with females. From that perception they may have difficulty validating themselves, depending on external sexual reinforcement for their sense of well-being.

31. *Control issues.* Many perpetrators of incest have significant issues regarding control of themselves as well as significant others. This may have originated in their own victimization as children.

32. *Dysfunctional guilt.* Sexual offenders may direct significant amounts of emotional blaming at themselves often in the form of a psychologically dysfunctional guilt response. This effort may represent attempts to do penance for sins committed; however, the actual effect is often to waste energy, leaving offenders stuck in their behaviors.

33. *Rigid moral or religious values.* Perpetrators may have very rigid moral and religious values and demand strict compliance with little or no flexibility. Their own sexual irresponsibility is highly inconsistent with this position.

34. *Sexualization of emotions.* Stress, anger, fear, insecurity, and other emotional states may be tied to offenders' sexual states. As these emotions rise so do their needs for sexual release. After heated arguments with their wives, they may suggest going to bed and making up by having sex. If these sexualized emotions are not resolved sexually with spouses, husbands may turn elsewhere, perhaps to children.

CONCLUSION

While the intent and focus of this chapter has been to provide current and prospective incest treatment providers with a realistic, but sobering (and not particularly encouraging), picture of undertaking such a professional course, it is critically important to reaffirm the pressing need for many more capable, committed, and qualified clinicians to join the ranks.

Although the challenges are significant, there could hardly be a field of mental health that offers a greater sense of contribution. Incest inflicts a devastating and often long-term blow to everyone directly and even indirectly involved. A choice to provide services to this pop-

188

TREATMENT

ulation is a decision to help realize a day when children can grow up
in homes that are safe and secure. We can only imagine what inevitable
benefits to society will result from such a change.

REFERENCES

Benson, R. M. (1985). *Sexual addiction as it relates to incest perpetrators, spouses, and survivors.* Unpublished masters thesis, Brigham Young University, Provo, UT.

Broderick, C. B. (1983). Keynote address at the Association of Mormon Counselors and Psychotherapists, Salt Lake City, UT.

Carnes, P. (1983). *The sexual addiction.* Minneapolis, MN: Compcare.

Cormier, B. M., Kennedy, M., & Sangowicz, J. (1962). Psychodynamics of father-daughter incest. *Canadian Psychiatric Association Journal,* 7(5), 203–217.

Crewdson, J. (1988). *By silence betrayed: Sexual abuse of children in America.* Boston: Little, Brown.

Deighton, J., & McPeek, P. (1985). Group treatment: Adult victims of childhood sexual abuse. *Social Casework: The Journal of Contemporary Social Work,* September, 403–410.

de Young, M. (1982). *The sexual victimization of children.* Jefferson, NC: McFarland.

Dietz, C. A., & Craft, J. L. (1980). Family dynamics of incest: A new perspective. *Social Casework: The Journal of Contemporary Social Work,* December, 602–609.

Finkelhor, D. (1984). *Child sexual abuse: New theory and research.* New York: Free Press.

Ganzarian, R., & Buchele, B. (1986). Countertransference when incest is the problem. *International Journal of Group Psychotherapy,* 36, 549–566.

Giarretto, H. A. (1981). A comprehensive child sexual abuse treatment program. In P. B. Mrazek & C. H. Kempe (Eds.), *Sexually abused children and their families.* Elmsford, NY: Pergamon.

Groth, A. N. (1979). Sexual trauma in the life histories of rapists and child molesters. *Victimology: An International Journal,* 4(1), 10–16.

Herman, J. L. (1981). *Father-daughter incest.* Cambridge, MA: Harvard University Press.

Haugaard, J. J., & Reppucci, N. D. (1988). *The sexual abuse of children.* San Francisco: Jossey-Bass.

James, B., & Nasjleti, M. (1983). *Treating sexually abused children and their families.* Palo Alto, CA: Consulting Psychologists Press.

Justice, B., & Justice, R. (1979). *The broken taboo: Sex in the family.* New York: Human Sciences Press.

Mayer, A. (1983). *Incest: A treatment manual for therapy with victims, spouses and offenders.* Holmes Beach, FL: Learning Publications.

Miller, A. (1986). *Thou shalt not be aware: Society's betrayal of the child.* New York: Farrar, Straus, & Giroux.

Mrazek, P. B. (1981). *Sexually abused children and their families.* New York: Pergamon.

Rogers, C. (1951). *Client-centered therapy.* Boston: Houghton Mifflin.

Roundy, L. M. (1988). *Sexual abuse problem checklist: Form V.* Provo, UT: Author.

Russell, D.E.H. (1982). The incidence and prevalance of intrafamilial and extrafamilial sexual abuse of female children. *Child Abuse and Neglect,* 6(10), 20.

Ryan, T. S. (1986). Problems, errors and opportunities in the treatment of father-daughter incest. *Journal of Interpersonal Violence, 1*(1), 113–124.

Sanford, L. T. (1982). *The silent children.* New York: McGraw-Hill.

Sege, I. (1989). Agony of child abuse cuts across class lines. In *The Boston Globe, 235* (58), 1, 4.

Solin, C. A. (1986). Displacement of affect in families following incest disclosure. *American Journal of Orthopsychiatry, 56,* 570–576.

Steele, B. F., & Alexander, H. (1981). Long-term effects of sexual abuse in childhood. In P. Mrazek & H. Kempe (Eds.), *Sexually abused children and their families.* New York: Pergamon.

Williams, L. M., & Finkelhor, D. (1988). The characteristics of incestuous fathers: A review of recent studies. In W. L. Marshall, D. R. Laws, & H. E. Barbaree (Eds.), *The handbook of sexual assault: Issues, theories and treatment of the offender.* New York: Plenum.

Yalom, I. D. (1985). *The theory and practice of group psychotherapy.* New York: Basic Books.

12

Where Do I Start? *Guidelines for Clinicians*

Nodie Cox Davis
Vicki D. Granowitz
Deena D. Levi

INTRODUCTION

Therapists routinely assess their clients for suicidal tendencies, chemical dependency, and other potentially dangerous behavior. The potential for initial or recurring incest should be routinely assessed as well. Often, an incest perpetrator does not fit our currently held stereotypes; the people involved in incest may be attractive, likeable, and intelligent.

Perpetrators often present themselves as the general population of clients with a seemingly typical range of initiating problems and diagnoses. Since the danger of incest is a multifaceted issue, it is imperative that an evaluation for the potential of incest be undertaken with virtually every client. This assessment is an ongoing process and should remain in the therapist's thoughts, not only in the initial sessions, but throughout the course of treatment. These offenders are certainly a considerable danger to others if not detected.

The process for assessing the general client population for the potential of an incest situation is delineated in the section following the description of a case study. Primary prevention involves the identification of a potential for incest, and therapists may find themselves asking, "Where do I start? What indicators do I look for?"

The following vignette will identify some of the issues involved in assessing family situations for the potential of incest.

CASE EXAMPLE

A male client was referred for therapy following treatment in an inpatient chemical dependency program. During the initial evaluation, he talked about how hard it had been for him since his wife had been promoted at work and had started working longer hours. He was angry at his wife, feeling neglected and depressed, and suffering from low self-esteem. He had no friends since he had given up his drinking buddies. And, he felt that, since he had stopped drinking, he had done more than his wife toward preserving the family unit. In the first few years of their marriage the couple had intercourse every day. Now, the wife was seldom interested in sex. The client stated that his 10-year-old daughter was the only one who seemed to care about him.

Through several sessions with this client, it became clear to the therapist that the client had grown up in a dysfunctional home. His father was an adult child of an alcoholic and his mother was emotionally unavailable. He became jealous of the special attention that his sister received from their father. In therapy, the client began to suspect that the father had molested his sister. The client also disclosed that he had started masturbating when he was 11 and was currently masturbating several times a day. He eventually came to identify himself as a sex addict. Through therapy, he was able to recognize how much his wife reminded him of his mother, discovering that much of the anger at his wife was unresolved anger at his emotionally unresponsive mother. The client had identified with his father whom he saw as a victim of his mother's coldness.

The client's wife was invited to join in marital counseling, where she disclosed that she had been molested by her brother when she was a child. Her husband's demands for sex renewed her feelings of victimization and she had shut down. As a result, she had emotionally withdrawn from him and from their children.

In this case, the 10-year-old daughter was at high risk to be molested by her father. The mother was working long hours, leaving father and daughter alone frequently. The daughter was expected to help take care of her younger siblings and do much of the cooking and cleaning. She had little time for friends outside the home. She felt close to her father and detached from her mother, who was unavailable to her. The father was angry and feeling abandoned by his wife. Roles and boundaries had eroded, and there was little communication between the client and his wife.

Through identification and intervention, the therapist was able to point out the danger signs to this client and his wife. Through the use of individual, marital, and family therapy, it was possible to appropriately realign the boundaries and roles within the family. In addition, all of the children were educated in child sexual abuse prevention.

Presently, the father continues to attend AA and work on his sexual addiction. The mother is receiving treatment for her incest issues. The daughter is no longer performing as a parentified child and is participating in age-appropriate activities with friends.

The following sections will provide a guide to appropriate diagnostic questions, which reflect the issues necessary for detection and treatment. The potential for incest will be evaluated on two levels: (a) the potential for the initial occurrence of incest, and (b) the potential for recurrence of incest. These suggestions and techniques are based on considerable library research, group brainstorming, and extensive clinical experiences with members of the incest population. Information and research gathered on the background and characteristics of incest perpetrators, nonoffending spouses, victims, and incest family dynamics have been used by the authors to develop additional assessment guidelines to aid clinicians.

USING THE ASSESSMENT GUIDELINES FOR PRIMARY PREVENTION

Responses to these guidelines will help the therapist discriminate when an individual or family may be at high risk for initial or recurring incest. As therapists collect information, they may initially look for signs that indicate a healthy family versus a dysfunctional family with a high probability of incest. In a family that displays clear emotional and physical boundaries—individually, in interaction with each other, and with people outside the family—incest is less likely (incest involves a violation of these emotional and physical boundaries).

Appropriate roles within the family are important as is a clear, but flexible, separation between adults and children. Parentification of a child, or an adult who behaves like a child, would be a warning sign. Incest involves secrecy; therefore, the potential for incest is lessened in a family that does not keep secrets. This openness within the family will allow for social contacts outside it, eliminating the isolation that is often a dynamic of incest families. The ability of each member to see others as separate from him/herself implies the ability to separate his/her own needs and the needs of others. High self-esteem and respect, individually and as a family unit, indicate reduced potential for incest.

The following diagnostic questions emphasize the behavioral, historical, and dynamic components that are often present in incestuous families. It is necessary to gather information on each family member that may be common to several members as well as information that is specific for an individual member. The assessment is done by taking a careful and detailed history, and through ongoing observation by the therapist. Utilization of information from personnel at other agencies or institutions may be of assistance.

An affirmative finding on any single factor is not necessarily in and of itself indicative of the probability of incest. But, as therapy unfolds and evidence presents itself, a therapist should be prepared to initiate whatever actions may be indicated. Because incest occurs within a family context, the guidelines include an assessment of the perpetrator, the nonoffending spouse, the child(ren), and relationships within the family.

PRIMARY PREVENTION ASSESSMENT GUIDELINES FOR PERPETRATOR AND NONOFFENDING PARTNER

1. What are the personality styles of the clients? The most common personality styles of incest perpetrators include rigid and authoritarian, passive or dependent, hostile, misogynistic, and narcissistic. Personality styles frequently found in nonoffending partners include borderline or histrionic personality disorders, and passive or dependent, controlling or rigid styles. Sociopathic or psychotic personalities need to be identified as quickly as possible, because the assessment guidelines may not prove valid with this population.

2. Are the clients sexual addicts or co-addicts? Are immediate family members addicts? What are their addictions? If so, what is the degree of addiction? (See Chapter 9 on addiction.)

3. Are the clients adult children of dysfunctional families (e.g., where there was alcoholism, drug abuse, mental illness)? What role did the clients assume in the dysfunctional families?

4. Are the clients chemically dependent or otherwise addicted? What is the nature of the addiction(s)? How do the clients' addiction(s) affect other family members?

5. Are the clients co-dependent with family, coworkers, or friends? How do the clients carry out the co-dependent role?

6. Were the clients physically or emotionally abused or neglected as children? Was the style of the family of origin disengaged, rigid, or enmeshed? Was the discipline in the family harsh and authoritarian, or overly permissive?

7. Were the clients molested as children? Who was the perpetrator? Was it within the family? At what age did the incident(s) occur? Was it disclosed, and if so, what was the outcome? Were the incidents denied within the families?

8. Were siblings in the families of origin sexually abused? Who were the perpetrators? Were the clients aware of the incidents, and if so, what were the clients' reactions to them?

9. What are the body images and physical characteristics of the clients? How do the clients dress? Is it age-appropriate or do the clients appear to be much younger than the stated age? Do the clients appear childlike or older than their partner? Do they appear highly sexualized or asexual?

10. Do the clients feel that the development of their secondary sexual characteristics was delayed or accelerated? Do they think that their sexual characteristics were different or unusual?

11. Are the clients easily threatened or defensive? Are denial, minimization, and disassociation the primary defense mechanisms?

12. Do the clients lack personal boundaries and limits? Do they feel whole only when enmeshed with others? Are the clients able to respect others' privacy and personal space?

13. What are the clients' religious backgrounds? Are they rigid and punitive? What messages about sexuality are conveyed from their particular religious backgrounds?

14. What are the clients' sexual histories? Have they ever perpetrated a molestation, rape, or incest? If so, at what age did this occur? Who were the victim(s)? Have there been other sexual assaults or inappropriate sexual behaviors? When were the clients' first sexual experiences? What memories and feelings do the clients have about them? How many sexual partners have the clients had? Have the clients contracted any sexually transmitted diseases? What are the clients' current sexual behaviors? What are their sexual fantasies? Are the clients' at a developmentally appropriate stage of sexual functioning?

15. Do the clients have children or plan to have them? Do the clients have ready access to children either their own, through the extended family, neighborhood children, professional or volunteer activities?

16. Have there been significant crises that have resulted in a loss of self-esteem for the clients, for example, loss of a job, health problems, death of a family member?

"Direction" and "directness" are bywords when pursuing this background information. Clients may then respond to this directness when they would seldom volunteer abuse information in any area.

PRIMARY PREVENTION ASSESSMENT GUIDELINES FOR CHILDREN

The following questions pinpoint areas that the authors have found to be indicators of the potential for victimization:

1. Is the child needy, insecure, or lacking in appropriate love and nurturing?
2. Does the child perceive him/herself as powerless in the family?
3. What type of sex education has been provided in school and at home? What education has the child received about child sexual abuse?
4. Is the child allowed to have friendships and social activities outside of the family?
5. Has the child been previously molested by someone outside the family?
6. Is the child assuming an adultlike role with either or both of the parents, or siblings?
7. Is the child physically or mentally handicapped?
8. Has the child been physically or emotionally abused?
9. Is the child able to say "no," and is that "no" respected?

PRIMARY PREVENTION ASSESSMENT GUIDELINES FOR RELATIONSHIPS WITHIN THE POTENTIAL INCESTUOUS FAMILY

A good history on each individual is important, but individual assessment is only the first step. While the individual's characteristics introduce the potential personality makeup for perpetrators, nonoffending partners, and victims, it is the relationships or dynamics within the family that lead to the potential incest situation. To assess the relationships, the following questions are suggested.

1. How long have the adults been in their current relationship? How did they meet, and what most attracted them to each other?
2. Are the adults married or living together?
3. Are both sexual and nonsexual intimacy a part of the adult relationship?
4. How is the power distributed within the adult relationship? Is there an emotional, sexual, or financial imbalance?
5. What are the adults' former relationship histories? Have either been involved in sexually, physically, or verbally abusive relationships?

6. What are the parenting styles? How do the adults discipline the children? Who is the primary care giver? Do the adults share parenting responsibilities? Do they triangulate, infantilize, or parentify their children?

7. What are the clients' major concerns and fears about the relationship? Are the threats, concerning abandonment or retaliation, real or implied?

8. How do personality styles interact within the family unit? Are one or more of the family members disengaged and unavailable, or overly involved and enmeshed?

9. Are there clear distinctions between the roles of the children and the adults within the family?

10. How do family members communicate with each other? Is there an identified patient within the family? If so, what roles does he/she serve in the family?

11. Are family members socially isolated? Do they have friends individually, as a couple, and/or as a family?

MAKING USE OF DIAGNOSTIC QUESTIONS

It is from the information gathered by the use of these questions that potential for incest can more accurately be predicted. Although there may be circumstances that prevent access to some information included in the assessment, the authors consider the assessment to be thorough enough to allow for missing information and still be able to evaluate the potential for incest.

USING THE DIAGNOSTIC GUIDELINES FOR SECONDARY PREVENTION

Secondary prevention is an assessment of the "potential" for the recurrence of incest and includes the implementation of measures designed to avoid recurrence. In a situation where incest has been disclosed (and the therapist is treating the perpetrator, spouse, or victim), the dilemma for the primary therapist is in assessing when the family can be reunified and when treatment can be safely terminated. The assessment guidelines include two basic questions: (a) Have all the secrets been disclosed and dealt with? (b) Have the individuals and the situation changed sufficiently so that the possibility of relapse is minimal?

This assessment, too, is an ongoing process. For the child-protective worker and the court, the danger of reunification may be a one time evaluation; while, for the therapist, it is an ongoing part of the treatment process. However, in the perpetrator's case it is a life-long process: The danger of recurrence is always there, but that danger is diminished if the perpetrator, victim, and family understand the dynamics of incest. A perpetrator who cannot identify his own incestuous danger signals—taking initial steps in setting up the victim, feeling out of control or overwhelmed, or feeling the need to control and use power—is in real danger of relapse. From the authors' clinical experience, indications that a family is still at high risk include, but are not limited to, (a) a nonoffending spouse who refuses to deal with the incestuous assault, (b) prevalence of denial and minimization, and (c) a victim whose role is to care for the adults. It is critical that these dynamics change before a perpetrator can safely reunify with the original family.

If the perpetrator moves to another primary relationship, his therapist must be assured that this new relationship does not carry the potential for recurrence of incest. This evaluation takes place under the guidelines described in the Primary Prevention section.

CONCLUSION

Because assessment of the potential for initial and recurring incest is a multi-faceted issue, it is an ongoing process for the therapist and all concerned. The general client population, as well as identified perpetrators and their families, need to be evaluated. The information gathered using the assessment guidelines provided in this chapter can help the therapist place families along a continuum of dangerousness for the likelihood of incest.

REFERENCES

Finkelhor, D. (1984). *Child sexual abuse: New theory and research.* New York: The Free Press.

Froth, A. N. (1979). *Men who rape: The psychology of the offender.* New York: Plenum Press.

Knapp, F. H. (1984). *Retraining adult sex offenders: Methods and models.* Syracuse: Safer Society Press.

13

Current Treatment Providers

Annette Plyer
Cydney S. Woolley
Troy K. Anderson

INTRODUCTION

An important question that most inexperienced clinicians ask initially in working with incest perpetrators is, "What to do?" With the rise in incest reporting nationwide, offenders are entering various treatment programs, which are attempting to help this population. Due to the nature of this problem and the serious repercussions it causes for so many families, it is extremely important for professionals to have proper training, knowledge, and attitudes with regard to incest perpetrators in order to help them. Currently, treatment providers at all levels are actively engaged in answering the question posed above.

However, little is actually known about the training, preparation, and approaches of those currently treating the incest perpetrator. Groth (1978) asserted that treatment providers "have not been prepared in their academic training to work with incest perpetrators." Overall, in addition to lack of preparation, allegations have been made that these helpers are unmotivated and have little desire to work with this population.

For the reader's convenience, this chapter has been divided into two parts. Part I discusses the treatment providers, addressing their own expressed interest and desire to work in this area, their education, training, preparation, and personal experiences. Part II outlines the treatment modalities, approaches to treatment, duration of services, and clinical suggestions for working with offenders.

PART I: TRAINING, KNOWLEDGE BASES, AND ATTITUDES

Herman (1981) indicated that the dynamics involved with incest perpetrators are very complex. Mrazek (1981) noted that treatment providers must be "alert" and have a clear understanding of the incestuous system so as not to be manipulated by the sexuality of the family. Treatment providers with limited experience and understanding regarding the perpetrators are very disadvantaged, and may be misled.

In a study conducted by Dietz and Craft (1980), it was found that treatment providers believed their training and skills to be lacking for working with incestuous families. Most of the treatment providers obtained knowledge on their own by outside reading. Ninety-five percent reported needing more "information, training, and skills" to help incestuous families.

Because treatment for offenders is currently in the initial stages of development, those clinicians in practice today are making critical program and treatment decisions for incest perpetrators. Since it is such a controversial topic, it is important to take as much guesswork out of treatment issues as possible. It is critical to know who the clinicians are, and what they are doing. In an effort to explore those who are providing treatment, our research team examines the following areas: (1) background characteristics of treatment providers, (2) reported levels of education, training, and personal experiences, (3) desired traits and skills, and (4) desire to work with Perpetrators.

Social and Demographic Profiles of Treatment Providers

The sample consisted of 67 treatment providers from Parents United, 13 from private practice settings, 14 from prisons, and 4 from forensic mental health centers. (See Appendix for more details and methodology.) Table 13.1 shows a social and demographic profile of the treatment providers who participated in the study.

The combined group of 98 treatment providers contained 53.1% males and 46.9% females. The mean age of the treatment providers was 40.4 with ages ranging from 23–73. As would be expected, 90% of treatment providers were Caucasian, with other minorities representing only 10%.

Only 10.4% of treatment providers reported being volunteers, with 69.8% reporting to be full-time staff. Income per month ranged from $200 to $6500 per month, with $2438 being the mean income. About

Table 13.1 Social and Demographic Profile of Treatment Providers

Variable		Percent
Sex (N = 98)		
Female		46.9
Male		53.1
	Total	100.0
Age (N = 98)		
20–29		11.2
30–39		41.9
40–49		29.6
50–59		11.3
60–74		6.0
	Total	100.0
$\bar{X} = 40.4$		
Race (N = 98)		
Caucasian		90.8
Black		3.1
Other (Hispanic, Asian)		6.1
	Total	100.0
Marital Status (N = 98)		
Single		13.3
Married		64.3
Separated		1.0
Divorced		11.2
Widowed		6.1
Living together		3.1
Other		1.0
	Total	100.0
Religion (N = 94)		
No preference		28.7
Catholic		18.1
Protestant		33.0
Jewish		8.5
Other		11.7
	Total	100.0
Highest degree completed (N = 98)		
Associate		1.0
Bachelor's		19.4
Master's		67.3
Doctorate		11.2
Other		1.1
	Total	100.0

(*continued*)

Table 13.1 (Continued)

Variable		Percent
Field of study (N = 97)		
Social Work		33.1
Psychology		30.9
Other (Ed. Psych., MFT)		36.0
	Total	100.0
Volunteer or paid professional (N = 96)		
Volunteer		10.4
Part-time		19.8
Staff		54.2
Director		15.6
	Total	100.0
Income per month (N = 84)		
under $999		8.0
$1000–1999		28.0
$2000–2999		30.0
$3000–3999		17.0
$4000–4999		8.0
$5000–5999		6.0
$6000–6999		3.0
	Total	100.0

$$\bar{X} = \$2438.21$$

NOTE: The N's in Table 13.1 are not identical because of missing data.

43% of treatment providers reported they had been with their organization five or more years. Forty percent reported their time with the organization as being one to five years.

Reported Levels of Education, Training, and Experience

Approximately 79% of the treatment providers held Master's degrees or higher. Fields of study were equally represented by Social Work 33%, Psychology 30.9%, and 36% reported related or unrelated fields of study (i.e., MFT, Ed. Psych.). Table 13.2 presents treatment providers' reported levels of education, training, and experience.

Seventy-one percent of the treatment providers reported having prior professional experience preparing them to work with incest perpetrators. About 41% reported their experience came from workshops, 21.9% from internships, 25% from actual experience with incest perpetrators, and 12.5% from the classroom. Treatment providers

Table 13.2 Reported Levels of Education, Training, and Experiences

Variable		Percent
EDUCATION		
Last grade completed (N = 96)		
12–15		2.2
16–19		65.9
20 and over		30.9
	Total	100.0
Highest degree completed (N = 98)		
Associate		1.0
Bachelor's		9.4
Master's		67.4
Doctorate		11.2
Other		1.0
	Total	100.0
TRAINING		
Specific agency required training (N = 87)		
Yes		27.4
No		71.6
	Total	100.0
Inservice training provided by agency per month (N = 50)		
1–3 (hours)		48.0
4–6		26.0
7–9		8.0
10 and over		18.0
	Total	100.0
$\bar{X}$ = 4.8 hours		
Type of training within agency (N = 87)		
None		23.0
New worker		2.3
Inservice		6.9
Team meetings		5.7
Workshops		29.9
Readings		13.8
One on one		5.7
Hands on		3.4
Other		9.3
	Total	100.0
Regular inservice training within agency (N = 91)		
Yes		44.6
No		54.4
	Total	100.0

(*continued*)

Table 13.2 (Continued)

Variable		*Percent*
EXPERIENCE		
Prior professional experience/preparation for work with perpetrators (N = 93)		
Yes		71.0
No		29.0
	Total	100.0
Type of experience (N = 64)		
Workshops		0.6
Internship		21.9
Classroom		12.5
Prior work experience		25.0
	Total	100.0
Years of experience working with perpetrators (N = 94)		
1–5 (years)		62.7
5–10		31.9
over 10		5.4
	Total	100.0
Personal experience with incest in own family (N = 96)		
Yes		14.6
No		85.4
	Total	100.0

Note: The N's in Table 13.2 are not identical because of missing data.

reported an average of 5.1 years of experience working with incest perpetrators.

In regard to training, 72% reported their agency had no specific training for work with perpetrators, and 54.3% reported no ongoing training or inservice in their agency. Eighty-five percent reported no training was required of them before treating the incest perpetrator. Those who did receive training got it from workshops (29.9%) and reading the literature (13.8). Over half (53.1%) of the treatment providers reported no use of time during the week for preparation and education regarding incest perpetrators. Even though the prison and mental health sample was quite small, it was interesting to note that the prison and mental health settings reported the least amount of training within and without their particular organization. All (100%) of the prison and mental health sample reported no specific training for treatment providers.

About 85% of treatment providers reported having no personal experience with incest in their own families. Those treatment providers who did report incest in their families had received an average of 6.5 years of treatment.

Clinical Observations on Social Information and Professional Experience

Males and females were represented nearly equally among the treatment provider sample. Traditionally, it had been assumed that males should treat the perpetrator. This idea originated from the fact that in institutional settings treatment providers mostly consisted of males. But, obviously females are treating perpetrators and should not be discouraged from doing so.

The findings also indicated that treatment providers are a mature, seasoned group of individuals, since the average age is 40. There is also some stability in work with incest perpetrators as about one-half of respondents reported being with their organization five or more years. This contradicts assumptions made in the literature that treatment providers were unmotivated. Providers must be motivated to some degree in order to stay with their work for an extended period of time. This stability could suggest that these treatment providers working with perpetrators are motivated and committed to this population.

It is impressive to find the levels of education and experience that treatment providers reported. This information contradicts what is currently found in the literature, such as treatment providers having little experience and being poorly educated. However, treatment providers are not gaining their experience through the classroom, which validates Groth's (1978) point about academic deficiencies.

It is clear from this data that treatment providers are well-educated and experienced. This is encouraging information since experts and potential experts are entering this area of work. A high level of education and experience sets a strong foundation for the development of expertise. It would appear that this "lack of experts" (Sgroi, 1982) is currently being replaced by experts and potential experts.

While it was found that treatment providers are a well-educated group, training is an obvious weak point. This supports Quinsey (1977) and Edelson (1984) in that treatment providers appear to have little training or support for training within their organizations. This is especially interesting because treatment providers themselves suggested training as a qualification/preparation guideline for others working with incest offenders. While treatment providers may be well-educated and experienced, individual and ongoing agency training is lacking.

It is difficult to target the reasons why training is not occurring or available to treatment providers. It has been reported in the literature that updating and training are necessary for working with perpetrators. Perhaps training is assumed to be the treatment provider's responsibility. Some treatment providers suggested reading materials they had used individually for training purposes.

A majority of treatment providers reported having no personal experience with incest in their own families. This data differs from that found by Moulton (1981) who was concerned about victims becoming treatment providers. Many treatment providers disagreed with the idea that victims should not treat perpetrators. However, they did express a strong opinion that the victim treating the perpetrator must "work through their victim issues" before effective treatment could occur. Transference and countertransference are seen as critical points of concern still needing clinical clarification.

Desired Traits and Skills

Several experts have attempted to outline desirable qualities and skills necessary for treatment providers to work effectively with the incest perpetrator (Fein & Bishop, 1987; Giarretto, 1981; Herman, 1981; James & Nasjleti, 1983; Justice & Justice, 1979; Mrazek, 1981; Topper & Aldridge, 1981). In general, a vital quality necessary for treatment providers is that they be "skilled in a variety of therapeutic techniques" (James & Nasjleti, 1983) and have a good understanding of treatment and incest.

Recurring themes of importance focus on various aspects of sexuality with an emphasis on the need to be comfortable in discussing openly and honestly all aspects of human sexuality. It is essential that the treatment provider be "secure" with his/her own sexuality as well (Fein & Bishop, 1987; James & Nasjleti, 1983). Mrazek (1981) pointed out that someone with a "puritanical repressive upbringing" or personal experience of sexual assault as a child or adult may find work with incest "difficult or impossible" unless the individual has thoroughly worked through their issues. Moulton (1981), during an inservice training program for 60 social service workers, found that 25% of the females and 15% of the males had been sexually assaulted as children. Moulton pointed out that, with victims working as treatment providers, the dilemma of "who is receiving treatment" arises. These treatment providers may have a need to resolve their own issues during therapy sessions with clients. Issues such as transference and countertransference may become barriers to effective intervention.

Although there is a "lack of experts" in the field of child sexual assault (Sgroi, 1982), according to Herman (1981), incest perpetrators should never be permitted to become treatment providers, or leaders of group therapy or self-help groups.

In addition, it is important that the treatment provider communicate in an "open, honest, warm manner" (James & Nasjleti, 1983), and at the same time be confrontive and assertive (James & Nasjleti, 1983; Justice & Justice, 1979). According to Herman (1981), treatment providers must be "authoritative and somewhat charismatic." She also stated that the treatment provider should not "enjoy, excuse, or condone the perpetrators behavior."

The treatment provider must feel comfortable working with the perpetrator, which often times means resolving angry feelings toward the incest perpetrator. Giarretto (1981) believed that it is normal to respond to the perpetrator with disgust or anger, but that such feelings must not continue; "hateful reactions must be replaced with productive interventions."

Giarretto (1981) also believed that treatment providers are not working in the best interest of the child [nor the family] if they are out to "destroy the father." Angry reactions or unresolved personal issues may result from transference or countertransference and may prevent the treatment provider from responding appropriately to the perpetrator (Mrazek, 1981).

Justice and Justice (1979) agreed that anger must be resolved in order for the treatment provider to be effective, but, at the same time, the provider must be cautious so as not to rationalize or minimize the perpetrator's offenses. As stated so clearly by Justice and Justice, "those who reject are inclined to punish, those who rationalize, to dismiss."

Topper and Aldridge (1981) added that the treatment provider must review and assess from time to time feelings, values, and level of comfort when working with incest perpetrators. It is important to frequently examine oneself in the therapeutic process. Giarretto (1981), an expert in treating incestuous families and founder of the Child Sexual Abuse Treatment Program (CSATP), believed that the success of his program was largely dependent on whether the treatment providers had adopted a "humanistic attitude" in dealing with the perpetrators.

Treatment is a difficult process as Fein and Bishop (1987) indicated. The treatment provider must always remember that the perpetrator is a criminal so as to safeguard the child, but, at the same time, must promote an "empathetic, understanding environment." And while a key factor for the perpetrator in treatment is to admit responsibility for actions, frequent confrontation is necessary. Those working with incest can easily become too emotionally involved, and a treatment provider who feels animosity towards a perpetrator may find it very difficult to remain neutral during treatment.

Finally, treatment providers get few rewards from their work and, thus, they must be "highly self-motivated" (James & Nasjleti, 1983). Financial support from communities for treatment programs is lacking, and treatment providers get minimal encouragement or feedback for their work—in fact, it is often belittled. Mrazek (1981) stated what one treatment provider experienced when working with incestuous families: "It is as though I were treating lepers. The rest of the world is relieved someone else is doing it, but they would prefer not to know about it."

The Desire to Treat and Interests of Treatment Providers

Because motivation, enthusiasm, and a belief that mental health components are important in the change process, these areas are discussed as essential in the prevention of clinicians' "burnout." Clinicians pointed out that first-hand experience does promote a strong interest in this field and, while not every counselor would select this population, those that do express a high desire to do so and a high level of competence.

These beliefs were strongly supported by the clinicians interviewed. Their suggestions and expertise were invaluable. On a scale of one to five, with one representing "not at all satisfying" and five representing "very satisfying," most treatment providers rated their level of satisfaction as four; 26% reported their level of satisfaction at three, and 16.8% reported five. Approximately 81% of treatment providers reported their level of comfort working with offenders as "very comfortable" or "as comfortable as with any other client."

It was also found that 7% were working with offenders because they wanted to, 29% because they were interested in abuse, 22% because

Table 13.3 Responses to Questions on Desire to Work with Perpetrators

THOSE WITH HIGH DESIRE
  "I felt they were long neglected."
  "They are the most needy family member in the incest population."
  "I had good clinical skills in sex therapy and hoped for a positive connection and contribution."
  "I saw this essential to good family therapy, which is ultimately the most successful form of working with incest families."
THOSE WITH MODERATE DESIRE
  "I want to work with all areas of incest families."
  "It is a tremendously challenging field, where little is known."
  "It is necessary to understand other family members."
  "Needed trained worker and I became local expert."
THOSE EXPRESSING LOW DESIRE
  "Had history of working with other offenders. I was asked."
  "More social workers needed in this aspect of the program."
  "Opening existed and I respected other workers."
  "Fascination and curiosity."

they found it challenging, and one-third because it was part of a larger job, or a job opening existed. Contrary to the belief that these clinicians were younger, inexperienced, or not well-trained, the average age was 40, with prior experience in the field, and a personally estimated success rate of:

    0 - 3 not successful at all = 7%
    4 - 6 moderate success = 29%
    7 - 10 high success = 64%

The treatment providers also felt that the treatment of incest was the province of:

    law/criminal justice = 2.5%
    psychotherapy = 12%
    combination = 84.5%

The high rate of combined treatment verifies the need for understanding and respect between these two disciplines, as effective treatment will demand a working partnership between the two.

Beginning Clinician's Desire and Interest

Troy Anderson, MSW (see Appendix), did an interesting survey of new clinicians who were just completing graduate degrees and what their preferences were. Not surprisingly, these neophyte counselors did not desire to work with incest perpetrators, and they ranked this category in the top five "unpopular." This demonstrates a real resistance to this population. However, this study did demonstrate that those students who had more classroom training, field experience, and personal experience rated them significantly higher. Again, familial or personal experience was high and may well cause transference and countertransference problems, particularly with those clinicians who were unseasoned and often unaware of the potential impact of their own experiences.

It was also encouraging to find treatment providers' levels of comfort and satisfaction working with incest perpetrators. This is interesting to note since experts in the literature (Giarretto, 1981; Fein & Bishop, 1987; James & Najleti, 1983; Mrazek, 1981; Topper & Aldridge) have placed much emphasis on the importance of treatment providers feeling comfortable with perpetrators, incest, and the dynamics involved.

However, considering the stability of the work and the levels of comfort and satisfaction treatment providers reported, some interesting implications can be identified. Even though treatment providers may not necessarily want to work with perpetrators initially, when they do they find it satisfying and comfortable work. Often, treatment providers reported that they were pleasantly surprised that by being situationally inducted into services, they grew to enjoy it as their experience increased.

Conclusion

It is important to note that the qualifications the treatment providers suggested directly support what experts have outlined as desirable qualities and skills necessary for effective work with perpetrators. There is consensus among the experts and treatment providers themselves as to what qualities, experiences, preparation, and training are desired in treatment providers of incest perpetrators.

While Finkelhor (1986) indicated that the current literature has little to offer treatment providers in the way of training materials, many suggested readings were reported by treatment providers.

Many of these have been included in the resource section at the end of this book. While there may be a deficit of incest perpetrator literature, treatment providers are locating, using, and sharing what they can find.

Treatment providers of incest perpetrators have been labeled as being poorly trained, unmotivated, inexperienced, uneducated individuals who are not meeting the therapeutic needs of their clients. Treatment providers who participated in this study have been found to be highly educated, experienced individuals who are motivated and committed to their work. These treatment providers also express a high level of comfort and satisfaction with their work. Training is a weak point, both individually and within organizations, but some treatment providers are taking the initiative to train themselves with current literature.

Future research in this area might explore why training is such a deficit and what measures are necessary to improve training possibilities. It might also be beneficial to explore how treatment providers work through their initial issues with incest perpetrators, and how they obtain their high level of comfort with them.

PART II: TREATMENT MODALITIES, APPROACHES, AND SUGGESTIONS FOR CLINICIANS

Although little research has been done to better understand and treat the offender, there have been more reporting, media coverage, and policy changes, and thus a greater need to "correct" perpetrators thrust on the criminal justice system. Because of prison overcrowding, a perceived low threat of dangerousness to the community and the familial focus of these crimes, community-based treatment, specifically family oriented treatment, now seems a desirable (and cost-effective) option for certain offenders (Finkelhor, 1986; Groth, 1978). But little is currently known about these resources, their programs, or their successes. Therefore, very few practitioners or referral sources (including the courts) are aware of the treatment options available, and they have little concept of the effectiveness of the programs in their communities.

A sense of crisis in our society and criminal justice system has demanded that new, untried, and innovative treatment be applied to incest perpetrators. This study looked critically and carefully at the types of treatment programs offered and applied, and the directions taken by treatment providers as they gained experience and expertise with this special population.

The question of what constitutes "good" practice with incest offenders needs empirical, in-depth study. Although the treatment process is highly complex, when broken down into specific components it becomes more relevant and provides the therapist with practical treatment guidelines. Because we are beginning from scratch, we will look at the very basic, but essential, practice and process elements: treatment modalities, treatment approaches, length of treatment (both recommended and actual), and, perhaps of greatest importance, the suggestions these clinicians have to offer.

Treatment Modalities

Findings

Group therapy was the treatment modality most often reported to be used by both the community-based and institutional treatment providers—97.5% and 88.9% respectively. Individual therapy was reported to be used by 76.3% of community-based treatment providers and by 50% of institutional providers. Couple/conjoint therapy was reportedly used by 68.7% of community-based providers and by 44.4% of providers in the mental health centers and prisons. It is interesting to note that only 57.5% of treatment providers in community-based settings and 44.4% of providers in the institution-based settings reported use of family therapy.

Discussion

The topic of treatment modalities is particularly relevant to all treatment providers working with incest. Because each discipline varies in its emphasis and approach and because many clinicians have not been trained specifically to work with this population (Groth, Hobson & Gary, 1982; Larson & Maddock, 1986), a study of its application and current usage will be helpful to both the treatment provider and the client.

Family advocates argue that reunification of families after incestuous abuse is an appropriate, feasible, and highly desirable goal of intervention. These advocates argue that offenders who have been treated are capable of being safe and positive family members (Finkelhor, Hotaling & Yllo, 1988). Despite this and the assertions of Finkelhor and Associates (1986), Trepper and Barrett (1986), and Larson and Maddock (1986) that a family emphasis is a practical necessity when dealing with incest families, it was found that group and individual therapies were used by more providers than was family therapy (96% and 71% as compared to 55% in all settings). This discrepancy may be accounted for by the relative youth of family therapy as a specialty—more providers are trained in group and individual therapies (which have a more clinically recognized reputation) than in specific, effective methods of family therapy. Because of the high level of desire on the part of the clients, this area needs more attention.

In certain settings, it may be difficult to conduct family sessions for administrative and logistical reasons—many families are disadvantaged by the distance to the institution. Also, it is interesting to note that Horton (1987) reported that over 60% of community-based perpetrators and approximately 35% of institutionalized perpetrators are married. This may account for the fact that treatment providers in community-based settings report using couple/conjoint and family therapies more often than those in institutions (67.8% and 57.5% compared to 44.4% and 44.4%, respectively). Perhaps a greater emphasis on the importance of these sessions, in addition to training the clinician to provide these sessions, might narrow this unfortunate gap.

Treatment Approaches

Findings

Treatment providers in both settings reported that they most often used a combination of treatment approaches in the treatment of the incest perpetrator. The most frequently used approach—cognitive therapy—was reported by 63.8% of the community-based and 72.2% of the institutional providers. Behavioral therapy was next with 57.5% community-based and 55.6% institutional providers reporting use. Other approaches were reported less frequently and may be examined in Table 13.4.

Of community-based treatment providers 11.2% and of institutional providers 5.3% reported that using only a single type of therapy is the least successful approach to treatment. The most surprising report was that 13.8% of community-based and 11.2% of institutional treatment providers reported specifically that a Rogerian or humanistic approach to treatment is not successful. Insight therapy was reported by 10% of community-based providers and by 11.2% of providers in the prisons and mental health centers to be unsuccessful, and 9% of community-based treatment providers reported that the psychoanalytic approach is not successful.

Table 13.4 Treatment Approaches Used to Treat Incest Perpetrators

Approach	% Community-based	% Institutionalized	% Total
Cognitive	63.8	72.2	65.3
Behavioral	57.5	55.6	57.2
Humanistic	21.3	0.0	17.4
RET	17.5	11.2	16.4
Structural	17.5	0.0	14.3
Education	16.3	44.5	21.5
Reality	15.0	16.7	15.3
Gestalt	12.5	11.2	12.3
Other	6.3	11.1	7.1

Note: These do not total to 100 because respondents were asked to list all treatment approaches they used.

Discussion

Finkelhor et al. (1988) asserted that treatment of incest perpetrators is controversial. They stated that the public, media, and politicians call for harsher sanctions for the offender, and that at the same time treatment providers argue that current criminal justice practices of punishing the perpetrator do little to effectively protect the public. Treatment providers state that some form of therapeutic intervention needs to be provided to both institutionalized and community-based perpetrators. It is encouraging to note that many of the currently existing treatment programs for perpetrators are based in part on this assumption (Finkelhor et al., 1988; Groth, 1978).

Although treatment providers endorsed a wide range of therapeutic approaches, cognitive and behavioral approaches were by far the most frequently mentioned by both sample groups (65.3% and 57.2%, respectively). The third most preferred approach of community-based providers was "humanistic" (21.3%), while institutional providers' third choice was "educational" (44.5%). This is not surprising, as cognitive, behavioral, and educational approaches lend themselves comparatively well to criterion-based monitoring, or relatively objective assessment of progress and goal attainment. This characteristic would likely be of great interest to institutional providers, and of less interest to providers based in the community (see Table 13.1 for comparison of both populations' use of treatment approaches). Treatment providers in both settings showed little agreement on which approaches to avoid in the treatment of incest perpetrators. This is consistent with the literature that reports treatment providers are not in agreement with regard to what approaches to use or not use in treating the offender (Devine, 1978; Finkelhor, 1984; Finkelhor et al., 1988). The most striking disparity among those surveyed involved the use of a humanistic approach: While 21.3% of the community-based providers reported using this approach, with incest perpetrators, 13.8% of this same group listed humanistic approaches under the "least successful" heading (none of the institutional treatment providers reported using this approach, and 11.2% reported that they considered it to be least successful). Clearly, if we are to effectively treat the incest perpetrator, we must conduct studies on the outcomes of treating offenders with a variety of approaches, and develop more systematic and consistent ways of providing treatment.

Length of Treatment

Findings

In regard to the suggested length of treatment, community-based treatment providers recommend a length of treatment ranging from 3 months to 5 years, with a mean of 26.1 months. In comparison, the treatment providers in the prisons and forensic mental health centers recommend anywhere from 2 to 5 years, with a mean length of 29 months. Community-based treatment providers reported that on the average incest perpetrators are actually staying in treatment for the recommended length: 25.9 months. On the other hand, the mean reported duration of treatment in institutional settings was 24 months — on the average, 5 months less than that recommended by the institutional treatment providers.

Discussion

The issue of the length of treatment that incest perpetrators should receive is controversial. Treatment providers vary on recommend treatment length. Treatment providers in institutional settings recommend that treatment should be longer (an average of 29 months) than do community-based treatment providers (an average of 26 months).

The length of time that perpetrators remain in treatment, compared to recommended lengths of treatment, showed a notable disparity only in the institutional sample. Institutionalized perpetrators tend to remain in treatment (on the average) five months less than the mean length recommended by the institutional treatment providers, and nearly two months less than that recommended by their community-based counterparts. It may be that pressures to release inmates, prioritize cases, and provide treatment to "more dangerous" offenders are factors in this finding. More research is needed to determine how much time the perpetrator actually stays in treatment and what factors work to influence this.

It is currently not known how effective existing programs are in working with offenders, but it is known that the perpetrators remain at risk for a very long time after release from supervision (Finkelhor et al., 1988). With this being the case, it makes sense to look into why the institutionalized offenders are not remaining in treatment for at least the average recommended length.

Treatment Providers' Recommendations

Findings

Treatment providers had many recommendations and suggestions for improving the treatment of incest perpetrators. The treatment providers from the community-based sample reported that there needs to be more family work done and that they saw a need for after care or follow-up treatment to be done once the perpetrator terminates from their facility. They also suggested that the treatment providers of incest perpetrators are lacking in education about normal sexual development. Other complaints of the community-based treatment providers were that not enough individual therapy services are available to perpetrators, and that the spiritual aspect of treatment is missing with this population.

Treatment providers in the institutional sample also reported that more time needs to be spent treating the family, and that individual therapy services are lacking. Many of the treatment providers in this sample complained that not enough resources (e.g., training materials and behavioral interventions) are available to them in their specific agencies. They also stated that there is an unmet need for after care and follow-up once a perpetrator is released to the community. Both the community-based and the institutional treatment providers reported that they are concerned about the criminal justice system's inconsistency and slowness to act in the matter of incest.

Discussion

There is currently a great need to find out what is being done to treat the incest perpetrator (Conte, 1984), yet the treatment providers of both community-based and institutionalized incest perpetrators are a rich resource that has rarely been tapped with regard to making suggestions for treating the offender. As could be expected, the clinicians currently working with this population have a variety of recommendations and concerns about the needs of the incest perpetrator.

Treatment providers in both settings had specific concerns and suggestions about what services needed to be provided or improved on in order to better meet the needs of the incest perpetrator. They reported that family treatment is lacking and suggested that more time be allowed for working with incestuous families. This is particularly interesting because the literature reports that most of the currently existing programs include family therapy (Finkelhor, 1986), and because Parents United advocates so strongly for the family.

Treatment providers in both the community-based and institutional settings also suggested that more education about normal sexual development and human sexuality needs to be provided to the incest perpetrator. This may imply that treatment providers believe that the perpetrator is uneducated about normal sexual development and responses, and that more education may help him better understand his sexuality, thus leading to a more appropriate definition of his sexual boundaries.

Another recommendation that treatment providers in all settings made was for greater legal expediency and fairness. They stated that legal services with regard to incest perpetrators were not consistent or timely. This may be a direct result of poor communication between the criminal justice system and the treatment community. Although the courts and related agencies are depending more on treatment providers to suggest lengths and methods of treatment (Finkelhor, 1986; Groth, 1978; Holmes, 1983), programs designed to specifically meet the needs of the incest perpetrator have been slow to develop.

Further, the community-based treatment providers as well as the institutional providers stated that they were concerned about the unavailability of after care and follow-up for the offender. In fact, Finkelhor, et al. (1988) stated that a two- or three-year follow-up would be beneficial, but a one-year follow-up is too short, and a five-year minimum would be best. It is apparent that this kind of intensive after care or follow-up would require that treating agencies and institutions employ additional staff and allocate additional money. This presents quite a problem since money available for treatment is tight.

CONCLUSION

This study has helped to identify specifics of treatment currently being provided to incest perpetrators (including treatment modalities, length of treatment, approaches to treatment, and recommendations of experienced treatment providers) in the various community-based treatment settings, prisons, and mental health facilities reflected in our sample. This data will enable treatment providers to compare their treatment approaches and offerings, to develop new treatment programs, to modify existing programs, and to investigate new treatment forms that may prove to be significant in the treatment of incest perpetrators. It will also help treatment providers, the courts, and other legal systems to draw guidelines for treatment, and will provide important information to policymakers. At present, judges sentence offenders with little information about existing treatment programs; data generated by this study will help in the development of guidelines for effective alternatives to incarceration.

REFERENCES

Conte, J. R. (1984). The justice system and sexual abuse of children. *Social Science Review*, December, 556–568.

Dietz, C., & Craft, J. L. (1980). Family dynamics of incest: A new perspective. *Social Casework: Journal of Contemporary Social Work*, December, 602–609.

Devine, R. A. (1978). Incest: A review of the literature. *Psychoanalytic Quarterly*, 27, 485–500.

Edelson, J. (1984). Working with men who batter. *Journal of Social Work*, 29, 237–242.

Fein, E., & Bishop, G. V. (1987). Child sexual abuse: Treatment for the offender. *Social Casework: Journal of Contemporary Social Work*, 68, (123–124).

Finkelhor, D. (1984). *Childhood sexual abuse: New theory and research*. New York: Free Press.

Finkelhor, D., & Associates. (Eds.). (1986). *A source book on child sexual abuse*. Beverly Hills, CA: Sage.

Finkelhor, D., Hotaling, G. T., & Yllö, K. (1988). *Stopping family violence: Research priorities for the coming decade*. Newbury Park, CA: Sage.

Giarretto, H. (1981). A comprehensive child sexual abuse treatment program. In P. B. Mrazek & C. H. Kempe (Eds.), *Sexually abused children and their families* (pp. 179–189). New York: Pergamon.

Groth, A. N. (1978). Guidelines for the assessment and management of the offender. In A. W. Burgess, A. N. Groth, L. L. Holmstrom, & S. M. Sgroi (Eds.), *Sexual assault of children and adolescents*. Lexington, MA: Lexington Books.

Groth, A. N., Hobson, W., & Gary, T. (1982). The child molester: Clinical observations. In J. R. Conte & D. A. Shore (Eds.), *Social work and child sexual abuse* (pp. 129–144). New York: Haworth Press.

Herman, J. L. (1981). *Father-daughter incest.* Cambridge, MA: Harvard University Press.

Holmes, R. M. (1983). *The sex offender and the criminal justice system.* Springfield, IL: Charles C Thomas.

Horton, A. L. (1987). *Incest perpetrators: The family member no one wants to treat.* Paper presented at the 1987 Annual Conference of National Council on Family Relations, Atlanta, GA.

James, B., & Nasjleti, M. (1983). *Treating sexually abused children and their families.* Palo Alto, CA: Consulting Psychologists Press.

Justice, B., & Justice, R. (1979). *The broken taboo: Sex in the family.* New York: Human Sciences Press.

Larson, N. R., & Maddock, J. W. (1986). Structural and functional variables in incest family systems: Implications for assessment and treatment. In T. S. Trepper & M. J. Barrett (Eds.), *Treating incest: A multimodal systems perspective* (pp.27–45). New York: Haworth Press.

Moulton, J. (1981). Personal communication of P. B. Mrazek, June 7, 1979. In P. B. Mrazek & C. H. Kempe (Eds.), *Sexually abused children and their families.* New York: Pergamon.

Mrazek, P. B. (1981). Special problems in the treatment of child sexual abuse. In P. B. Mrazek & C. H. Kempe (Eds.), *Sexually abused children and their families* (pp. 160–165). New York: Pergamon.

Quinsey, V. L. (1977). The assessment and treatment of child molesters: A review. *Canadian Psychological Review, 18,* (3).

Sgroi, S. (1982). Child sexual assault: Some guidelines for investigation and assessment. In B. Schlesinger (Eds.), *Sexual abuse of children: A resource guide and annotated bibliography* (p.70). Toronto: University of Toronto Press.

Topper, A. B., & Aldridge, D. J. (1981). Incest: Intake and investigation. In P. B. Mrazek & C. H. Kempe (Eds.), *Sexually abused children and their families.* New York: Pergamon.

Trepper, T., & Barrett, M. J. (1986). Treating incest: A multimodal systems perspective. *Journal of Psychotherapy and the Family, 2.*

14

Integrated Treatment: *The Self-Help Factor*

Henry Giarretto
Anna Einfeld-Giarretto

INTRODUCTION

Integration of interventions in father-daughter incest cases fostered since 1971 by the Child Sexual Abuse Treatment Program (CSATP) of San Jose, California, will be the subject of this chapter. The CSATP is based on the following premises: (a) The child-victim is best served if she can be returned to her own family; (b) to accomplish this aim, the family system must be changed from an abusive to a nurturing one; and (c) to expedite the return of the child to a healthy familial environment, systematic collaboration is required among police, legal-judicial personnel, social workers, therapists, and the family members themselves (through their professionally guided self-help groups, Parents United and Daughters and Sons United).

BACKGROUND

From our contacts with over 2000 participants in workshops conducted in San Jose and nationwide, there appears to be little disagreement, in principle, with these premises of the CSATP. However, on closer examination of the actual interventions of law enforcement and legal-judicial personnel, we often find they do not act on the basic premise that the child is best served if she is returned to her family. Police and prosecuting attorneys, in particular, are likely to believe that the vic-

AUTHORS' NOTE: Only those aspects in the early development of a CSATP that pertain to initial steps toward integration of community services in father-daughter incest cases have been described in this chapter. ICEF has amassed considerable printed and electronic materials on the CSATP and its training program. For a list of these materials write to: ICEF, P.O. Box 952, San Jose, CA 95108.

tim was betrayed by both parents and that the family is beyond repair. In certain instances, they may concede that her mother may be salvageable, but the father has abdicated his rights as parent, is beyond treatment, and must therefore be punished.

Moreover, the above groups believe that incarceration of the perpetrator will protect other potential victims, teaching the victim and other family members to become law-abiding citizens. It is not uncommon to hear from law enforcement officials the admonition that they are not social workers; their primary duty is to uphold the law. Therefore, they must concentrate on obtaining admissable court evidence of the father's guilt from the victim. This attitude is also often held by social workers and probation officers who investigate incest cases.

These personal observations, admittedly anecdotal, are supported by the findings of a study by Saunders (1988). He surveyed the attitudes of five professional groups in an urban community and reported, "Statistically significant differences were found among child welfare social workers, police officers, district attorneys, public defenders and judges."

Therapists, also, are not free of personal bias, despite agreeing, in principle, with the dictum that they must not be judgmental in therapeutic transactions. The results of another study indicate that the gender of therapists strongly influenced their reactions to intrafamilial child sexual abuse. In response to a series of vignettes involving family members, female therapists expressed 20% more anger toward the adult perpetrator than the male therapists did. However, male therapists showed more anger toward, and attributed a higher degree of responsibility to, the victim than did female therapists (Strano & Kelly, 1988).

Prejudicial reactions of all sorts have surfaced in our workshops, which have been attended by legal-judicial and human services professionals from various parts of the United States. In the discussion portion there has been little intellectual disagreement with the humanistic, but pragmatic, approach of the CSATP (Giarretto, 1978). This rationale is tested through role-playing exercises, in which some of the trainees act as nonoffending parents, offenders, and victims, while others take on the roles of interviewing social workers or therapists. Considerable disparity becomes evident between a trainee's intellectual understanding of the needs of the clients and his/her emotional reactions during the simulated face-to-face contacts with the clients.

In the exercises with the perpetrator and the nonoffending parent, the trainees were instructed to ventilate their normal feelings freely. Anger was quickly aroused and often became strident. In the enactments with the victims, the reactions of the trainees tended toward pity and mawkishness rather than empathy for the underlying emotional feelings of the victims.

In another exercise, the trainees were asked to form groups of five and were instructed to "become" the offender. Each should have expressed, spontaneously, the feelings of the offender at the time he is facing the first investigator. ("What will become of me and my family? I've destroyed the people I love the most. Who will support my family while I am in prison" and so on.)

These exercises indicated that intervenors who are connected with the investigation, prosecution, and adjudication of the offenders, and who have minimal contact with the victim, are less likely to empathize with the plight of the victim and the family as a whole. Better able to sense the emotional duress of the victim are the intervenors who are specifically directed by juvenile or family courts to protect the victims, such as the social workers and the police who interview the victim and mother, as well as the juvenile court prosecutors and judges. Best able to empathize with the needs of the victim are case managers in Child Protective Services and therapists with experience derived from frequent contacts with all members of the families.

In an article entitled "Beyond Selfishness," Kahn (1988) stated "that you are more likely to help others not only if you feel their pain, but also if you understand the way the world looks to them." To feel and understand what is going on in the members of incestuous families, the intervenor must also be continually aware of his/her own feelings and biases, especially those triggered during client contacts. The processes are interdependent and must be attended to simultaneously for the therapist to do what is best for the child.

START-UP OF AN INTEGRATED CSATP

Community-based programs that follow the CSATP model are usually spearheaded by social workers and therapists who have completed the nine-day workshops conducted by the Institute for the Community as Extended Family (ICEF) in San Jose. The workshop, conducted as a teaching clinic, enables trainees to interact with CSATP clients personally and to participate in the self-help groups. On returning to their community, a social worker and a therapist agree to act as partners in implementing a procedure similar to that which led to the establishment of the CSATP in San Jose. The social worker refers a sufficient number of father-daughter incest cases to the therapist to allow him/her to gain knowledge of the unique treatment needs of these families.

A typical family of four members will be engaged in a therapeutic regimen, which generally proceeds as follows:

- The mother and daughter are immediately provided individual therapy.
- Dyadic therapy for the child and her mother is begun as soon as the child feels comfortable with the arrangement. She will want to meet with her mother if she is convinced that the mother believes her story and will give her unequivocal support.
- The perpetrator is provided therapy if he has removed himself from the home and is acknowledging responsibility for the sexual offenses.
- The sibling is also given individual therapy since he/she often feels emotionally neglected believing that the victim is his/her father's favorite child and has little time for him/her.
- Conjoint family therapy, including the perpetrator, is started when the therapist deems this appropriate.
- Marital therapy is begun if the wife confides that she wants to salvage the marriage and the therapist believes that the partners have progressed sufficiently in their individual therapy.
- Dyadic therapy involving the victim and perpetrator is started in the later stages of the program, provided the victim feels comfortable in doing so and the perpetrator is ready to relate to his daughter as a nurturing father.
- Conjoint family therapy including all family members becomes the principal treatment modality and continues through completion of the therapeutic program.

During the early phases of a CSATP the therapeutic progress of parental incestuous families rarely proceeds as smoothly as may have been suggested in the example. Especially in a community in which the criminal justice system is reputed to be extremely punitive, the parents are fearful of the consequences if they support the victim's allegations. Thus, they resort to denial and will urge the victim to recant her story. They will paint a foreboding picture of what will happen if she sticks to her allegations. She will be forced to live with strangers and her father will be sent to prison for many years where he will be beaten severely and possibly murdered. Her father promises to never abuse her again, and it will be far better if she will allow the family to deal with the problem privately.

In many American communities this dire prediction of what may befall an incest family will, at least in part, materialize. During this past decade the temper of the average community, reflected by that of its officials, toward lawbreakers has become increasingly unforgiving and retributive. Parental incest perpetrators are dealt with even more harshly than hardcore felons.

The therapist is caught in a quandary. She realizes that the family cannot be treated effectively if they persist in the denial. If she is successful in convincing the victim and her mother to admit to the authorities that the abuse did indeed occur, will she be placing the family in greater jeopardy than if they support the lie? Nevertheless, she will soon discover that the family cannot survive under a mantle of deception. The victim and her parents must be made to admit that the family is severely ill and cannot recover without long-term treatment, and this necessitates full exposure of the abuse to the authorities.

The therapist can draw some comfort from knowing that the courts usually are more lenient with cooperative families, especially if the judges can be assured that the perpetrator is taking full responsibility for the abusive situation and has left the home. The mother is clearly protective of her daughter, and the family as a whole is making progress in its therapeutic program.

The therapist also discovers that the perpetrators, and also many of the mothers, harbor deep-seated emotional problems stemming from their own sexual, physical, or emotional abuse during childhood (Giarretto, 1989). The therapist senses that the therapeutic plan for the family must include treatment of the parents as abused children before they can become effective parents.

THE START-UP OF THE PEER-SUPPORT GROUPS

It must be restated that most families are in severe emotional crisis by the time they come to the therapist, their original troubled state having been further aggravated by the inept handling of earlier intervenors. Even if the therapist has only four or five families with which to cope, she soon will find that traditional in-office sessions do not meet the tremendous therapeutic needs of the families.

As instructed and demonstrated in the workshops through personal contacts with CSATP clients, the therapist starts to form the Parents United self-help groups. To initiate this process, the therapist enlists the assistance of a family in which the father and the mother are beginning to fulfill their roles as parents and the family is on the path toward reconstruction. This family helps sponsor the new family and gives them someone with whom to initially return. The mother, victim, and father of this sponsoring family are given training in peer crisis counseling: They are asked to recall their painful emotional states during their own crisis period and to participate in role-playing exercises. They practice the art of empathetic listening and reflecting on the feelings of their counterparts in a hypothetical family in the early throes of crisis. They also confide in them how they coped with this crisis, and what they are doing now to save their family. This family helps sponsor the new family and gives them someone with whom to initially network.

In the first session, the therapist suggests to the parents that their anxieties would be lessened if they were to talk with the parents of another family who will be pleased to contact them by phone this very evening. The incoming parents will usually comply with this recommendation, and the therapist makes the necessary arrangements. He/she will continue to pair new and old clients and in a few months will have a sufficient number of clients for a parents' group and a separate group for the victims. These early groups are usually co-led by the therapist and his/her partner the social worker.

It soon becomes apparent to the partners that, by allowing the families to help one another, the essential prerequisites for effective therapy are being established sooner: The father stops denying or minimizing the offenses and assumes full responsibility for the troubled state of his family; the mother provides unqualified support for her daughter. Once these prerequisites have taken place, therapeutic progress becomes clearly evident. Perhaps the most gratifying effect of increasing parental responsibility is manifested by the victim whose guilt subsides and, thus, who is less inclined toward self-abusive behavior. The tangible outcomes of professional therapy complemented by peer support can also be discerned in the parents whose self-esteem is strengthened as they see improvement in their child's mental health and in the salutary effects of their peer-support efforts with the new families.

INVOLVING THE CLIENTS IN THE
INTEGRATION EFFORT

The opportunity for peer support constitutes the first step in the evolution of the CSATP and its core component, Parents United. The therapist takes the next step when he/she involves her clients in the effort to convince law enforcement and legal-judicial personnel of the advantages of the CSATP approach over their present ways of coping with incestuous families. The therapist had been forewarned in the training program that meetings with police, district attorneys, and judges will seldom convince them that the empathic treatment of incestuous families as practiced by CSATP will produce more immediate and long-term benefits to the community than retributive handling.

Law enforcement people, in particular, are wary, if not cynical, of psychological remedies to criminal behavior. As was underscored to the trainees in the workshops, the efficacy of the CSATP approach must be demonstrated. The people responsible for investigation, prosecution, and adjudication of incest cases must be given the opportunity to observe firsthand the outcomes of the CSATP approach. It must be demonstrated to them convincingly that as a result of the treatment most of the perpetrators are taking full responsibility for the offenses, the mothers are primarily concerned with the welfare of their children, and, most importantly, the mental health of the victims has improved under the stewardship of the CSATP.

To prove to the authorities that CSATP methodology is effective the therapist and/or the social worker will invite key community intervenors to attend individually the adults' and the children's groups. Many therapists are reluctant to invite strangers to the groups since they have been taught that to do so will breach the rules of confidentiality and interfere with the group process. But those who have attended the workshops and have spoken individually with CSATP clients and participated in the groups have seen that Parents United members, particularly those in advanced stages of therapy, are eager to communicate with intervenors, individually and through their self-help groups. They wish to show the authorities that when they are dealt with as worthwhile human beings, rather than pariahs, they are better prepared to return to the community as productive citizens. Seasoned group members discover they can help themselves when they help other members, and realize they further add to their personal growth if they can help future victims and families coming to the attention of the authorities to be treated decently.

The CSATP becomes increasingly effective as more legal-judicial and human-services intervenors in intrafamilial child sexual abuse cases integrate and orient their services toward the goal of returning victims to their own families. By involving family members in the development of the CSATP, interdependent benefits are realized through accelerating both the progress of family therapy and the integrative process.

REFERENCES

Giarretto, H. (1978). Humanistic treatment of father/daughter incest. *Journal of Humanistic Psychology, 18,* (4), 59–76.

Giarretto, H. (1989). Community-based treatment of dissociative disorders in the incest family. In R. P. Kluft (Ed.), *Psychiatric Clinics of North America.* Symposium on the Treatment of Victims of Sexual Abuse.

Kahn, A. (1988, October). Beyond selfishness. *Psychology Today,* p. 38.

Saunders, E. J. (1988). A comparative study of attitudes toward child sexual abuse among social work and judicial system professionals. *Child Abuse and Neglect, 12,* 83.

Strano, J. J., & Kelly, R. J. (1988, September). *The significance of therapist bias in issues of child sexual abuse.* Paper presented at the VII International Conference on Child Abuse & Neglect, Rio de Janeiro.

15

A Model Program for Incestuous Families Demonstrating Cooperation Within the Military Community

Charlotte H. Shuler

INTRODUCTION

Fort Knox, Kentucky, is not only a major military training base but a large city as well. With a daytime population of nearly 20,000 soldiers, 15,000 family members, and 8,000 civilian employees, Fort Knox is often referred to as Kentucky's fifth largest city (Provost Marshal Office, 1989). Like most military installations, Fort Knox has a multidisciplinary team, the Family Advocacy Case Management Team (FACMT), that oversees all child and spouse abuse cases relating to military members or their families on or off post. Although commanders, police investigators, and social workers are the first response team, the FACMT monitors and makes recommendations on all child sexual abuse cases.

At Fort Knox, during the fiscal year 1988 (October 1987–September 1988), there were a total of 53 reported cases of child sexual abuse, of which 24 were substantiated (Social Work Service, 1988). In the past, the effort to punish the perpetrator and protect the child often resulted in further damage to the victim. Typically, the child was required to testify against the father; the father was sent to prison; the family lost their housing and benefits and had to leave the military-sponsored schools and community. The child faced enormous pressure to either recant or accept an ever-growing cognitive distortion of her responsibility in the destruction of her family.

Unique within the U.S. Army at this time, the Fort Knox Child Sexual Offender Rehabilitation Program is an effort to offer family treatment options where none were available before. Of 24 cases substantiated in 1988, five families have participated fully in the rehabilitation program. Three families are currently participating in the treatment program, and two others have left the military for administrative reasons and are no longer eligible for treatment services. There have been no reports of recidivism among the families in treatment.

CHILD SEXUAL OFFENDER REHABILITATION PROGRAM

Based on the premise that certain child sexual offenders can be successfully treated, the rehabilitation program operates on dual tracks. The criminal justice process and the treatment program are integrated for a more effective approach to treatment.

CRIMINAL JUSTICE PROCESS

At Fort Knox, the incest perpetrator is typically a soldier whose behavior is subject to the Uniform Code of Military Justice (UCMJ). His commander and those in his supervisory chain of command have the authority and responsibility for deciding the course of action relative to the soldier's offenses. The Fort Knox military criminal justice system adopted legal options for entry into the Sex Offender Rehabilitation Program with the publication of U.S. Army Armor Center's (1988) USAARMC Regulation 608-1.

LEGAL OPTIONS FOR ENTRY INTO THE REHABILITATION PROGRAM

As long as there is no repetition of abuse and treatment is ongoing, offenders may be permitted to enter the rehabilitation program using one of the options listed below:

1. Deferral of prosecution.
2. Court martial with pretrial agreement to suspend all or part of the sentence.
3. Court martial, sentence, then a grant of clemency by the Commanding General to suspend all or part of the sentence.

The soldier/offender's commander may also take other actions, such as not preferring charges at all or simply discharging the offender from the Army. In off-post offenses, civilian legal systems may also prosecute the soldier/offender, but most have deferred their prosecutions as long as the military was proceeding on charges.

CRITERIA FOR ADMISSION INTO THE REHABILITATION PROGRAM

Criteria for admission into the rehabilitation program represent ten areas of concern, which are used in an effort to select perpetrators who (a) can benefit from treatment and (b) can also be tolerated by their coworkers in their work environments. Offenders and their families must meet all of the criteria for admission before they can be legally recognized as a part of the rehabilitation program. The following criteria are quoted from USAARMC Regulation 608–1:

1. "The victim(s) is a family member, who is the opposite sex of the offender, and no bizarre or ritualistic acts were involved in the child sexual activity." Incest perpetrators seem to have lower recidivism rates when compared with perpetrators of other types of child molesting (Finkelhor, 1986) and may be more amenable to treatment (Groth, 1982). Sex offenders of boys are among those who are most likely to repeat their behaviors (Finkelhor, 1986). Additionally, the homosexual stigma of a same-sex offense makes such a perpetrator intolerable within the military community.

2. "A determination that the offender is not a fixated pedophile (i.e., that the offender's primary sexual attraction is not toward children)." Groth (1982) stated, "Sexual offenders against children may be divided into two basic types with regard to their primary sexual orientation and level of sociosexual development." Fixated pedophiles have a primary attraction to children and seem to identify sociosexually as a child. Regressed pedophiles, on the other hand, retain their primary sexual orientation with adults and substitute the child in a pseudo-adult role (Groth, 1982). Because their primary sexual orientation is with adults, regressed pedophiles seem to experience molesting behavior as somewhat ego-dystonic, especially after the addictive process is experienced, and are therefore more motivated to change.

3. "The offender is motivated to undergo treatment, as assessed by the offender's willingness to admit to the child sexual activity, stated desire and willingness to participate in treatment, and concern for the victim and family. In order to meet this criterion, the offender must have made a complete admission to the Criminal Investigation Division (CID) and cooperate fully with Social Work Service (SWS), before any

guarantee of acceptance into the program. To encourage self-referral, the admission may be accomplished as part of a pretrial negotiation process." Prior to entry into treatment, most perpetrators in this program gave statements that were even more detailed than the statements given by their child.

4. "The offender has no other significant mental or personality disorder." Offenders and their wives are assessed by means of psychological evaluations, which include the MMPI and interviews by a psychologist. Those with severe difficulties in reality testing, or with personality disorders such as sociopaths, would not be accepted into the program. Finkelhor's (1986) review of the research indicated that those with personality disorders are more likely to reoffend.

5. "There are not prior reported child sexual offenses involving the offender." Verification is made by assessing family history, by querying the worldwide records of the FACMT's central registry, and by checking police records through Military Police and CID files.

6. "The victim and other family members are willing to participate in the treatment program and desire rehabilitation of the family unit." This requirement serves two functions: (a) Serving the stated needs and desires of the victim seems to satisfy some judicial goals concerning victim advocacy and justice, and (b) treatment prognosis is more positive for both victim and perpetrator when family issues can be resolved. Groth (1982) stated, "As frequently is the case in incest, the inappropriate sexual activity appears to be in part the result of and a symptom of family dysfunction." Participation in treatment by family members does not relieve the perpetrator of his responsibility for his own inappropriate behavior.

7. "There is sufficient time remaining on the offender's service obligation for effective participation in the treatment program (in most cases, 1 year or more from the inception date of treatment)." When a soldier leaves the Army, military benefits, including the treatment program, cease. Also, the military judicial system would be nearly impossible to enforce after the soldier has left military service.

8. "The offender has a good military record (with no prior court-martial or civilian felony convictions) and, in the judgment of the offender's chain of command, demonstrates potential for continued service." The chain of command must have sufficient positive regard for the soldier to tolerate his being identified as a child molester and his subsequent two- to four-hour absences each week while he participates in required treatment modalities.

9. "A positive recommendation for admission into the program by the installation FACMT" is required. After admission into the rehabilitation

program, the sex offender and his family will have their case periodically reviewed for progress and needed assistance by the FACMT. The
evaluations will consider (a) if the incest has been repeated, (b) failure
to progress, (c) unexcused absences, and (d) additional felon crimes.

10. "Acceptance of the FACMT's recommendation for admission into the
program by the appropriate court-martial convening authority" is required. One of the supervisors in the soldier/offender's chain of command, probably his battalion commander, brigade commander, or the
commanding general of Fort Knox, must formally admit the offender
into the Sex Offender Rehabilitation Program.

CRISIS MANAGEMENT FOR FAMILIES IN DISARRAY

With the initial report of child sexual abuse, the legal authorities automatically become involved. CID begins its investigation and, within
24 to 72 hours, the clinician contacts the family. Working as both a
child protection worker and as a therapist, the clinician interviews all
family members and makes preliminary assessments concerning their
potential for treatment. The dual role as both investigator and clinician
sometimes confuses the family and has the potential for blocking trust.
However, making early supportive contact and hearing the unadorned
statements during that brief period when the defenses are in disarray
compensate for the potential difficulties. The early contact can be critical for relationship building with the mother and the child. Also, observing the family's behavior during crisis gives important clinical im-
pressions, which are not available even a week later when the family
has begun to reassemble its defenses.

Usually, the father is ordered by his commander to leave the home
and to have no further unsupervised contact with the victim. Typically,
he returns to live in the barracks where other soldiers can monitor his
whereabouts, remaining out of the home for three months to one year.
With the father removed from the home, the mother is left completely
in charge of the children—this at a time when she is likely feeling most
inadequate and frightened. The children also feel disorganized and
confused. This disruption for all family members necessitates substantial therapeutic support during the initial weeks of crisis.

SUPERVISED FAMILY VISITS

Nothing will quickly relieve the family's pain, but supervised visits will
provide reassurance and safety, especially for the children seeking con-

tinuity within their family. Weekly visits, supervised by social workers, are initiated as soon as the father has physically separated from the family. And, although the father is not allowed unsupervised contact with his daughter, couple contact without the children is allowed in an effort to encourage rebuilding of that dyad.

PERPETRATORS' GROUP

Led by a male and a female cotherapist, the Perpetrators' Group meets weekly during duty hours. Perpetrators are released from their work assignments for the group sessions, but are expected to remain effective at these jobs despite their absences.

Even though the offender has already made a confession to CID, initial entry into the Perpetrators' Group requires him once again to describe his behavior with his child. This is done for the purpose of assessing levels of denial and minimization.

Therapeutic intervention is loosely organized around Finkelhor's (1986) description of:

> theories that attempt to explain why adults become sexually interested in and involved with children. These theories are organized into four basic categories: (a) emotional congruence—why the adult has an emotional need to relate to a child; (b) sexual arousal—why the adult could become sexually aroused by a child; (c) blockage—why alternative sources of sexual and emotional gratification are not available; and (d) disinhibition—why the adult is not deterred from such interest by normal prohibitions.

Experiential techniques, such as the "empty chair," are used to counter the offender's emotional congruence with the child. Cognitive reframing and behavioral changes are also emphasized. Encouraged to relinquish the view of themselves as helpless victims, perpetrators reframe their views as they gain greater internal validation and, consequently, more self-esteem and sense of personal adequacy.

To offset the offender's sexual arousal to children, because of conditioning or modeling from earlier childhood abuse experiences, experiential techniques are used to help him reexperience a trauma and then release himself from its hold. As noted earlier, an offender whose sexual arousal seems to be primarily toward children (fixated pedophile) is excluded from this treatment program.

To remove the perpetrator's apparent blockage to other, more appropriate, sources of sexual and emotional gratification, therapeutic intervention has included training in assertiveness, communication, and parenting skills. A female therapist is used to alleviate difficulties in relating to women, and couple therapy has included the issues of sexual dysfunction, appropriate family roles, intimacy, and dominance.

To counter the perpetrator's disinhibitions for incestuous acts—perhaps because of impulse disorder, alcohol, or situational stress—the threat of punishment through the military is ever present. In addition, the same therapist works with each of the family members, gaining intimate knowledge of the family system, and becomes better able to ascertain if incest recurs. Alcohol has not been documented as playing a role in disinhibiting behavior for this group, but situational stress and the resulting sense of aggressive frustration has. Group members work to recognize periods of vulnerability to recurring incest and to establish behavioral contingency plans for overcoming them. In treatment, emphasis is on the recovering aspect of being a perpetrator— one is never "cured."

MOMS' GROUPS

The mother seems to be a key to family recovery. Without her, the progress of the perpetrator and the child moves slowly. Nevertheless, her therapeutic tasks are enormous. She needs unconditional positive regard as she begins to sort through her dual failed roles of being "both 'cuckold' and failed protector" (Pittman, 1987). Typically dependent, she may need to lean rather heavily on therapeutic support in order for her to avoid initial rejection of her daughter or of dissolving "into pitiful ineptitude" (Pittman, 1987).

Group work begins with the mother describing details of all sexual behavior between father and daughter. Such a description is necessary for her to begin to acknowledge the reality and the irrevocable nature of past deeds. It is not unusual for the mother to respond, initially, as a protector of her daughter and then to struggle with the rage and jealousy felt toward the daughter as the "other woman" (Bass & Davis, 1988). Sometimes, reading her husband's confession helps the mother to maintain her perspective as a protective parent.

The Moms' Group provides support for the mothers through understanding and confrontation. It is in this safe environment that they are able to reduce their social violation by expressing their feelings freely.

Typically emerging from disengaged or enmeshed families, these women face the necessity of setting personal limits, or boundaries, within their family relationships. Before the incest became known, the mother may have expressed her enmeshment by becoming the "family maid," gluing everyone together with her helpfulness, or she may have described a disengaged family dynamic by having an extramarital affair and withdrawing emotional support. Now, however, before she can become an adequate protector of her children, she must experience her own personal boundaries as well as connectedness within the family. That is, she must moderate both disengagement or enmeshment. Building self-esteem and self-concept, as well as learning specific skills of assertion and parenting, are basic before the family can be safely reunited.

INDIVIDUAL COUNSELING FOR CHILDREN

Individual counseling with the child begins as soon as possible after the incest is discovered. Ideally, the therapist meets the child during the initial police investigation and participates in the early interviews. It is here that the child gives a detailed description of her father's behavior as well as her own. Familiarity with the therapist is important as the child needs support from someone who has heard the details, believes her, and does not turn away in distaste.

Once the trust has been established, the relationship between the therapist and child takes a directional turn in an effort to learn what the abusive behavior meant to the child. For example, one child appeared to have been impacted more by her loss of respect for her father because he begged for her permission than by his actually performing cunnilingus on her. Without reinforcing her sense of helplessness and victimization, the child must be validated as she accepts that she is not responsible for her father's actions. Overprotection of the child, especially an adolescent, can create new pathology in which she shrugs off all responsibility for acting-out or self-destructive behavior by blaming others.

When the Sex Offender Rehabilitation Program first began, the children were grouped together for weekly sessions. But the ages and the degree of pathology of each varied too widely, and, consequently, group cohesiveness and productivity could not be established. The children now attend groups at Parents United and continue in individual therapy. Interventions are individualized using some of the following techniques: sand play, psychotherapeutic games, art therapy, collages describing self, mutual storytelling, gestalt techniques, imagery, assertiveness, and communication skills.

PARENTS UNITED

As an adjunct to the weekly groups, Parents United provides an opportunity for the Fort Knox families to meet a variety of other families and individuals affected by incest. The organization provides an additional means of cutting through denial and minimization (used by both parents), and assists them in owning their responsibility in the incest dynamics of the family. After the initial crisis is calmed and the family seems more stabilized, weekly meetings in Louisville, 35 miles away, are required for the entire family. There may be anger confrontation groups for offenders and spouses, and support groups for victims and their siblings.

STRUCTURED CLASSES

As a part of comprehensive therapy, parents attend structured classes in parenting skills, assertiveness, financial counseling, and stress management. Attendance is dependent on the client's needs and the availability of classes. Learning these skills reinforces other aspects of therapy.

COUPLE THERAPY

While the family is separated, couple therapy begins in an effort to rebuild the bonds between the couple. Issues of trust, infidelity, sexuality, and anger are usually addressed. Loss of trust by the wife must be acknowledged, grieved, and accommodated. Renewal of blind trust is emphatically discouraged, but emphasis is placed on a realistic partnership in which both acknowledge inadequacies and devise ways to compensate for and protect the newly placed limits. For example, some couples have devised contracts of having both parents present during activities with the children.

FATHER-DAUGHTER SESSIONS

Father-daughter therapy sessions have been attempted with mixed results. Too often, the mother feels threatened by being left out, and the child may respond with behavioral difficulties if she perceives herself without a protector. Any therapeutic objective for a father-daughter session could probably be met in a family session, thus sidestepping issues of secrecy and alliance building in a family that has a dysfunctional history concerning such issues.

FAMILY THERAPY

About three months to one year after entering treatment, family therapy begins. At this point, the child seems better able to tolerate the intensity of the family, individuals have made progress, and the perpetrator has begun to make unsupervised home visits. Apologies to the daughter and other family members are required of the father, but acceptance of his apology is determined by each family member. With individual boundaries already in place, family therapy goals include: (a) cohesion without collapse of boundaries, (b) emphasis of rituals that add structure (Hartman & Laird, 1983), (c) resolution of conflict (taught through family council meetings), and (d) resolving the differences between secrecy and privacy, retaining respect for individual privacy.

SUMMARY

In an effort to prevent continued victimization in incestuous families, Fort Knox, Kentucky, a large military training base, has established a rehabilitation program for incest perpetrators and their families. The Child Sexual Offender Rehabilitation Program operates on dual tracks for effectiveness. The criminal justice process and the treatment program are integrated. With either prosecution deferred or sentence suspended, an incest perpetrator may enter the treatment program only after meeting strict criteria. The treatment program includes the offender and family members, with the therapeutic focus on acceptance of individual responsibility within a family systems base. The program is small and new, but the families involved seem to have made remarkable progress. More particularly, the children appear optimistic—beginning to trust again.

REFERENCES

Bass, E., & Davis, L. (1988). *The courage to heal.* New York: Harper & Row.
Finkelhor, D., & Associates. (Eds.). (1986). *A sourcebook on child sexual abuse.* Beverly Hills, CA: Sage.

Groth, A. N. (1982). The incest offender. In S. M. Sgroi (Ed.), *Handbook of clinical intervention in child sexual abuse* (pp. 215–241). Lexington, MA: Lexington Books.

Hartman, A., & Laird, J. (1983). *Family-centered social work practice.* New York: Free Press.

U.S. Army Armor Center and Fort Knox. (1988). *Child sexual offender rehabilitation program* (USAARMC Reg 608–1). Fort Knox, KY: Author.

Pittman, F. S., III. (1987). *Turning points: Treating families in transition and crisis.* New York: W. W. Norton.

Provost Marshal Office. (1989). Unpublished raw data. United States Army Armor Center, Fort Knox, KY.

Social Work Service. (1988). Unpublished raw data. Ireland Army Community Hospital, Fort Knox, KY.

16

Confidentiality Issues with Incest Perpetrators: *Duty to Report, Duty to Protect, and Duty to Treat*

Robert J. Kelly

INTRODUCTION

One of the many reasons the incest perpetrator constitutes "the family member no one wants to treat" is that the clinician often feels placed in the uncomfortable role of legal watchdog rather than treatment provider. In most nonforensic therapist-client dyads, the therapist can encourage full client disclosures and listen to these while focusing on their implications for the client's treatment. The clinician treating an incest perpetrator, however, often finds him/herself listening to a disclosure and focusing, instead, on whether that disclosure must be reported to authorities. Some therapists find themselves stopping incest perpetrators in mid-sentence before they disclose clinically important but legally reportable information. By doing so, these therapists may be leaving vulnerable children unprotected. Other therapists cavalierly encourage full disclosure and report all of it to authorities without adequately preparing the client for what is likely to feel like therapist betrayal. In these cases, future therapy sessions are certain to find the incest perpetrator spending much energy censoring further disclosures.

THE THERAPIST'S DILEMMA

As Sherlock and Murphy (1984) have suggested, the effective treatment of a child molester is one of our best hopes for protecting chil-

AUTHOR'S NOTE: The author is grateful for the helpful comments of Spencer Eth, M.D., Louise Evans, M.A., John Lundberg, J.D., Mark Mills, J.D., M.D., Joe Simanek, J.D., Ann Redisch, J.D., and members of the UCLA Sexual Abuse Project. The work described in this paper was supported in part by the grant IT32 MH17118–02 from the National Institute of Mental Health.

dren from future abuse. Effective treatment requires the establishment of therapeutic rapport, a process that usually requires holding client disclosures confidential. A clinician treating an incest perpetrator must be able to balance a client's right to confidentiality with society's right to have its children protected. For an incest perpetrator, the right to confidentiality is a limited right that should be curtailed when children are in danger. Nonetheless, confusion about current laws and protective service operations may unnecessarily inhibit even this limited confidentiality. Perhaps these laws and systems can be clarified and modified to optimize our ability to protect children while also protecting the incest perpetrator's right to limited confidentiality and, in turn, therapeutic rapport. To explore this possibility, consider how you as a clinician would protect your client's right in the following scenario.

Gavin P., age 32, has been a well-respected grade school teacher for the past 11 years. Upon coming to you for therapy, he has disclosed, for the first time, that he was sexually abused at age 7. He has also disclosed that at age 13 he frequently fondled his 6-year-old sister, Nancy. Mr. P. has voluntarily sought therapy to deal with his impulses to molest his 4-year-old daughter, Karen. He also has weekly access to his 9-year-old son, Timmy, his only other child from his first marriage.

As Mr. P's therapist, you may feel some rapidly growing anxiety about your legal and ethical responsibility to tell someone else about these issues. But whom do you need to tell, what do you need to tell them, and how do you go about telling them while maintaining therapeutic rapport with Mr. P.? It may be useful to examine these questions as they relate to a therapist's duty to report and duty to protect, and the aspects of these duties that currently may hinder the therapeutic alliance.

DUTY TO REPORT

The duty to report refers to a therapist's legal responsibility to notify the appropriate legal and protective services whenever that therapist has knowledge or reasonable suspicion that a child has been abused. Thus, as Mr. P's therapist, you may first wonder whether you need to report that Mr. P. himself was abused as a child. Unfortunately, there is some controversy about whether the answer to that question can be found in current child abuse reporting laws.

California law provides a representative example. It requires therapists to report abuse of a child, but it makes no mention of whether past abuse of an adult during childhood must be reported. On the one hand, there is no statute of limitations on a therapist's duty to report; some therapists have taken this to mean that the abuse still needs to be reported. On the other hand, Children's Protective Services handles cases involving current minors, and there is a six-year statute of limitations on the criminal prosecution of child abuse offenses.

State laws need to address this issue directly before a therapist is unnecessarily dragged through a legal ordeal. As a clinician treating adults molested as children (AMAC), I strongly support state laws that do not require a therapist to report past abuse of an adult during childhood. The spirit of child abuse reporting laws is to protect children who cannot speak for themselves. An adult who was molested as a child should have the right to choose whether to proceed with a potentially traumatic investigation of an already traumatic abuse experience, much the same way that an adult rape victim is given that choice.

Following this rationale, as Mr. P.'s therapist you would not be required to report Mr. P.'s own abuse at age seven. However, you should discuss with Mr. P. whether he wishes to take some action against the abuser and, most important, whether the abuser still poses a risk to children. If the abuser does still pose a risk, I believe the clinician should be able to use clinical discretion in reporting this risk after considering the vulnerability of both the adult who was molested as a child and any potential child victims.

You also need to decide whether to report Mr. P.'s abuse of his sister Nancy. If Nancy were still a minor, you would be legally required to report the abuse. But since Nancy is now an adult, you may want to allow her the right to choose for herself whether to report that past abuse. If so, you would treat Mr. P.'s disclosure about this abuse the same way you would treat a client's disclosure that he assaulted a woman yesterday, that is, keep it in confidence while exploring the issues and assessing whether he poses a risk to others. You may wish to report Mr. P. as a past juvenile sex offender in a manner that does not infringe on Nancy's privacy. However, the current system of mandated child abuse reporting is set up to help known victims, not to monitor pedophiles who have abused anonymous victims years ago.

The most pressing issue concerns your decision whether to report Mr. P.'s impulses to molest his daughter Karen. If Mr. P. admits to any sexual act with Karen, you are legally required to file a child abuse report. You should realize, however, that after filing an initial child abuse report you are not required and, in fact, may not be allowed to disclose actual statements made by Mr. P. during therapy. The law requires therapists to make reports of suspected child abuse, but it has taken steps to safeguard the therapeutic alliance by recognizing actual client disclosures as confidential. As argued by Judge Mosk of the California Supreme Court in *People v. Stritzinger* (1983), "If the psychiatrist is compelled to go beyond an initial report to authorities regarding a suspected child abuse and must thereafter repeat details given to him by the adult patient in subsequent sessions . . . it is impossible to conceive of any meaningful therapy."

If Mr. P. does not communicate that he has molested Karen, you cannot file a child abuse report unless you have a "reasonable suspicion" that he has done so. The standard of reasonable suspicion is usually based on the assessment that other colleagues with similar credentials would make given the same facts. Similarly, you cannot file a child abuse report regarding Mr. P.'s son, Timmy, or Mr. P.'s students unless this standard of reasonable suspicion is met.

DUTY TO PROTECT

So far you have only filed a child abuse report if you know or have reasonable suspicion that abuse has already occurred to Karen, Timmy, or Mr. P.'s students. Have you done enough?

A second major legal obligation that tests the therapist's limit in maintaining confidentiality is the duty to protect (also interpreted as the duty to warn). The duty to protect refers to the implications of the famous *Tarasoff vs. University of California Regents* (1976) ruling and related case-law decisions holding that when a therapist has reasonable suspicion that a client may endanger another person, the therapist must use "reasonable care" in protecting the other person (*Hedlund v. Superior Court*, 1983; *Jablonski by Pahls v. U.S.*, 1983; *Tarasoff v. University of California Regents*, 1976). Many therapists fear that these case-law decisions will be interpreted so broadly as to make therapists legally responsible for any aggressive act perpetrated by their patients. As a consequence, some therapists, understandably concerned about malpractice suits, prematurely choose to break therapeutic confidentiality to warn people who might be only remotely in danger.

Sonkin (1986) has noted that these case-law decisions do not currently require therapists to protect "unidentifiable victims." Thus, if you did not know of any specific child with whom Mr. P. had contact, you would probably not be held responsible for failing to warn a currently unidentifiable child whom Mr. P. someday molests. It would be truly unfair for you to be expected to directly warn and protect all of the children with whom he might one day interact (*Brady v. Hopper*, 1983; *Thompson v. County of Alameda*, 1980).

However, Mr. P. has access to Karen, Timmy, and his students. You must therefore decide whether Mr. P. has communicated to you a serious threat to those children. The key interpretation seems to involve what constitutes a "communication" by the client that leads you to believe there is a threat. Your duty is clear when a client voices specific threats, but state laws vary in their inclusion of other indicators, such as a client's innuendoes or the presence of pathology that might impinge on a patient's ability to control dangerous impulses.

Clinicians' judgments in this case would vary widely. Many would say that Mr. P. is at risk to abuse children simply because he was abused himself as a child, yet most men who are sexually abused do not go on to sexually abuse children (Lew, 1988). Some would say that he is at risk to abuse because he abused his sister while he was a teenager, yet we do not have clear-cut data on the likelihood of adolescent perpetrators molesting as adults. Some therapists would feel that Timmy is not at risk because Mr. P. has only shown attraction to females, and that Mr. P.'s students are not at risk because his impulses are incestuous rather than extrafamilial. However, recent studies suggest that child molesters sometimes abuse children of both gender and that they often abuse out of the home as well as in the home (Abel, Becker, Cunningham-Rathner, Mittelman, & Rouleau, 1988). This issue is further complicated by the probability that the client may be withholding personal information out of fear that it will not be kept confidential, thus making the prediction of dangerousness even less clear-cut.

If you do assess Mr. P. as communicating a serious threat to Karen, Timmy, or his students, you must then act to protect them. One way to fulfill this duty is through direct warnings to potential victims, their guardians, and law enforcement officers. In some cases, however, you can fulfill your duty to protect without warning anyone and, thus, preserve confidentiality to some extent. For example, if you were able to convince Mr. P. to resign from his position as school teacher, you would not have to warn authorities at his school.

RECOMMENDATIONS

The case scenario just presented may raise many confusing legal and ethical questions for clinicians treating incest perpetrators. The following recommendations are offered to help clinicians become clearer about their duties and to support them in their efforts to provide such treatment.

1. Become knowledgeable about the legal parameters of limited confidentiality, which vary somewhat from state to state, and which change with new laws and new case-law decisions. Keep clear the oft-confused duty to report and duty to protect.

2. Clearly explain these parameters to your client and be consistent in your enforcement of them. The client has a right to know what the therapist's legal responsibilities are and how they will affect the confidentiality of personal disclosures. Being direct from the initial intake interview will minimize feelings of betrayal and a subsequent lack of rapport.

3. Distinguish between "legal confidentiality" and "clinical confidentiality." When an incest perpetrator is in treatment, his/her spouse and children are often in parallel treatment. At times you may feel a clinical need to disclose to those family members information supplied by the perpetrator. For instance, in a family meeting, you may need to confront a perpetrator when he/she is denying or minimizing the extent of the abuse. Be clear with your client about information that you might disclose to family members, but that you would not disclose to legal authorities.

4. Become clear on why you would or would not report an adult having been molested as a child by establishing what you consider to be the parameters of the adults molested as children or "AMAC right" to confidentiality. In California, for example, Attorney General Van de Kamp has suggested that clinicians report such abuse if the perpetrator currently has access to children. One clinical issue to keep in mind is that AMACs often have issues related to powerlessness and betrayal, and reporting their abuse without their consent may complicate these issues. When possible, help the AMAC to feel that he/she has taken a "power regaining" step by assisting in these reports.

5. Keep in mind the distinction between self-referred and court-referred incest perpetrators, both in terms of the client's freedom to leave therapy if trust is not established and in terms of any additional court-mandated evaluations that may threaten therapeutic rapport. Whenever an evaluation must be made, the therapist should discuss the entire

process with the client and explore the client's feelings about the effect of the report on the therapeutic alliance.

6. As Sonkin (1986) has suggested, there is a need for specific, empirically based guidelines for assessing the dangerousness of a child molester. It is neither fair nor accurate to assess all child molesters as equally dangerous to all children in all environments and for all time. Even if we cannot "cure" child molesters, we have had some success in making them less dangerous to children (Kelly, 1982). It would certainly be safer if we could be sure that they would never be in a setting with children, but such a solution is not a viable option.

   Unless we permanently incarcerate every known pedophile (a move that would be especially oppressive to people with pedophilic urges but no history of pedophilic behavior), we must make some clinical judgments about which ones are least dangerous to children. However, it is not realistic to assume that a therapist will take the societal and legal risk of assessing a pedophile as less dangerous unless some empirically based criteria have been developed in such areas as impulse control, environmental supports, and sexual arousal patterns.

   Cases in which a client is erroneously assessed as *not* dangerous and then molests a child are truly tragic. On the other hand, great psychological pain, social ostracism, familial upheaval, and loss of employment can occur in cases in which a client *is* erroneously assessed as dangerous. Empirically based guidelines will never be infallible, but they can increase our predictive accuracy (Monahan, 1981).

7. Case-law decisions must not become so broad that therapists become powerful legal watchdogs and impotent clinicians. We might first want to advocate that case laws continue to hold a therapist not responsible for harm committed to unidentifiable victims (California Civil Code, 1985). In addition, the therapist needs to maintain the power of clinical discretion in assessing and reporting dangerousness. This would include clinical discretion in choosing which personal client disclosures can be kept confidential without endangering children. If specific, empirically based guidelines for assessing dangerousness are developed, and a therapist combines these guidelines with reasonable clinical judgment in assessing a client as not being dangerous, it would seem unjust for a court to hold the therapist responsible if the client harms another person.

8. Whenever you must decide on whether or not you have met the criteria for "reasonable suspicion" of abuse or threat, consult with other well-informed colleagues without disclosing your client's identity. Make sure you then document these consultations in case notes along with your process for arriving at your particular judgment.

CONCLUSION

There are other ethical, legal, and clinical dilemmas inherent in balancing an incest perpetrator's right to limited confidentiality with society's right to protect its children. For example, we need to further consider the implications of a therapist's duty to disclose client records if a case does reach court (*In re Lifschutz*, 1970). We also need to examine our new awareness of young children who have been abused and then proceed to abuse their siblings and others while they are still children. Should these abuse-reactive children be assessed as dangerous to other children, and should we then report them and warn all of their peers? As Mr. P.'s case illustrates, there are no simple solutions. But it is hoped that clinicians will continue to recognize their own rights and responsibilities while they seek to protect their position as effective therapists, a position that must be fortified if we are to protect our clients and our society's children.

REFERENCES

Abel, G., Becker, J., Cunningham-Rathner, J. Mittelman, M., & Rouleau, J. (1988). Multiple paraphilic diagnoses among sex offenders. *Bulletin of the American Academy of Psychiatry and the Law, 16*(2), 153–168.

Brady v. Hopper, 570 F Supp 1222 (Denver 1983).

California Civil Code, Section 4392 (1985).

Hedlund v. Superior Court, 34 Cal 3d 695 (1983).

In re Lifschutz, 2 Cal 3d 415 (1970).

Jablonski by Pahls v. United States, 712 F 2d 391 (1983).

Kelly, R. J. (1982). Behavioral reorientation of pedophiliacs: Can it be done? *Clinical Psychology Review, 2*, 387–408.

Lew, M. (1988). *Victims no longer: Men recovering from incest and other sexual child abuse.* New York: Nevraumont.

Monahan, J. (1981). *Predicting violent behavior: An assessment of clinical technique.* Beverly Hills, CA: Sage.

People v. Stritzinger, 2.34 Cal 3d 437 (1983).

Sherlock, R., & Murphy, W. (1984). Confidentiality and therapy: An agency perspective. *Comprehensive Psychiatry, 25*, 88–95.

Sonkin, D. J. (1986). Clairvoyance versus common sense: Therapist's duty to warn and protect. *Violence and Victims, 1*, 7–22.

Tarasoff v. University of California Regents, 17 Cal 3d 425 (1976).

Thompson v. County of Alameda, 27 Cal 3d 741 (1980).

Appendix: The Incest Perpetrator Project: *Overview and Methodology*

During the fall and winter of 1987, our research team completed a book, *Abuse and Religion*, which was published in February 1988. In gathering data for this publication, it was necessary for the research team to do a comprehensive national study of incest perpetrators' responses and needs in respect to their caretakers and treatment providers. The research team's review of the literature revealed that the incest perpetrator has not received much direct empirical notice except as an element in the treatment of victims. Thus, our original proposal for that study was designed to be ambitious, including a large number of important variables to the clinical, legal, and research communities.

Therefore, the Incest Perpetrator Project set out to prepare a book on incest perpetrators for the treatment community (i.e., mental health workers, social service agencies, criminal justice facilities, marriage and family therapists, the clergy, and anyone working with these offenders). This project reflects the findings of several major studies of the incest perpetrator and combines them with the knowledge of other experts in the field to produce a unique and proscriptive book in an area that has received little research attention. Its purpose was to research findings and translate them into practical applications with guidelines and strategies for the clinician.

Material for this book was drawn from three extensive national studies in four different treatment settings and reflects the work of the major investigator, two coeditors/coauthors, and ten research assistants. Fourteen outside experts contributed focused material in their area of expertise. While the material is by no means exhaustive, it does represent new empirical findings from many sources. These studies will be referred to throughout the book in the chapters provided by the research team. Members of the research team receive individual credit for the work they researched under the close supervision of Dr. Johnson and Dr. Horton. A brief overview of their methodologies is reported here to explicate the references, observations, and findings reported elsewhere in the text with references to the appendix for the avid researcher. Copies of all instruments are available upon request.

OVERVIEW OF PROJECTS AND METHODOLOGY

National Perpetrator Study (1987–88)

Principal Investigators: Anne L. Horton, Barry L. Johnson, Gary D. Blair, David T. Ballard, Sterling Deveraux, Logan K. Valentine, and Doran Williams

Overview. At present, incest perpetrators are very limited in their choice of professional help. There is little empirical data about them, thus their needs are being generally ignored by the treatment community. Few therapists are willing to work with them and none are being specifically trained to work with them. Yet, as a key family member who is required to make major changes in order to retain a family role, clinical information must be gathered. This research project, therefore, is exploratory in nature and examines the following dimensions.

1. Who are the perpetrators? Basic demographic material: age, education, family composition and history, job and income, and so on.
2. What help did they seek for themselves—formal and informal support and treatment attempts that they pursued (counseling, clergy, friends, family, and so on). How satisfied were they with the help they received?
3. When do abusers recognize they have a problem? What are the phases of problem identification from denial to treatment?
4. What recommendations and reactions do they have with respect to support systems, treatment modalities, and resource availability?
5. What characteristics determine the treatment selection for incest perpetrators? A comparative look at the perpetrators in prison, mental health facilities, outpatient self-help groups (Parents United), and private therapy.

Methodology

Samples. All participants for each study were volunteers, were currently involved in some type of treatment program, and met the project's criteria for an incest perpetrator. For the purposes of this study, "incest" was defined as any intimate *sexual behavior or contact* between non-married members of a family, and included intercourse, sexual fondling, touching, and homosexual behavior between family members.

Phase I: Parents United Study

After a pilot test in March of 1987, questionnaires were mailed to 155 Parents United chapters and affiliated treatment centers throughout the United States. The addresses were obtained from the March 1986 Chapter Contact List: Child Sex Abuse Treatment Program. Detailed packets outlining the projects, along with guidelines for administering the 306 item questionnaire were mailed to the directors of these programs for disbursement to the proper treatment providers working with this special population. A total of 278 perpetrators, in 27 of the programs, agreed to participate and completed questionnaires for the study.

Phase II: Prison Study

In May 1988, following a pilot study conducted at the Utah State Sex Offenders Unit, Utah State Prison, 110 copies of the National Perpetrator Study questionnaire, along with the appropriate explanatory materials were mailed to all of the maximum security prisons listed in *Services for Adult Sex Offenders*, 1986. This publication, supposedly, included all of the private agencies, prisons, and forensic mental health centers that offered treatment to incest perpetrators. A total of 61 questionnaires were completed and returned from this population.

Phase III: State Hospital Study

The procedures for this population were comparable to those of Phase II. On May 1, 1988, questionnaires were mailed to the forensic mental health facilities identified in *Services for Adult Sex Offenders*, 1986. Forty-two completed questionnaires were subsequently returned from this population.

Phase IV: Private Practice Study

This phase basically used the same instrument and method as the Parents United sample. It was mailed on July 1, 1988, to the private agencies listed in the *Services for Adult Sex Offenders*, 1986. However, instead of sending questionnaires to a "group leader," they were distributed to all private agencies and therapists currently listed as offering services to incest perpetrators. Forty completed questionnaires were returned from this population.

Instrument: The Incest Perpetrator Questionnaire. Although the populations studied varied somewhat, the main instrument was "The Incest Perpetrator Questionnaire." This 304-item questionnaire was designed as a focused, retrospective-introspective instrument and included (a) basic demographic data, (b) abuse and sexual histories, (c) relationship assessments, (d) identification and referral information, and (e) choice of and description of the victims. In addition, there were a few short answer questions designed to explore the offender's strategies, program recommendations, and referral information.

STUDY OF TREATMENT PROVIDER'S QUALIFICATIONS EXPERIENCE AND PROFESSIONAL TRAINING (1988)

Principle Investigators: Anne L. Horton, Barry L. Johnson, Annette Plyer, Lynn M. Roundy, and Cydney Woolley

Overview. The purpose of this study was to examine the qualifications of treatment personnel working with incest offenders and to explore their therapeutic training, choice of treatment, and personal histories. As has been previously noted, the incest perpetrator usually only has access to a very poorly trained and unmotivated group of care providers. This study was designed to examine the care providers giving direct service to the incest perpetrator in each of the following settings: Parents United, the private practice area, prison, and state hospitals. Key issues included in this section of the research are:

1. basic demographic information / education / experience (both clinical and personal) of treatment providers in all settings;
2. use of volunteers / paid professionals / salary range;
3. treatment approaches / length of treatment / range of program costs;
4. referral services / auxiliary treatment;
5. basic agency treatment policy / philosophy / funding; and
6. level of satisfaction of care providers with the treatment provided and population served.

Methodology

Samples. A survey of treatment providers for perpetrators was conducted in mental health, prison, private practice, and Parents United settings throughout the United States. Only those treatment providers involved in direct treatment of the incest perpetrator were asked to participate. Questionnaires for the treatment providers were included and mailed to each of the treatment programs where the Incest Perpetrator Questionnaire was administered.

Phase I

In March 1988 surveys were sent to all 155 Parents United chapters and affiliated treatment centers in the United States registered in the *Chapter Contact List for Child Sex Abuse Treatment Programs*, March 1988. Parents United was chosen because it is currently the largest organized and recognized community-based treatment provider for incest perpetrators.

Phase II

During the summer and fall of 1988, a sample of treatment providers in private practice, prisons, and forensic mental health facilities was contacted. A cover letter explaining the study, along with a copy of the questionnaire, was mailed to the director of each institutional, private, and community-based organization. The director of each institutional or community-based organization was asked to deliver a questionnaire to each treatment provider working directly with perpetrators. Each treatment provider choosing to participate in the study received a copy of the questionnaire and a self-addressed, stamped, return envelope. A total of 97 treatment providers chose to participate.

Instrument. The instrument, "the Perpetrator Treatment Provider Survey," was used for data collection. This was a straight-forward, focused, 128-item, retrospective/introspective measure covering (a) basic demographic information—education, age, gender, and experience (both clinical and personal) of the treatment provider in the settings; (b) basic agency information—salary range, funding sources, use of volunteers, and paid professionals; (c) treatment approaches, length of treatment, and variety of programs; and (d) level of satisfaction of treatment providers and the specific treatment provided to incest perpetrators.

Several questions on the instrument required the respondents to check the alternative best describing themselves, and a few required a brief written answer. Some of the open-ended questions allowed the respondents to relate and rank order their preferences, as well as to reflect and offer suggestions for other treatment providers working with incest perpetrators.

TREATMENT POPULATION PREFERENCE STUDY

Principle Investigators: Anne L. Horton, Barry L. Johnson, and Troy Anderson

Overview. This study addressed the suggested crisis in providing trained caretakers for certain underserved, dysfunctional populations. Recently, the NIMH targeted treatment research and training toward increased support for training professionals to work with certain particularly challenging populations, such as incest perpetrators. Our study focused on determining:

1. Are graduating MSW students less willing to treat certain populations (i.e., incest perpetrators) than others?
2. Will the better prepared students decide not to work with these perpetrators?
3. Are these students prepared, either in the classroom, field, or through personal experience, to treat these perpetrators?
4. How much inservice training do agencies need to provide for themselves?

Methodology

Sample. A pilot study of 20 Brigham Young University graduating MSW students was administered a questionnaire in preparation for a national mailing. Then, on April 1, 1988, a packet of questionnaires was mailed to the Dean of each of the 100 university training programs offering an MSW degree, along with the necessary instructions for their administration. Ninety-three of the training programs were accredited by CSWE, with the remaining seven pending accreditation. One thousand sixty-three students from fifty-two of the graduate training programs chose to participate in the study.

Instrument. A brief survey instrument, "The Treatment Population Preference Survey," was a two-page checklist of 155 items, which measured students' preferences, classroom training, and personal and professional experience in the various treatment areas. The survey also asked the students if their personal experience helped or hindered their ability to work with certain populations. A brief demographic section identified students' age, sex, race, and G.P.A. These items were used to help examine preferred and least favored populations.

Limitations. While the methods used were the most cost-effective and allowed us to obtain data from a large number of people in a relatively short period of time, they are somewhat limited because of the sampling procedures that were used. In-depth interviews would have been extremely useful, but also very costly. Many institutions and agencies we approached had policies concerning research that made it very difficult, if not impossible, to obtain data.

The populations studied also presented problems of credibility because they obviously could and would reveal only what and how much they wished. The questionnaires were extensive, but not exhaustive, and although pilot-tested, still invited some confusion from the respondents. Again, while the face validity was good, the lie factor among the offenders remains unknown. This large sample of offenders and the in-depth information offered provide a springboard for additional exploration and research concerning incest perpetrators, their characteristics, and their treatment needs.

Resource Directory

ORGANIZATIONS:

AlexAndria Associates, 911 S.W. 3rd Street, Ontario, OR 97914.

Center for the Prevention of Sexual and Domestic Violence, N. 34th St., Suite 105, Seattle, WA 98103.

Channing L. Bete Co., Inc., 200 State Road, South Deerfield, MA 01373-0200, (800) 628-7733.

Child Sexual Abuse Curriculum for Social Workers, 9725 East Hampden Avenue, Denver, CO 80231-4919, (303) 695-0811.

Child Help USA, 6463 Independence Avenue, Woodland Hills, CA 91367, (818) 347-7280.

Effectiveness Training, Inc., 531 Stevens Ave, Solana Beach, CA 92075.

Ending Men's Violence National Referral Directory, To RAVEN, P. O. Box 24159, St. Louis, MO 63130, (314) 725-6137.

National Adolescent Perpetrator Network, Denver, CO 80231, (303) 321-3963.

National Self-Help Clearing House, Graduate School, City University of New York, 33 W. 42nd St., Rm. 1222, New York, NY 10036, (212) 840-1259.

Parents Anonymous (P.A.). To locate a P.A. group in your area, call toll free outside California (800) 421-0353. Inside California, call (800) 352-0386.

Parents United—treatment and self-help. Call to locate a P.U. group
    in your area. (409) 280-5055.

Society's League Against Molestation, 524 S. 1st Ave., Arcadia, CA
    91006, (818) 445-0802.

PUBLICATIONS:

Caparulo, F. (1988). *A comprehensive evaluation of an intellectually
    disabled sex offender.* The Center for Sexual Health and Educa-
    tion, Inc., P.O. Box 595, Orange, CT 06477-0595.

Fried, E. R. (1986, May). *A multimodal treatment of developmentally
    disabled sex offenders.* Paper presented at the Fourth National
    Conference on the Sexual Victimization of Children, New Or-
    leans, LA. Available through The Safer Society Program, Or-
    well, VT 05760, (802) 897-7541.

Giarretto, H. (1982). *Integrated treatment of child sexual abuse.* Palo
    Alto, CA: Science and Behavior Books.

Heinz, J. W., Gargaro, S., & Kelly, K. G. (1987). *A model residential
    juvenile sex-offender treatment program: The Hennepin County
    Home School.* Orwell, VT: Safer Society Press.

Knopp, F. H. (1982). *Remedial intervention in adolescent sex offenses:
    Nine program descriptions.* Orwell, VT: Safer Society Press.

Knopp, F. H. (1984). *Retraining adult sex offenders: Methods and
    models.* Orwell, VT: Safer Society Press.

Knopp, F. H. (1985). *The youthful sex offender: The rationale and
    goals of early intervention and treatment.* Orwell, VT: Safer So-
    ciety Press.

Knopp, F. H. (1987). *Female sexual abusers: A summary of data from
    44 treatment providers.* Orwell, VT: Safer Society Press.

Lackey, L. B., & Knopp, F. H. (1989). *A summary of selected notes
    from the working sessions of the First National Training Confer-
    ence on the Assessment and Treatment of Intellectually Disabled
    Juvenile and Adult Sexual Offenders,* Columbus, OH. March
    25–27, 1988.

Lew, M. (1988). *Victims no longer.* New York: Nevraumont.

Longo, R. E., & Bays L. (1988). *Who am I and why am I in treatment?* Orwell, VT: Safer Society Press.

Longo, R. E., & Gochenour, C. (1981, July/August/September). Sexual assault of handicapped children. *Journal of Rehabilitation,* 24–27.

Parsons, H. (1987). *The intellectually handicapped sexual offender.* Ross, Loss & Associates, P.O. Box 666, Mystic, CT 06355-0666.

Rosenberg, J. *Fuel on the fire: An inquiry into "pornography" and sexual aggression in a free society.* Orwell, VT: Safer Society Press.

Safer Society Program (1989). *Selected bibliography; Sexual offenders identified as intellectually disabled.* Orwell, VT 09760.

Salter, A. C. (1988). *Treating child sex offenders and victims: A practical guide.* Newbury Park, CA: Sage.

Smith, T. A. (1987). *You don't have to molest that child.* National Committee for Prevention of Child Abuse (NCPCA), Chicago, IL.

Index

lover, 185; of legal watchdog, 238; of suitor, 88; of the therapist, 165; playing exercises, 224; relationships, 71–72,90; victim, 49, 128, 197; within the family, 192, 233

Rules, absence of, 69; exceptions to, 45; normative, 58; social, 56, 58; violation of, 69

Seduction(s), aimed at victims, 49; manipulative, 172; maternal, 186; within clinical setting, 104

Self-esteem, as factor, 49; building, 234; feelings of, 56, 105; high, 192; improvement in, 60; loss of, 194; low, 96, 105, 174, 186, 191; of juvenile offender, 102, 105; poor, 21, 58; rebuilding, 159; strengthened, 224

Service, agencies, 152, 159–160, 163, 247; changes in available, 106; charitable, 162; child care, 160; clinicians who offer, 170–171, 187; community, 164; human, 155, 220; legal, 162, 216, 220, 239; military, 230; need for, 150, 153; perpetrators suggest, 161; planning, 44; protective, 99, 101, 103, 117, 162, 221, 239; providers, 250; social, 24–26, 37, 152, 168, 205, 227, 229, 247; use of community, 56, 58

Sex, addiction, 59, 127–128, 130–133, 138–141, 183, 192; addicts, 46, 127–129, 131–132, 134–138, 140, 142, 191, 193; as most important need, 130; clinicians of either, 172; commonplace, 92; confusing with love, 58–59, 183; crimes, 139; education, 58, 105–106, 162, 195; heterosexual, 46; object, 69; offenders, 28, 44, 59, 121, 153, 228–229, 231, 240; of victims, 23, 69; partner, 90, 111; oral, 94; preoccupation with, 81, 83, 129; psychogenetic makeup of each, 109; role, 67, 116, 118; intercourse with same, 101; talking about with daughters, 88; violent, 22, 28, 101; with a child, 19, 22, 27–28, 68

Sexual abuse, allegations of, 36–37, 40;

and the family, 28; by bio-fathers, 66–67; by noncustodial fathers, 69; by paternal caretakers, 65; by stepfathers, 65; cases of child, 19; contributing factor to, 67; data collected on, 70; disclosure of, 32, 181, 186; discovery of, 37; divorce-related, 36; duty to report, 40; entree to, 91; explanation for, 67–68, 111, 113–114; incestuous, 20, 23, 27, 179; interest that drives, 23; intrafamilial, 66, 99, 108, 220, 226; isolation factor in, 86; issues in, 40; juvenile, 99; legal reforms in, 40; ongoing, 96; of children, 23, 114; of daughter, 23; perpetrator 38–39, 74–75, 77, 86; problems associated with, 25, 27; prosecution, 38; protect victim from future, 72; rates of admission to, 71; recognition of female, 109–114; reporting, 160, 183, 231; studies on reported, 100; tie-in between physical and, 49; victim of, 32, 111, 164

Sexual access to children, 25

Sexual activities, 89, 92–94, 100, 103, 134, 230; with prepubescent child, 20

Sexual arousal, 21–25, 44, 66, 106, 232, 244

Sexual assault, 19, 31, 40, 205–206

Sexual attraction, 69, 229

Sexual orientation, 22, 70, 106, 134–135, 229

Sexual preferences, 28, 67, 71

Sexual relationship, 21, 26, 66–67, 83, 89, 100, 105

Sexual response, 106

Sexual satisfaction, 46

Sexual urges, 20

Sexual perpetrators/offenders, characteristics, 194; classifying, 23, 171; experiences of sexual abuse as a child, 70–71, 131, 223; guilt of, 187; incarcerated sample of, 22; look like everyone else, 19; low self-esteem, 186; needs of, 27; treatment of, 28; types of, 20; women as, 108–123

About the Editors

ANNE L. HORTON is Assistant Professor in the School of Social Work at Brigham Young University. She received her Ph.D. in Social Welfare from the University of Wisconsin-Madison (1983). As a Licensed Clinical Social Worker, she focuses her research and private practice in the area of domestic abuse. She has over 15 years of clinical experience and has spent 8 years as a crisis intervention specialist and program director. In 1989 she received the Susa Young Gates award for her outstanding service to women and dedication to the cause of women's rights and humanitarian service. She is a member of the American Association of Marriage and Family Therapists, the Council on Social Work Education, the National Association of Social Work, National Council on Family Relations, International Pediatric Social Service Workers, and Utah Association of Marriage and Family Counselors. She has written numerous professional articles and textbooks; her most recent book, *Abuse and Religion: When Praying Isn't Enough*, was published in 1988.

BARRY L. JOHNSON is Associate Professor at Brigham Young University with a joint appointment in the Department of Sociology and the School of Social Work. He received his Ph.D. in Sociology from the University of North Carolina-Chapel Hill (1977). He currently serves on the board of directors of The Utah Valley Family Support Center, an agency aimed at reducing the amount of domestic abuse in families. He is actively involved in The Religious Research Association, the Association for the Sociology of Religion, the Rural Sociological Association, the Western Social Science Association, the American Evaluation Association, the Utah Sociological Association, and the Utah Academy of Sciences, Arts, and Letters. He has published in the areas of marital happiness and adjustment, spiritual and social well-being, religious change and religiosity, and now in the area of sexual abuse.

LYNN M. ROUNDY is Executive Director of the Central Utah Sexual Abuse Treatment Program and Professional Coordinator of Parents United of Utah Valley. He received his M.Ed. in Counseling and Guidance from Brigham Young University in 1983 and is now pursuing a Ph.D. in Counseling Psychology. He is a charter member of the Utah County Child Abuse Council and a member of the Child Abuse Prevention Team of Utah County. He has written several articles on child sexual abuse and incest and published the *Sexual Abuse Problem Checklist*, an assessment tool for measuring the effects of prior sexual abuse in adolescents and adults.

DORAN WILLIAMS is an outpatient therapist at Timpanogos Community Mental Health Center. He received his M.S.W. from Brigham Young University. He has done group therapy for Parents United of Provo for three years and is a member of the National Association of Social Work. He coauthored a chapter in *Abuse and Religion: When Praying Isn't Enough*, published in 1988.

About the Contributors

CRAIG M. ALLEN is Associate Professor of Family Environment at Iowa State University. He received his Ph.D. from the University of New Hampshire. He has published articles on power and violence in families, and his professional interests include family violence, intrafamilial communication, and intergenerational value transmission.

TROY K. ANDERSON, M.S.W., is a psychiatric social worker at Aspen Crest Hospital in Pocatello, Idaho, where he works primarily with victims and perpetrators of sexual abuse. Before assuming his current position, he was involved in research in the area of incest perpetrators at Brigham Young University. His clinical interests include marital and family therapy, and treatment of those affected by abuse.

DAVID T. BALLARD, M.S.W., C.S.W., is a Case Manager for Human Affairs International, a wholly owned subsidiary of Aetna Life and Casualty. He also does private contract and consulting work for Intermountain Sexual Abuse Treatment Center, specializing in treating adolescent and adult sex offenders. Prior to his graduate training, he worked for five years in Japan and the United States in international business.

GARY D. BLAIR, M.S.W., C.S.W., is a social worker at the Utah State Hospital. His graduate degree is from Brigham Young University. He provides therapy for perpetrators, victims, and their families at Intermountain Sexual Abuse Treatment Center. His clinical interests also include mental health and geriatrics.

REED H. BLAKE, Ph.D., is Professor of Social Work and Sociology at Brigham Young University. He is a social psychologist whose research interests range from individual stress, such as that related to incest, to large-scale disasters. He is the author of five books and numerous professional articles. He teaches in the research methodology track in the graduate school of social work at BYU.

FRANK G. BOLTON, JR., is in private practice in Phoenix, Arizona. He is the author of more than 40 articles and 5 books. His other Sage books in family violence and related areas are *The Pregnant Adolescent: Problems of Premature Parenthood* and *When Bonding Fails: Clinical Assessment of the High Risk Family.*

SUSAN R. BOLTON, J.D., is an Arizona Superior Court Judge in Phoenix, Arizona. She received her law degree from the University of Iowa. Before her judicial appointment, she was in private practice in Phoenix. She and her husband are the coauthors of Sage's *Working with Violent Families.*

PATRICK J. CARNES, Ph.D., is Senior Fellow at the Institute for Behavioral Medicine. He is also the primary architect of an inpatient program for sexual dependency at the Golden Valley Health Center and, as a pioneer in the understanding of addictive processes, he is considered the leading expert in the field of sex addiction. He is the author of *Out of the Shadows* and *Contrary to Love.*

JOHN R. CHRISTIANSEN, received his Ph.D. from the University of Wisconsin (Madison) in sociology. Presently, he is Professor of Social Work and Sociology at Brigham Young University. He has published books and articles in sociology, civil preparedness, and family relations. He teaches research methodology for social workers, and is involved in research projects dealing with delivering social services in crisis environments, international civil-defense systems, and family relations.

TERESA M. CONNOR, M.S.W., is a social worker in the Program for Healthy Adolescent Sexual Expression (PHASE) at East Communities Family Service in Maplewood, Minnesota. She received her degree in 1988 from the University of Minnesota School of Social Work in Minneapolis. Professional interests include qualitative research on the development of sexually abusive behaviors in both adolescent and adult perpetrators of child sexual abuse. With Jane F. Gilgun, she recently coauthored "How Perpetrators View Child Sexual Abuse," in the *Journal of Social Work.*

JON R. CONTE, Ph.D., is Associate Professor at the School of Social Service Administration at the University of Chicago. The Founding Editor of the *Journal of Interpersonal Violence,* he is a member and past President of the American Professional Society on the Abuse of Children. He is the author of numerous publications dealing with various aspects of child sexual abuse, and is a frequent lecturer at national and international meetings. Dr. Conte has conducted research on the effects of childhood sexual experiences on child and adult survivors, the etiology of sexual violence, professional practice in child sexual abuse, and the effects of programs to prevent the sexual victimization of young children. A clinical social worker and researcher by training, Dr. Conte maintains a private practice working with the victims of interpersonal violence, and consults to treatment providers and other private and public agencies.

NODIE COX DAVIS, Ph. D., is an organizational/staff psychologist for the Department of Social Services Children's Services Bureau of the County of San Diego. She also has a private practice, primarily treating adults from dysfunctional families. She frequently lectures on incest dynamics to professional organizations, community agencies, and student groups, and she was a presenter at the National Conference on Sexual Addiction and Compulsivity.

STERLING DEVEREAUX, M.S.W., is a psychotherapist at Heritage Residential Adolescent Treatment Center in Provo, Utah. He received his degree from Brigham Young University and plans to pursue a doctoral degree in the near future.

KATHLEEN COULBORN FALLER, M.S.W., Ph.D., is Associate Professor in the School of Social Work and Codirector of the Interdisciplinary Project on Child Abuse and Neglect, the University of Michigan. She is the author of *Social Work with Abused and Neglected Children, Child Sexual Abuse: An Interdisciplinary Manual for Diagnosis, Case Management and Treatment,* and *Child Sexual Maltreatment: A Sourcebook for Mental Health Professionals.* She conducts research and engages in clinical work with sexually abused children and their families.

ANNA EINFELD-GIARRETTO, a Ph.D. candidate in counseling psychology, is a licensed marriage, family, and child counselor and group leader/trainer for lay and professional groups. On behalf of the Child Sexual Abuse Treatment Program (CSATP) (developed with Hank Giaretto), she has given numerous presentations at seminars in the United States, Canada, West Germany, and Australia, and has appeared frequently on radio and television.

HENRY GIARRETTO, Ph.D., is founder and Executive Director of the Institute for the Community as Extended Family and of Parents United, International. In 1971 he founded the first community-based program to offer professional and self-help treatment to the victims of incest and family members. This treatment approach, widely known as the Giarretto model, is practiced by over 150 treatment centers in the United States and other countries.

JANE F. GILGUN is Assistant Professor in the School of Social Work at the University of Minnesota, Twin Cities. She received her Ph.D. in Family Studies from Syracuse University, her Master's in Social Service Administration from the University of Chicago, and a licentiate in Family Studies and Sexuality from the University of Louvain, Belgium. For almost ten years, she has done research in the area of child sexual abuse, and has studied the development of sexually abusive behavior toward children for the past four years.

VICKI D. GRANOWITZ, M.S.W., L.C.S.W., Diplomate in Clinical Social Work, is in private practice in San Diego, California. She received her degree at San Diego State University where she did research on male incest victims. Her divergent experience in the areas of child abuse and sexual assault include providing in-home support services for families at risk for violence and treating sex offenders and their significant others. Currently, she specializes in treating survivors of incest and molestation.

ROBERT J. KELLY is Assistant Research Psychologist in the UCLA Psychology Department, where he is Co-Principal Investigator and Project Coordinator of a federally funded study on the effects of child sexual abuse in day care. He received his Ph.D. from the State University of New York at Buffalo. A licensed clinical psychologist, he has run therapy groups for male perpetrators, male survivors, and female survivors of child sexual abuse.

DEENA D. LEVI, M.A., is a Marriage, Family, and Child Counselor in private practice in San Diego, California. She has worked at the Child Sexual Abuse Treatment Program in the County of San Diego doing individual and family psychotherapy with victims, nonoffending spouses, and perpetrators in incestuous families, and she has led Parents United and Daughters United groups. Her clinical interests include treatment of members of incest families, including individual and group work with Adults Abused as Children.

KEE MacFARLANE, Ph.D., is associated with the Children's Institute in Los Angeles. She is a nationally known author and lecturer in the area of abuse.

LOIS H. PIERCE, Ph.D., is Associate Professor of Social Work at the University of Missouri-St. Louis. Her graduate degree is from Washington University. Prior to her university appointment, she worked in several child mental health settings providing services to emotionally disturbed children and their families. Her current research and clinical interests include adolescent sex offenders and adult survivors of child sexual abuse.

ROBERT L. PIERCE, Ph.D., is an Associate Professor of Social Work at the George Warren Brown School of Social Work, Washington University, St. Louis, Missouri. Prior to receiving his graduate degrees from Washington University, he was a child protective service worker for San Bernardino County (California) Public Welfare Department. His current research and clinical interests include adolescent sex offenders, examining the relationship between race and various forms of violence, and the history of Black children in America.

ANNETTE PLYER, M.S.W., is a graduate of Brigham Young University. She is associated with Charter Canyon Hospital and Charter Counseling Center in Provo, Utah. She is currently working with women and adolescents with plans to pursue another degree.

CHARLOTTE H. SHULER, M.S.W., A.C.S.W., is a social worker with the Social Work Service at Ireland Army Community Hospital, Fort Knox, Kentucky. She received her M.S.W. from Brigham Young University in Provo. Her clinical interests include family therapy, as well as child and spouse abuse issues. Currently, she is the clinical director of the Fort Knox Sex Offender Rehabilitation Program.

LOGAN K. VALENTINE, M.S.W., is a psychotherapist with Heritage Residential Adolescent Treatment Center in Provo, Utah. He received his degree from Brigham Young University and completed research on a nationwide study of the social skills of the incest perpetrator. For the past 12 years, he has worked with emotionally and behaviorally disturbed children. His clinical interests include treatment of stepfamilies, adolescents and their families, and group psychotherapy with adolescents.

CYDNEY S. WOOLLEY, M.S.W., received her graduate degree from

Brigham Young University, Provo, Utah. She has worked as a therapist with children, adolescents, and adults. Her professional interests include individual and group therapy, couple therapy, and research in the area of family violence.